READING PARFIT

'Derek Parfit's *On What Matters* is a major contribution to moral philosophy. The timely essays of this wonderful volume both clarify and evaluate Parfit's central arguments. Anyone interested in Parfit's work should study them carefully.'

Jussi Suikkanen, *University of Birmingham, UK*

'*Reading Parfit* features an impressive group of ethicists and metaethicists offering well-aimed critiques of Parfit's many arguments from his book, *On What Matters*. Parfit reacts in his characteristic style in a long response essay. The discussion illuminates many of the most important features of his argument and position.'

Mark van Roojen, *University of Nebraska–Lincoln, USA*

Derek Parfit was one of the world's leading philosophers. His *On What Matters* was the most eagerly awaited book in philosophy for many years. *Reading Parfit: On What Matters* is an essential overview and assessment of volumes 1 and 2 of Parfit's monumental work by a team of international contributors, and includes responses by Parfit himself. It discusses central features of Parfit's book, including the structure and nature of reasons; the ideas underlying moral principles; Parfit's discussions of consequentialism, contractualism and Kantian deontology; and his metaethical ideas and arguments.

Reading Parfit will be central reading for students of ethics and anyone seeking a deeper understanding of one of the most important works of philosophy published in the last fifty years.

Contributors: David Copp, J.L. Dowell and David Sobel, Julia Driver, Simon Kirchin, David McNaughton and Piers Rawling, Julia Markovits, Derek Parfit, Douglas W. Portmore, Kieran Setiya and Philip Stratton-Lake.

Simon Kirchin is Reader in Philosophy at the University of Kent. He is the author of *Metaethics* (2012) and is the editor of *Arguing about Metaethics* (with Andrew Fisher) (Routledge, 2006).

Derek Parfit (1942–2017) was for many years a Fellow of All Souls College, Oxford, retiring as Senior Research Fellow in 2010, whereupon he became an Emeritus Fellow. He also held visiting professorships at New York University, Harvard and Rutgers.

READING PARFIT

On What Matters

Edited by Simon Kirchin

LONDON AND NEW YORK

First published 2017
by Routledge
2 Park Square, Milton Park, Abingdon, Oxon OX14 4RN

and by Routledge
711 Third Avenue, New York, NY 10017

Routledge is an imprint of the Taylor & Francis Group, an informa business

© 2017 Simon Kirchin for selection and editorial matter; individual chapters, the contributors.

The right of Simon Kirchin to be identified as the author of the editorial material, and of the authors for their individual chapters, has been asserted in accordance with sections 77 and 78 of the Copyright, Designs and Patents Act 1988.

All rights reserved. No part of this book may be reprinted or reproduced or utilised in any form or by any electronic, mechanical, or other means, now known or hereafter invented, including photocopying and recording, or in any information storage or retrieval system, without permission in writing from the publishers.

Trademark notice: Product or corporate names may be trademarks or registered trademarks, and are used only for identification and explanation without intent to infringe.

British Library Cataloguing-in-Publication Data
A catalogue record for this book is available from the British Library

Library of Congress Cataloging-in-Publication Data
A catalog record for this book has been requested

ISBN: 978-0-415-52949-5 (hbk)
ISBN: 978-0-415-52950-1 (pbk)
ISBN: 978-1-315-22553-1 (ebk)

Typeset in Goudy
by Sunrise Setting Ltd, Brixham, UK

To the memory of Derek Parfit (1942–2017)

"An undisputed pillar of the contemporary canon of Western analytic philosophy."
— Cody Fenwick, *New York City Patch*

"In the estimation of many us, perhaps the greatest moral philosopher in our midst."
— David Shoemaker, *PEA Soup*

"Of all the people I have met, no one comes closer to embodying the ideal of a questioning philosopher than did Derek Parfit."
— Tyler Cowen, *Marginal Revolution*

"Clear, precise, rigorous, unpretentious and ingenious."
— *The Times*

"A British philosopher whose writing on personal identity, the nature of reasons and the objectivity of morality re-established ethics as a central concern for contemporary thinkers and set the terms for philosophic inquiry."
—*The New York Times*

"A philosopher who ingeniously created intellectual context and complication for others to freely move about within."
— Christian Munthe, *Philosophical Comment*

"It takes just two words to capture what made him worthy of the respect and attention even of those who profoundly disagreed with him: 'what matters'."
— Julian Baggini, *Prospect*

"He wrote only two books… but their originality, brilliance and provocativeness not only inspired philosophers all over the world, but also influenced discussion of practical and political strategies in tackling poverty, inequality, welfare economics, ageing and global warming."
—*The Guardian*

CONTENTS

Notes on contributors ix
Acknowledgements xii

Introduction 1
SIMON KIRCHIN

1 **Reflections from Wolf and Wood: incommensurability, guidance and the 'smoothing over' of ethical life** 10
SIMON KIRCHIN

2 **Normative naturalism and normative nihilism: Parfit's dilemma for naturalism** 28
DAVID COPP

3 **On what it is to matter** 54
JULIA MARKOVITS

4 **The buck-passing account of value: assessing the negative thesis** 82
PHILIP STRATTON-LAKE

5 **Normativity, reasons and wrongness: how to be a two-tier theorist** 96
DAVID MCNAUGHTON AND PIERS RAWLING

6 **Wrong-Making Reasons** 123
KIERAN SETIYA

7 **Parfit on reasons and rule consequentialism** 135
DOUGLAS W. PORTMORE

8 **Advice for Non-Analytical Naturalists**   153
   J.L. DOWELL AND DAVID SOBEL

9 **Contingency and constructivism**   172
   JULIA DRIVER

10 **Responses**   189
   DEREK PARFIT

   Index   237

CONTRIBUTORS

David Copp is Distinguished Professor of Philosophy at the University of California, Davis. He is the author of *Morality, Normativity, and Society* (Oxford University Press, 1995) and *Morality in a Natural World* (Cambridge University Press, 2007) and he has edited several anthologies, including *The Oxford Handbook of Ethical Theory* (Oxford University Press, 2006). He is the editor of a monograph series with Oxford University Press called *Oxford Moral Theory*. He has published and lectured widely on topics in moral and political philosophy.

J.L. Dowell, an Associate Professor at Syracuse, has published in metaphysics, philosophy of language, philosophy of mind, philosophical methodology and metaethics. She is the 2014 winner of the Marc Sanders Prize in Metaethics and is currently working on a book on deontic modals, under contract with Oxford University Press.

Julia Driver is Professor of Philosophy at Washington University in St. Louis. She works primarily in normative ethics and moral psychology. She has published three books: *Consequentialism* (Routledge, 2012), *Ethics: the Fundamentals* (Blackwell, 2006), and *Uneasy Virtue* (Cambridge University Press, 2001).

Simon Kirchin is Reader in Philosophy at the University of Kent and is currently Dean of its Faculty of Humanities. He works mainly in ethics and metaethics and is a past President of the British Society for Ethical Theory. He is the author of *Metaethics* (Palgrave, 2012) and has edited the following volumes: *Thick Concepts* (Oxford University Press, 2013), *A World without Values* (with Richard Joyce; Springer, 2010), and *Arguing about Metaethics* (with Andrew Fisher; Routledge, 2006). He is currently finishing a monograph with the working title *Thick Evaluation*.

David McNaughton is Professor of Philosophy at Florida State University and Professor Emeritus at Keele University. He is the author of *Moral Vision* (Blackwell, 1988), *Forgiveness* (with Eve Garrard; Routledge, 2010) and of a number of papers on ethics, philosophy of religion and the relations between

CONTRIBUTORS

the two. He has recently finished editing Joseph Butler's moral writings for Oxford University Press and is currently writing a book with Piers Rawling on their approach to practical reasons.

Julia Markovits is Associate Professor of Philosophy at Cornell University. She joined the Cornell faculty in 2014, after spending five years on the philosophy faculty at MIT. Before that, she was a Junior Fellow at the Harvard Society of Fellows. Markovits researches and teaches in meta- and normative ethics, bioethics and the philosophy of law. More specifically, she has written about questions concerning the nature of moral reasons and about moral praiseworthiness and blameworthiness. She is the author of *Moral Reason* (Oxford University Press, 2014).

Derek Parfit (1942–2017) was for many years a Fellow of All Souls College, Oxford, retiring as Senior Research Fellow in 2010, whereupon he became an Emeritus Fellow. He also held visiting professorships at New York University, Harvard and Rutgers.

Douglas W. Portmore is Professor of Philosophy in the School of Historical, Philosophical and Religious Studies at Arizona State University. He works mainly in moral philosophy. He is the author of *Commonsense Consequentialism: Wherein Morality Meets Rationality* (Oxford University Press, 2011). He is currently working on another book with the working title *Opting for the Best: Oughts and Options*. The book concerns what is, perhaps, the least controversial normative principle concerning action: you ought to perform your best option – that is, the option that is most highly favoured by your reasons.

Piers Rawling is Professor and Chair of Philosophy at Florida State University. He has wide-ranging interests and has published papers on decision theory, ethics (with David McNaughton), philosophy of language, various other areas of philosophy, and quantum computing (with Stephen Selesnick). He is co-editor (with Alfred Mele) of *The Oxford Handbook of Rationality* (Oxford University Press, 2004) and is currently writing a book with David McNaughton on their approach to practical reasons.

Kieran Setiya is Professor of Philosophy at MIT. He works in action theory, ethics and epistemology and is the author of *Reasons without Rationalism* (Princeton, 2007) and *Knowing Right from Wrong* (Oxford University Press, 2012). His essays range from the nature of rational agency to the place of love in moral philosophy and the resolution of the midlife crisis.

David Sobel is Guttag Professor of Ethics and Political Philosophy at Syracuse University. His *From Valuing to Value*, a collection of his old and new work on subjective accounts of well-being and reasons for action, is forthcoming from Oxford University Press. He co-edits, with Peter Vallentyne and Steve Wall, *Oxford Studies in Political Philosophy*.

CONTRIBUTORS

Philip Stratton-Lake is Professor of Philosophy at Reading University. He is the author of *Kant, Duty, and Moral Worth* (Routledge, 2000) and editor of *Ethical Intuitionism: Re-evaluations* (Clarendon, 2002), W. D. Ross's *The Right and the Good* (Clarendon, 2002) and *On What We Owe to Each Other* (Blackwell, 2004).

ACKNOWLEDGEMENTS

I would like to thank all of the contributors for their papers and for their unfailing patience as I was putting this collection together.

Tony Bruce who first helped when I had the thought for this book has been unwavering in his commitment. I am also grateful to many of his colleagues at Routledge for their work and kindness. Rebecca Shillabeer, Sarah Gore and Tim Hyde were very helpful when the book was in its final stages. I am also grateful to three anonymous referees for their comments on the whole volume when it was in draft form.

The University of Kent, as always, provided me with a wonderful environment in which to work and think whilst I was working on this volume, and I am very grateful to it and my many colleagues. Penny, Freddie and Molly contributed in more ways than one, and I am forever in their debt.

As this book was going to press it was announced that Derek Parfit had passed away. Derek was not only a hugely influential philosopher and writer of philosophy, he was also a very kind and thoughtful man. My fellow contributors and I are grateful to him for the support he showed for this volume and the whole project. No matter whether you agree with him, his passing greatly diminishes the whole philosophical community. This book is dedicated to his memory.

Simon Kirchin
Kent, Winter 2017

INTRODUCTION

Simon Kirchin

Derek Parfit's *On What Matters* is a striking intervention into modern moral philosophy and was, it is fair to say, one of the most eagerly anticipated works of analytic philosophy published for a long time.

Parfit published *Reasons and Persons*, his first book, in 1984. This influenced a whole generation of thinkers, both within moral philosophy and far beyond it, in its arguments, its ideas and its style of working through philosophical problems. As such, whatever book Parfit published next would have found itself in the spotlight. However, *On What Matters* (hereafter OWM) deserves to be considered and admired on its own terms and for its own reasons. There are a number of distinctive and arresting views that Parfit articulates within its covers, with many topics discussed and numerous arguments offered that range from the subtle to the direct. Indeed, it is probably worth lingering on one detail. Although we may talk of *OWM* as *a* book, it is a book that, when it was originally published, came in two volumes that ran to just over 1,400 pages (a third volume was published in 2017).[1] Further, it is split into six parts (one comprising commentary from Barbara Herman, T. M. Scanlon, Susan Wolf and Allen Wood) plus appendices. One can justly describe it as 'a work' that is, in fact, a few books.

In this short introduction I do no more than offer a flavour of the topics and ideas that Parfit covers in *OWM* 1 and 2, roughly in the order in which he discusses them, whilst also summarizing the chapters in this volume.

Parfit begins by thinking about reasons. For him a reason is something conceptually fundamental, something that cannot be explained in, or reduced to, further terms and concepts, even if one can get a sense of what a reason is from various examples and by seeing how it sits with similar normative and evaluative terms and concepts. His key aim throughout Part One is to argue against subjective theories of reasons and to argue in favour of objective theories. Subjectivists about reasons think that what we have most reason to do is (solely) a function of our desires and aims. These may be our actual and present desires and aims, or some desires and aims we would have if we more carefully considered the known facts or were made aware of facts that we do not know. In contrast, objectivists about reasons think that what we have most reason to do is (solely) a function of the facts. For example, we may well have most reason to act in a particular way because it is this action that will bring about the most good. It is clear that subjectivism and objectivism will deliver different conceptions of what we have most reason to do and clear how they can diverge in their final recommendations across a number of situations. For instance, whilst you may think you have most reason to choose a certain career path because it is what you desire to do or be, in fact choosing a different career path would produce the most good. In this case, at least as described in this bare manner, subjectivism and objectivism would differ as to what you have most reason to do.

There are a number of arguments that Parfit offers against subjectivism, some of which parallel his thoughts in Part Six. One line of argument begins by simply stating that subjectivists need to ensure that they are making substantive claims about reasons. They can fall into the danger of dealing in concealed tautologies, moving from the target phrase to be understood (1) 'we have most reason to act in some way' to the phrase (2) 'this act would best fulfil our present fully informed telic desires' (and hence giving sense to 'reason') and then giving a spin on this latter phrase by saying that (3) 'we have most reason to do what would best fulfil our present fully informed telic desires'.[2] If subjectivists use 'have most reason' in the desire-fulfilment sense, then (3) is shown to be a concealed tautology, not a substantive claim: 'the act that would best fulfil our present fully informed telic desires is the act that would best fulfil these desires'. So subjectivists need to use words such as 'reason' in a normative sense and not just as a synonym for the descriptive or factual 'what is most desired'. This immediately creates trouble for them. We can construct scenarios involving the adoption of a course of action in which agents suffer a large amount of pain but where, for whatever reason, they desire to suffer in this way. Subjectivists are then committed to saying that there is most reason (in the normative, substantial sense) for the agent to adopt such a course of action, even when it seems obvious that experiencing such pain is dangerous, bizarre or just plain bad. It strains credulity to think that we would really, sensibly want to say that the agent has most reason to choose this course in most scenarios, and thus subjectivism fails.

Taking himself to have established objectivism's truth through a number of arguments, Parfit moves, in Parts Two and Three, to consider how normative ethicists might seek to advise us as to what we should do.[3] What principles and theories should we adopt in deciding what reasons we, in fact, have? His thoughts here are arguably the single most important contribution that OWM makes to modern debate. In the words of Samuel Scheffler, from his introduction to the whole work, "Parfit aims to rechart the territory of moral philosophy".[4]

Students and scholars alike routinely think that the normative ethical theories of consequentialism and Kantian deontology offer fundamentally different views of what we should do in our moral lives. Consequentialists are typically cast as thinking that the rightness of one's actions is (solely) a function of their consequences. In contrast, Kantian deontologists are typically cast as eschewing consequences and favouring instead a set of principles or maxims that forbid and encourage certain action-types in accordance with the overarching idea or ideas expressed by the Categorical Imperative. So, to take a simple example, we should not lie because lying treats another person as a means to an end.

Across Parts Two and Three Parfit challenges the assumption that we have fundamental opposition and argues instead that normative ethics contains far more unity than most assume. In order to do this he further refines the theories he is interested in, arguing that his refinements present the best of the broad positions that are part of normative ethics.

He deals with three positions: rule consequentialism, Kantian deontology and contractualism, specifically Scanlonian contractualism. He argues that these three positions will recommend and justify the same, more specific moral principles and actions, and blends them into what he calls the *Triple Theory*:

> TT: An act is wrong just when such acts are disallowed by some principle that is optimific, uniquely universally willable, and not reasonably rejectable.

He goes on to say:

> We can call these the *triply supported* principles. If some principle could have any of these three properties without having the others, we would have to ask which of these properties had most importance. But these three properties, as I have argued, are had by all and only the same principles.[5]

To be clear, Parfit does not advocate that by coincidence these three positions pick out all of the same specific moral principles. Rather, there is something about the nature of these theories and the high-level principles and ideas that are at their core which means they converge on the same specific principles. He thinks there are good reasons to believe the Triple Theory to be true.

Parfit focuses in Parts Two and Three on engaging with Kant's philosophy, Kant being one of the philosophical heroes of OWM. Despite his admiration for Kant, Parfit reworks Kant's position, often in radical ways. He rejects or reimagines many points that some commentators think of as central to Kantianism, most notably (I think) the notion of a maxim.[6] A maxim is assumed to be, roughly, the subjective principle or policy on which agents act. 'Subjective' here does not mean what it means above: we are not discussing desire-based principles. Nor is 'subjective' synonymous with 'relativistic'. 'Subjective' here means that something is primarily the agent's. Maxims are those fundamental aims and policies that guide the agent's actions or, to use a shorthand, they are the fundamental motives of the agent that help to explain – indeed help to constitute – his or her action. Kant thinks, roughly, that we can judge the wrongness of the act by whether the maxim can be universalized. However, there are notorious problems with this. First, if one makes the maxim narrow and detailed (Parfit's example is the theft of a wallet from a woman dressed in white who is eating strawberries whilst reading the last page of Spinoza's *Ethics*), then one can easily universalize without fear that anyone else will act in this way, thus providing oneself with an exception. Yet the action is clearly wrong. In contrast, some maxims are 'mixed', often because they are worded more generally: for example, 'Do what is best for me' and 'Never lie'. Sometimes acting on such maxims can be wrong, but often not, and Kant failed to account for this, according to Parfit. Parfit attempts to show through various examples that the best version of Kantian deontology should eschew maxims, at least on one understanding of that term. We should instead focus on what the morally relevant description of the action is. Focusing on what people are intentionally doing in a particular circumstance will help us to get at such a description, suggests Parfit. For example, in the first example above the person is intending to steal; the other details are irrelevant. In a different case, although I am doing what is best for me by putting on a jumper, I am doing so only to keep warm and hurting no one in the process. Acting in this way can hardly be considered to be wrong. And so on.

As mentioned, Part Four sees four thinkers engage with Parts Two and Three. Susan Wolf claims that in arguing for the Triple Theory Parfit misses much that is of value within the various theories he tries to bring together, for their differences are essential and important to them. Allen Wood raises profound worries about Parfit's philosophical methodology and also disagrees with him about Kant. Whereas Parfit thinks that the Formula of Humanity is not a practically useful principle, Wood disagrees. Barbara Herman also focuses on Parfit's Kantian exegesis, with much of her discussion revolving around the relation between an agent's motive and an act's effects on others. Whilst she is not against trying to see connections and even combinations between theories, she thinks Parfit goes too far in ignoring the importance of motives to the moral worth of actions and brings into question how we arrive at a morally relevant description of an action. Lastly, Scanlon claims that he is not a Kantian and that his position cannot be subsumed into the Triple Theory. He concludes that Parfit takes the production of optimific results to be most morally basic, whereas he himself thinks that what is most morally basic is agreement amongst people. Despite his discussions, thinks Scanlon, Parfit does not capture this type of agreement in the right sort of way. Part Five sees Parfit engage with these four colleagues in which he deepens his view, especially with regards to Scanlon's criticism. He argues that his recasting of Scanlon's view provides Scanlon with a more plausible theory that in turn makes possible the Triple Theory as Parfit conceives it.

This brief summary of Parts Four and Five comes nowhere near doing justice to the material therein and the differing viewpoints one finds. Whilst the details undoubtedly matter, it is worth stressing two themes that emerge strongly from these parts. First, the critics worry that Parfit's position is too consequentialist (that is, too concerned with the production of results) to accommodate the insights of the other theories satisfactorily. Parfit profoundly disagrees with this, arguing that the best versions of the other two theories are more concerned with the production of moral effects than many people acknowledge. Second, Parfit may well think as he does because of his style of moral reasoning: the main concern of moral philosophy, it seems, is to develop principles to guide our specific actions across all situations. We often refine such principles in the light of the results we get in certain situations (real or imagined) that we test them against. Wood in particular doubts whether this is the best way of proceeding.

In Part Six Parfit switches tack away from normative ethics and towards metaethics. He is a realist and cognitivist about value and normativity and also a staunch non-naturalist. So, for him, normative properties exist and can be things we can know. Furthermore, they cannot be reduced to natural phenomena that are, for example, studied by the natural and social sciences. They are *sui generis*. Parfit considers a number of metaethical positions and writers that seek to offer alternative views, and he argues against all of them. The leading three opposing views are all Ns: noncognitivism, naturalistic realism (both analytic and non-analytic) and nihilism (which incorporates error theory).

Like many other philosophical areas, metaethics has a huge amount of detail and complication as well as a number of chief positions that compete against each other to explain roughly the same phenomena. What is refreshing about Parfit's Part Six, in my view, is that much of the detail and complication is stripped away. He looks at the essential bones of each position in an attempt to make progress.

Parfit begins by echoing his thought from Part One. He argues that we have external reasons for acting – reasons that do not depend for their existence on any agent's desires or aims – and against those who think that the only reasons that exist are internal reasons – reasons that do so depend. He then moves to provide a battery of ideas and arguments against the positions listed above. A notable argument – the Triviality Objection – employed against non-analytic naturalism mirrors one from Part One.[7] To say that we ought to do something is to make a substantive normative claim. Non-analytic naturalism renders such claims trivial. How so? Take the following claim, which appears to be philosophically substantive:

> (U) when some act would maximize happiness, this act is what we ought to do.

U can be claimed by all sorts of utilitarians. Non-naturalist utilitarians such as Sidgwick (the other main philosophical hero in *OWM*) would claim that the property of maximizing happiness makes the act have the different or further property of being what we ought to do. Naturalist utilitarians claim that the maximization of happiness is the same property as the property of being what we ought to do. If this latter identification is made, says Parfit, then it renders a seemingly substantive claim such as U trivial, for we are then saying only that when some act would maximize happiness it is an act that would maximize happiness.

At the heart of this move is Parfit's general idea that some other metaethicists incorrectly conceive the subject matter they are trying to explain first of all. If one does not start in the right way, then one can be led into all sorts of failure, as Parfit attempts to show throughout Part Six. Fellow thinkers may render seemingly substantive claims trivial, as above. Or they may fail to explain what it is to disagree with others or how we can improve morally. (These are ideas he raises against noncognitivism.) Or they may have a curious account of reason that fails to do justice to our ethical lives and intuitions. (This is Parfit's main worry with Bernard Williams' thought, echoing the ideas of Part One.) Parfit's overriding concern is that unless one adopts the sort of cognitivist non-naturalism he espouses, then one cannot capture the idea that life and our existence matter, and it is surely right that we do this.

Throughout the whole of OWM there is a boldness in style and orientation which receives two main expressions. In Parts One and Six, where Parfit deals with conceptions of reasons and normativity, he presents an uncompromising account of the reality of the moral and the practical, and of what it takes for things to matter. In Parts Two, Three and Five he is similarly bold. In fashioning a position that seeks to remodel three main normative ethical theories so as to bring them together, he stakes out a position that shakes up the theoretical landscape. In doing so, he begins to give us some idea of how we can decide which things matter ethically. Given the boldness of these aims we will undoubtedly have to measure the success of OWM over a long period of time.

What of the commentators in this book?[28] We begin with my chapter. I discuss the commentary of Wolf and Wood, and Parfit's replies to them. I restate and further Wolf's criticism that the Triple Theory overlooks or unjustly eschews much that is valuable in the three theories Parfit considers. In doing so, I consider the few comments that Parfit makes in his defence. I then turn to Wood's attack on Parfit's philosophical methodology, in part because it strikes at the heart of Parfit's project, and also because Parfit himself prefers to focus on Kant in his reply. I bring the themes from both commentators together (whilst acknowledging their differences), showing how they can lend support to the other, developing points that Parfit needs to answer in order to show that the Triple Theory, or anything like it, is plausible.

Next up is David Copp's chapter. Normative naturalists hold that normative properties and facts are natural, contending that these are similar in all metaphysically important respects to other natural properties and facts. Parfit argues, however, that if normative naturalism were correct, normativity would be illusory and that normative naturalism is close to nihilism. Parfit's most direct argument for this is his Soft Naturalist's Dilemma. From this he concludes that normative naturalists are committed to Hard Naturalism. According to Hard Naturalism, we could get rid of normative terms and concepts without any cognitive loss. Copp argues that this is wrong, focusing on the idea that the naturalist can say,

INTRODUCTION

for example, that even if the property *wrongness* is identical to a natural property, N-wrongness, the proposition that torture is wrong is distinct from the proposition that torture is N-wrong. Hence if we lacked the normative concept of wrongness, there are true propositions we would be unable to believe, including the proposition that torture is wrong. Indeed, we would be unable to formulate the thesis of normative naturalism. There would be a cognitive loss. There is, moreover, argues Copp, additional complexity in our 'ways of thinking' (WOTs) of normative properties that is crucial to normative belief playing its characteristic role in motivating action. To explain this, Copp introduces the idea of an internal WOT of a normative property where 'internally represented' normative beliefs have a characteristic bearing on the motivation of action. This is a feature of internally represented normative beliefs that is not had by naturalistic beliefs, not even if the naturalistic belief has the same truth conditions as the internally represented belief. The upshot is that the naturalist can reject Hard Naturalism. Properly understood, Copp concludes, naturalism does not eliminate normativity. It aims to explain what normativity consists in.

In her contribution Julia Markovits notes the consensus-building of Parts Two and Three and contrasts it with Parfit's total rejection of subjectivism in Part One. She argues both that the difference between objectivism and subjectivism may not be as deep as Parfit presents and that any consensus-building should push us towards subjectivism. A crucial part of her project is to argue that we can have reasons for our desires and that identifying these is a collective project. This leads to an 'optimistic subjectivism', whereby we attempt to identify aims and goals we all have reasons to share, where such reasons are based on desires that we have in common.

In Part One Parfit mentions in passing his commitment to a buck-passing account of goodness, although he disagrees with Scanlon, its most notable defender. In short, Parfit endorses the positive thesis of buck-passing (roughly, that if X is good, then the properties that make X good give us various reasons to act in relation to X) but denies the negative thesis (that goodness itself is never reason-providing). In his contribution, Philip Stratton-Lake also considers buck-passing, and focuses in great detail on the refinement Parfit makes. He also discusses work on this topic by Mark Schroeder. The best case to be made on behalf of Parfit is of understanding X's goodness as a non-additive reason. Stratton-Lake argues that Parfit's view fails and that there is as yet no good reason to reject the negative thesis.

David McNaughton and Piers Rawling in their wide-ranging, joint chapter concern themselves with an overarching idea that emerges across all of *OWM*, namely Parfit's 'two-tier' view of practical reasoning. According to this view, practical reasons are cast as facts. Consider, for example, the following: the fact that you are hungry is a reason to eat some food. There are two facts here, hence why it is two-tier: the fact that you are hungry and the fact that you being hungry is a reason. McNaughton and Rawling trace Parfit's thought across a variety of topics: for example, whether normative notions other than reasons can be central and irreducible, and the issue of moral constraints in normative theory. This leads them to argue that Parfit should not be a constructivist about morality and should adopt a thoroughgoing non-constructivist two-tier theory.

Kieran Setiya focuses on Parfit's Kantian Contractualism – a crucial part of the Triple Theory – and asks how and whether it can guide action. Kantian Contractualism states that 'everyone ought to follow the principles whose universal acceptance everyone could rationally will'. This provides us with a clear sense of which acts are wrong: an act is wrong if it is deemed wrong by those principles that one accepts under this formula. Through a series of moves, most notably a focus on the idea of a Wrong-Making Reason, Setiya worries whether we can apply the Kantian Contractualist formula when we do not already know what we have reason to do. The formula may be redundant.

Doug Portmore makes trouble for rule consequentialism, another key element of Parfit's Triple Theory. He casts rule consequentialism as stating that agents have reason to act so long as the act is part of a set of acts that, if realized, would bring about the best consequences, and that this is so even if (1) the act itself does not have good consequences and (2) the agent cannot see to it that the set of acts (and their consequences) are realized. Portmore argues that an agent has reason to perform the act only if she can see to it that the set of acts and the consequences are also realized, thus denying (2). This then leads, absent any other sufficient reason to act, to the fact that agents lack sufficient reason to act. So, argues Portmore, this means either that rule-consequentialism is false, or that we often lack sufficient reason to act as morality requires. Both of these options damn Parfit's position.

In their joint chapter J.L. Dowell and David Sobel consider Parfit's argument – the Triviality Objection – against non-analytic naturalism (as considered by Copp). They argue that naturalism can meet the central challenge that Parfit offers. Non-analytic naturalism *can* make informative identity statements, and Parfit misses this because he relies on the mistaken assumption that the informativeness of such statements must be explained by their semantics rather than by the pragmatics of their use. Dowell and Sobel show that it is possible for non-analytic naturalists to make informative identity statements, and hence Parfit's objection is undermined.

Having raised a worry with Parfit's anti-naturalist stance and also considered one of his anti-naturalist arguments, we then change tack to consider what a naturalistic alternative might look like. In her contribution Julia Driver argues for a type of naturalism, whilst taking seriously Parfit's view that metaethical theories should ensure that they can make sense of things mattering. Her approach is broadly Humean. Within this broad approach she defends a view of 'constitutivism', which sees reasons as extractable from basic norms of agency. This can, of course, mean that the reasons that exist are contingent on features of humans and our agency, and this contingency may be unpalatable for certain realists, including, one can imagine, Parfit. Driver argues that this contingency does not in any way lead to a vicious arbitrariness and that this position can still make plausible sense of why it is that things matter. In this way it ties in nicely with Markovits' chapter.

At the end of the book Parfit replies to all our commentators, with the replies having varying lengths. I do not go into detail here about Parfit's replies. Two main points are worth highlighting, however. First, as one might expect, many of the themes from above appear: the nature and ground of reasons, the status and value of the Triple Theory, practical rationality, Parfit's arguments against naturalism, and others. Second, his replies are robust in his defence, although, as one would expect from Parfit's work, he is always at pains to ensure he gives as clear an answer as possible. It is also worth noting that where he agrees with a fellow writer, Parfit sometimes merely records this fact, whilst at other times he spells out why he thinks that a supposed disagreement is nothing of the sort and why there is some deeper agreement between himself and the writer he is responding to.

This searching for agreement has become a theme in Parfit's writing of late; the advance of the Triple Theory itself shows this. The writers in this volume hope that the various criticisms and ideas discussed here will help to show what (seeming) disputants can in fact agree on and help to underline what can remain as real disagreement.

Notes

All references to *On What Matters* in this volume are referenced as either *OWM* 1 or *OWM* 2, with the relevant page number, chapter or section. *Reasons and Persons* is referenced as *RP*.

1. In this collection we deal only with the first two volumes.
2. *OWM* 1, p. 72.
3. These two parts were first delivered, in different form, as Tanner Lectures in 2002.
4. *OWM* 1, p. xix.
5. *OWM* 1, p. 413.
6. See especially *OWM* 1, §42.
7. *OWM* 2, §95.
8. The order of commentators was suggested by Parfit himself because of how he wanted to structure his responses.

1

REFLECTIONS FROM WOLF AND WOOD

Incommensurability, guidance and the 'smoothing over' of ethical life

Simon Kirchin

Introduction

In *On What Matters* (hereafter *OWM*) Derek Parfit argues that the best versions of Kantianism, Scanlonian contractualism and rule consequentialism can be combined into a position – the Triple Theory – that shows us what sort of ethical principles we should adopt to guide our behaviour and moral judgement.

These three theories are traditionally thought to be rivals, with deep differences. The prospect of their convergence is one of Parfit's most exciting proposals in *OWM*. In this chapter I think about the very idea of combining these three theories. I do so by looking at Parfit's ambitions through the eyes of two of his commentators from Volume 2, namely Susan Wolf and Allen Wood.[1]

This may seem an odd step in a volume devoted to Parfit's work. But I do so because, in his interesting responses, Parfit doesn't engage with what I find most arresting about what Wolf and Wood say. Their criticisms connect with the heart of the whole *OWM* project, and part of my aim is to encourage Parfit to say something in his defence.

Wolf suggests that the attempt to synthesize Kantianism, Scanlonian contractualism and rule consequentialism is unwise, mainly because these theories see different features of our lives as being ethically significant and because they cast many of the same moral features differently. Having highlighted particular parts of Wolf's criticism, I extend her commentary by articulating the theoretical underpinning that Parfit seems to assume for his view. He assumes that normative ethical theories are good and decent only if they can provide clear, practical guidance, and in turn this requires an assumption that all values and things valued are commensurable. This has, in addition, connections with his metaethics in Part Six.

I believe his meta-normative ethic – that is, his theory about what normative ethics is about and how it should be conducted – is essential to the advancement of his Triple Theory, and yet it gets little if any articulation in OWM and certainly no detailed defence.

What of Wood? He criticizes Parfit's methodology, amongst other matters. Whilst both he and Parfit are interested in practical guidance, I use the differences between their methodologies and conceptualizations to illustrate and deepen Wolf's concern. Whilst that is a prime aim of mine, I also repeat and extend some of Wood's ideas to, again, encourage Parfit to reply.

Doubt is cast by both commentators not so much on the details of the Triple Theory itself but on Parfit's more general hope of drawing together much of what is important in the Western moral canon in order to advance our moral thought. What is embodied in the Triple Theory may have more narrow appeal and success than Parfit seems to think.

Wolf

In summarizing and discussing Wolf's ideas in this section and the next, I emphasize and extend three interrelated themes: incommensurability, the conception of action guidance offered by normative ethics and how these first two ideas relate to Parfit's concerns about disagreement and reality.

Wolf begins her rich and interesting commentary by articulating Parfit's ambition in OWM. It is not just that Parfit is picking and choosing what he takes to be best in the three main theories he focuses on. He aims, too, to systematize them individually and then synthesize them to show us that, perhaps imperfectly, proponents of these views are attempting to reach the same single true morality. Parfit shares the assumption or hope that there is a single true morality with "many if not all of the major figures in the traditions he claims to combine".[2] For Wolf, in contrast, it would not be such a "moral tragedy if it turned out that morality were not so cleanly structured as to have one".[3]

Wolf thinks that Kantianism, contractualism and consequentialism all capture something important about value and about how to lead and make sense of ethical life. Yet she worries that there is deep tension and disagreement between these theories, and that this is inevitable since what they say is of value and the way in which they capture the valuable differs, often fundamentally. Attempting to reconcile these theories will result in a dilution of their individual visions of what the ethical life is. Involved in this, I take it, is a worry that we may well lose some aspects of our ethical life that each may show us to be valuable, and that we may lose an appreciation, in part or whole, of why they are valuable.

Wolf's main example in this regard concerns autonomy and consent. She focuses on the tension between Kantianism and consequentialism, and specifically the tension that seemingly exists between a concern to respect autonomy and a concern to produce optimific results. In short, Wolf notes that Parfit's commitment to an objective, value-based account of reasons means that what many take to be important and morally significant about consent drops out of the picture. Under Parfit's construal, she thinks, when we think about whether to act in a way that will affect some person, we think not about how she has consented, or how she would consent were she able to, but only about the reasons that relate to our action, reasons that justify choices that she herself *could* (but not necessarily *would*) endorse.

This idea conflicts with the value of consent given by many theorists, including Kant.[4] As I read Wolf, it also conflicts with a prevalent, everyday understanding of consent. The idea is simply this. We may well be able to maximize best outcomes if we ϕ, but a (central) person in the situation has not consented to our ϕ-ing, or has expressly forbidden us to ϕ, or (we can reasonably imagine) would refuse to consent to our ϕ-ing if asked. Such refusals stand as important checks on our action. If we do decide to ϕ, then we would be overriding what this person has said she wants to happen, or would say if asked. According to Wolf, Parfit's treatment of consent, with its direct and explicit link to the reasons that exist, allows him to introduce a concern for optimific results and drop respect for what people choose and would choose. Wolf illustrates this with the example of *Means*. She says that there are things that count in both directions in this case, but that it would be odd to say that in saving White's life one had satisfied some Consent Principle.[5] The point is that there is no real acknowledgement of the respect that we should give to Grey, or anyone, in the exercise of their own practical reason.

At the end of her section 'Consent', Wolf says:

> The problem with [Parfit's] suggestion, as I have argued, is that it leaves what may be considered the moral point behind a consent principle behind. It leaves consent behind, and the respect for autonomy, from which the value of consent might be thought to derive. If one is concerned in the first instance not in formulating a supreme or decisive principle, but rather in registering and articulating important (but possibly competing) moral considerations, the need for unanimity would not be allowed to transform one's principles in this way.[6]

Consent drops out for Parfit, according to Wolf, but what is really interesting is why it does so. It drops out because of Parfit's aim to formulate a supreme principle involving as it does – to pick a label – the *smoothing over* of seemingly profound moral differences.[7]

We can push further. There is a feature of Wolf's criticism and Parfit's reply that reveals the nub of their discussion. At one point Wolf discusses a 'trolley' case. We are to imagine being in a position to push a man onto the tracks to stop some runaway trolley and hence save people on the track.[8] She claims that people are resistant to pushing the man not only because he is innocent. What is also involved – indeed what is "distressing" – is that someone else is deciding what to do with someone's life, even if many other lives could be saved as a result. Much of the appeal of autonomy lies in choosing what to do with your own life, where it is you who is "calling the shots", and Wolf imagines that we can project such a view onto other people and imagine what it is like for them. This is not a mere preference, for Wolf, as opposed to a value (her contrast). It should be classified as more important than that. She argues that this preference is something that everyone could adopt and that we should treat such a preference as rational. So, for example, it is perfectly rational to accept a principle that favours leaving some man on a bridge (where if we pushed we could save many) and prefer it to a principle that says we should push. She says:

> If it be granted, therefore, that a person may rationally prefer to maintain immediate control over his body and his life to minimizing his risk of loss of life and limb, then Parfit's argument that Kantian Contractualists must support a form of Rule Consequentialism will not go through. Even if we grant Parfit's claim that everyone could rationally accept optimific principles, as I am happy to do, we would also have to admit that everyone could rationally accept nonoptimific principles, in particular principles which would more strongly protect people against interference from others in the control of their own bodies.[9]

This continues her discussion, for in effect she draws a distinction between a preference for welfare and a preference for autonomy, and adds that some Kantians or Kantian Contractualists would further claim that preference for autonomy over welfare would be "uniquely rational". To Wolf's mind, the value of autonomy is 'irreducibly important' for some people and this is something Parfit fails to recognize. Given her main theme is to emphasize the complexity and variety of ethical life, we can readily class this as just one example of a difficult or impossible choice amongst many.

Parfit's response to this passage is revealing.[10] He casts Wolf as saying that "everyone could rationally choose that everyone accepts some such principle even though this principle would not be optimific" and says that both claims could not be true. Why not? When, as Kantian Contractualists, we ask which principles everyone could rationally choose, we presume they know all of the reason-giving facts. If these autonomy-protecting principles were not optimific, then they simply would not be chosen: people would have clear impartial reason to refrain from choosing them. In effect, Parfit sees no possibility of a clash between a rational preference for, or a valuing of, autonomy and a concern to adopt optimific principles. To rationally prefer some principle *simply is* to see it as an optimific principle, and vice versa.

Parfit goes further in sorting out Wolf's criticism by distinguishing welfare from optimificality.[11] Wolf seems to treat the two as synonyms, but Parfit is at pains to make clear that he is not committed (and is indeed not trying) to further a welfarist account of rule consequentialism. He is concerned only with those principles that make "things go best",[12] and, as he sees matters, if we had a situation where everyone rationally chose that everyone accept some autonomy-protecting principle, then, again, this is simply what it would be for everyone to accept the principles that are optimific, since such principles would make things go best in the impartial-reason-implying sense.

There is here a fundamental and revealing misunderstanding on Parfit's part. He uses 'rational' to indicate that one is responsive to reasons in an impartial sense. When Wolf uses 'rational', I believe she has a different, perfectly acceptable, conception of 'rational' in mind. When she imagines that people might prefer autonomy over something that could maximize welfare, she has in mind that it would be perfectly (morally) reasonable and understandable that people would make such a choice, for the reasons she gives, such as wanting to call the shots. (And not only *could* people have such a reasonable preference, but they *do*.) We can also note the connected point that whilst Parfit is right to indicate that he is not advancing a welfarist conception of 'best', his notion of 'best' does reveal a blind spot. He imagines that if everyone rationally chose for everyone to accept autonomy-protecting principles, then this is just what it would be to choose the best principles: that is, optimific principles. His notions of 'best' and 'optimific' are 'singular' notions, at least when discussing the Triple Theory. (More on that important qualifier in the next section.) Throughout much of OWM he is searching for the set of principles and moral ideas that tell us what we should do, seemingly singularly and uniquely (or, at least, for an overarching principle that helps to choose which substantive principles should guide our actions).[13] Wolf, on the other hand, wants to contrast choosing autonomy over welfare or other notions, whereby in some cases there is no obvious single solution and some cases that have significant moral 'residue'. This will mean there are tensions between various notions, some of which will be impossible to resolve, leaving us to render the value of such notions irreducible with respect to other values and things valued. In a particularly complex and fraught situation, it can be reasonable and rational to choose to protect autonomy but also reasonable and rational to choose to promote welfare, or keep one's promises, or whatever. A normative ethic can be decent and good whilst leaving such a tension in place. To always wish for some singular best set of principles to guide us is to distort the character of the ethical life. As Wolf says:

> For Parfit, appreciation of the different evaluative outlooks poses a challenge which he aims in this book to meet: to unify, systematize or otherwise combine the insights gleaned from these perspectives to reach a single, coherent moral view that can guide our actions in a way that is free from moral remainders and normative tensions. Though I think I understand the wish to reconcile the different traditions and transform their ideas into a single, unified whole, I am less gripped by it than many other philosophers.[14]

Wolf is not just emphasizing the complexity and variety of our moral lives, nor just that ethical theories perceive and cast what is valuable in different ways. Many people – including Parfit – can agree with that. She is arguing that many such theories are reasonable to hold in some sense because they each have some grain of truth in them. This is so since the ethical life contains many values, many of which are incommensurable. The word 'incommensurable' makes only one appearance in the whole of OWM, in Wolf's conclusion.[15] Parfit never uses it. But as far as Wolf is concerned, it is crucial to his account that values and things held to be valuable are commensurable.

Having now brought up the notion of incommensurability, we should begin to nail those three themes I introduced at the start of this section.

Three interrelated themes

Despite not using the word 'incommensurability' in OWM, Parfit does discuss matters pertinent to it.[16]

In Chapter 34, 'Agreement', he considers those that seek to attack moral realism or moral truth on the basis that there is a significant amount of moral disagreement. To cut a long story short, he runs through various features that may explain why there is so much disagreement and which in turn do not threaten the possibility of there being moral truth. As well as expected examples, such as ignorance of or disagreement about nonmoral facts, he also says:

> Some other moral disagreements are not about *which* acts are wrong but *why* these acts are wrong, or what *makes* them wrong. Different answers are given by different systematic theories, such as those developed by Kantians, Contractualists, and Consequentialists. Such disagreements do not directly challenge the view that we are able to recognize some moral truths .... [W]e would expect there to be more disagreement about these other questions [as to why acts are wrong]. As I have also argued, however, when the most plausible systematic theories are developed further, as they need to be, these theories cease to conflict.[17]

This passage occurs in §121, 'The Convergence Claim'. Whilst it clearly chimes with Parts Two and Three and therefore allows us to sustain Wolf's criticism, other parts of §121 may cut against the overall picture.[18]

I have floated the idea that Parfit thinks there should be a singular and unique sense of best, with which we could decide each problem. There is evidence for that in Parts Two and Three, but notice that I qualified this claim in the previous section. In §121 Parfit also discusses comparisons and makes two relevant points. First, he talks of precision. He thinks that it is a mistake to assume a universal linear model of best to worst for all judgements. Sometimes it is impossible to compare apples with oranges, or a job in one city with a different job in another city, and say definitively which one is best. Hence there may be apparent disagreement: a clash of views that, on Parfit's view of disagreement, does not constitute a (proper) disagreement. We can say in such cases that each of the things we are comparing is equally good where we mean 'imprecisely equally good' but not rank and give them a precise ordering. Further, it may sometimes be impossible to say with precision exactly how many times better one thing is (the really juicy apple, say) than another (the adequate orange). Often such precise comparisons make no sense. Second, he talks of indeterminacy: some questions may not have an answer. Parfit thinks, for example, that indeterminacy applies to the case of baldness. Whilst it may not be true that some man is bald, we cannot thereby conclude that the man is not bald. The world may not divide easily into the bald and the not bald. Parfit thinks that this point carries over to some moral matters. He thinks that there may be some difficult moral questions that have no moral answer; his examples are the ethics of population and the morality of war. This may also explain some apparent disagreements, for people may assume that there are always definitive answers as to whether an act is wrong. But perhaps there are no such answers. In which case, what seem to be proper disagreements are not. He ends this part of his discussion with this:

> If we give to the world's poorest people one hundredth of our income, that is too little, and we are acting wrongly. If we give nearly everything, that would be enough and we would not be acting wrongly. But this question may sometimes have no answer. If we give certain proportions of our income, such as one tenth, or one quarter, it may not be true that we are *not* acting wrongly. But it may also not be true that we *are* acting wrongly.[19]

This whole train of thought can be used to defend Parfit. Despite the whole tone of Parts Two and Three, which leads Wolf to her worries, we could argue that Parfit is not interested in providing us with normative ethical materials to construct a singular notion of 'ethical best'. We cannot have a clear, precise, determinate ranking of all options open to us in a situation, from morally best to morally worst (from good to bad, in other words, with some clear cut-off points for right and wrong). This, then, undercuts Wolf's criticism. As Parfit will admit, through dint of circumstance we sometimes have to pick an option. And if we have chosen one option but are not confident that it is obviously best, then this will leave some moral residue: some regret, some disappointment.[20] This will then bring Parfit a lot closer to Wolf than she realizes.

Although this seems a promising line, I doubt whether it will answer the depth of Wolf's criticisms. For a start, Parfit's thoughts about imprecision and indeterminacy do not stop him repeating his hope for the Triple Theory that I quoted above: that such theories should cease to conflict when developed further. So, second, perhaps we can see a tension or, at least, some gap that indicates more detailed reflection is required. Perhaps Parfit operates throughout with a *general* singular notion of 'best'. He still wishes to talk of what overarching theories and substantial principles make lives go best overall, even if, within that, when one gets down to *more specific* details and comparisons, we may find it hard to decide which job or course of action is best or morally best. That then opens up a way of recasting some of Wolf's criticisms in the light of what Parfit says. He is focusing his efforts at far too general a level. In order to make good on the hope that the three theories can be combined, much of the detail of what they cast as being of value is eschewed. We lose sight of the value of consent and how complex it can be; we lose sight of when consequences matter and why they do; and so on. Wolf's worry can be extended in this direction. When we get to the specifics of comparisons we can see that it is often hard to determine which option is best. If Parfit had thought more about that and why such decisions are difficult or impossible, he would have acknowledged that we have many competing values and things that are valued, and that they compete profoundly and irreducibly. That might well have had an effect on what he says at the more general level with our broad normative theories. This focus on the general at the expense of the specific is interesting but, ultimately, misguided, as it does not do justice to the moral life.

We have, therefore, a challenge to Parfit that remains, which can be summarized in terms of a choice. Either he does think that values and things valued are commensurable, in which case Wolf's criticism holds. Or he thinks that his comments about incomparability and imprecision are such that they undercut many or all of Wolf's criticisms, despite what I have just said. But in that case he owes us a detailed explanation to that effect. Throughout, what we want is some sense of what exactly Parfit thinks is meant by 'best': does it have this singular quality that it appears to have in Parts Two and Three, or is the situation more complex? As part of this account we need a clear sense of what this means for the Triple Theory. How far does Parfit want the Triple Theory to deliver principles that directly guide and justify what we do, such that we know which actions are right and wrong? Does the amount of indeterminacy that there could be threaten the Triple Theory's effectiveness?[21]

This first theme bleeds into the second, as will be soon apparent. In articulating the second theme, I keep to my main thought that Wolf is onto something and that value incommensurability is both seemingly a real phenomenon and that it makes trouble for Parfit.

What of that second theme, the guidance of action? I first repeat a point already made: through dint of circumstance sometimes we need to compare in a very ordinary sense and make a choice as to how to act. But that does not imply that there has to be some common measure. We may well have feelings of regret and upset to deal with once a choice has been made. Such feelings may well indicate that there is a significant loss from not taking the road we could have taken, which in turn is best spelt out by embracing incommensurability of a sort.

Of course, some deny that we can have rational and justified guidance of action if we think that the ethical life admits a significant amount of value incommensurability. On that consider these brief points.

If one adopts the view that ethical choice is justified only if one adopts a strategy or conception of maximization when deciding what to do, then this spells trouble for those who admit of value incommensurability: it is hard to see how one can coherently try to maximize with no common measure and hence how one can say that moral choices are justified. However, the notion of moral justification is itself up for grabs. At the very least, one could adopt a strategy or conception of optimization: a choice is justified only if it is at least as good as each alternative (where, I venture, the 'at least as good as' can be based on the assumption that both options are good of their kind, and not be based on some notion of common measure).[22] I am not arguing that Parfit is adopting a maximization strategy. (Perhaps he may be, in the end.) I introduce this debate to note that he is again silent here. And we can go further than this narrow debate between maximizers and optimizers. What this debate shows us is that the notions of intelligible choice and justified action are themselves up for grabs, and this is a point we can also draw out from Wolf's commentary. Recall my earlier thought that Parfit and Wolf may be working with different conceptions of 'rational choice'. For Wolf, one's choice can be (fully) rational or justified even if there is no overarching reasoning (based on some assumption of common measure between values) just so long as one's choice is supported by *some* reasoning that is reasonable to mature users of ethical concepts. Parfit would reject this view, I suggest.[23]

Inspired by Wolf, I detect in Parfit the idea that if we admit value incommensurability into our ethical life, we are unable to do what normative ethicists should be doing, namely providing ethical guidance. The thought is that ethical guidance can come only if there is a clear, singular sense of what should be done, with all loose ends tied up. Again, this is suggested in Parts Two and Three of OWM by the notion that there must be some idea of what it is best to do and that our three theories are all aiming to give us the best way in which things can be. Perhaps this is unfair to Parfit, but he needs to counter this view or, if it is his view, he needs to argue for it.

Further to this, and more fundamentally, it seems reasonable to suggest that in OWM he thinks that the prime or even only point of normative ethical theory is to provide practical guidance, ignoring any issue of incommensurability. The whole point of the Triple Theory is to bring together seemingly different traditions into one overarching principle that will enable us to choose substantive principles that tell us how life can go best. But where is the argument for the view that this is the point of normative ethics? Wolf, whilst not denying that ethical guidance is important, at least wishes to stress that description of the ethical life which leaves some of it 'intact' is also an important function. For her, this is part of why we have (at least) three valuable ethical traditions: because the ethical life admits of value incommensurability then our three theories focus on different aspects of this life and bring different aspects to the fore. This in turn means they will be in deep tension with each other. Whilst she wishes to admit the tension, Parfit wishes to smooth it away. Description of and the noting of (seeming) tensions is important, for him, but only in service of the prime aim of providing clear guidance. Again some argument for this idea is required.

Perhaps some argument for this *can* be given. This brings us to the third of my themes. One way in which Parfit seems to defend himself is by having recourse to the notions of reality and disagreement. Towards the very end of his responses to Wolf he picks up on her thought that "there is no reason to think it would be a tragedy if there were no moral principle, and it would not be a moral tragedy if it turned out that morality were not so cleanly structured as to have one".[24] He agrees that it would not be a tragedy if there were no single supreme principle. Yet he continues:

> it would be a tragedy if there was no *single true morality*. And conflicting moralities could not all be true. In trying to combine these different kinds of moral theory, my main aim was not to find a supreme principle, but to find out whether one can resolve some deep disagreement. As Wolf claims, it would not matter greatly if morality *turned out* to be less unified, because there are several true principles, which could not be subsumed under any single higher principle. But if we cannot resolve our disagreements, that would give us reasons to doubt that there are *any* true principles. There might be nothing that morality *turns out to be*, since morality might be an illusion.[25]

Parfit suggests that he is being driven to resolve disagreement because he wishes to protect the reality of the moral in some sense. I believe that his view of matters is wrong here. As far as Wolf – and myself – are concerned, if there is a variety of ethical values, and if they are incommensurable, one would expect disagreement – disagreement about what should be done. If one views a normative ethic as, in part, a description of what is of value – that is, what values exist – then it could easily be the case that different kinds of ethical theory could all be true, *contra* Parfit's second sentence in the quotation. One is led to believe what Parfit believes only if one thinks there is no incommensurability and also if, relatedly, one thinks that all normative ethics are in the business of providing clear, practical guidance as to what should be done. Description of the moral world is important, of course, but only in service of this ultimate end. Or, to put it another way, it seems to me that Parfit here imagines that ethical truth is possible only if there is the possibility of clear, simple, singular guidance. As I say, this strikes me as quite wrong.

Ironically, this may be shown by what Parfit says in §121. If there really is incomparability because of imprecision and the like, rather than humans lacking the epistemic abilities to make correct comparisons, then that does not threaten the fact that there are values. It is just that the nature of the values that exist is more complex than one might at first think.

Again, Parfit could challenge some of what I have said here. Perhaps his small passages in §121 can be built up to show that he has a more nuanced view of the guidance of action than I have saddled him with. But, again, we require detail of this more complicated picture.

One last substantial point in this section. In one way it is perfectly cogent to think that practical guidance can be given only if we have commensurability. If normative ethics as a whole is riven with difference and disagreement, then clear, simple guidance will not be forthcoming from it *as a whole*. But, it need be no part of Wolf's view that practical guidance cannot be given by any particular theory. Nor that some views, principles and particular injunctions cannot be ruled out as unreasonable, immoral or whatever. Nor – importantly – that one cannot gain guidance and thought from normative ethics even if there is deep difference. Simply by articulating the various differences and relations that exist between certain courses of action, one gains insight that can have a real bearing on what one does.

So we have three themes, and I hope that I have not only articulated them but also shown how they intertwine. (Indeed, pulling them apart and presenting them as three themes is artificial anyway.) The message is clear: Parfit may not believe everything that Wolf or I load him with. But that requires correction from him, and if he does believe anything here he owes readers a defence. Further, such a defence has urgency *for Parfit* given that OWM is built upon the premise that seemingly conflicting theories can and should be seen as having more in common than we thought. In order to advance the Triple Theory we require a defence of the assumptions that allow it – or any other similar, unifying theory – to be advanced.

One could end the challenge there, but we can see these themes at work in the comments of Allen Wood.

Wood on methodology

Two preliminaries. First, it may be a surprise that I cast Wood as illustrating the power of Wolf's criticism. After all, Wood can be construed as being interested in offering clear guidance of the sort that Parfit aims for. Further, Wolf could criticize Wood for not appreciating the incommensurability of the moral – or at least the variety of the moral – in the way she imagines. (I point out how below.) However, the bare fact that Wood disagrees with Parfit should itself show Wolf's point: there is much of value that Parfit misses. In addition, and more intriguingly, Wood's criticisms echo some of Wolf's in a way that may not be immediately apparent.

Second, in his responses Parfit focuses on what Wood says about Kant. Whilst interesting, I read Wood as primarily concerned with commenting on Parfit's methodology, through his discussion of trolley problems. So it is good, I think, to air these comments again.

Having stated these preliminary points, what does Wood say? For Wood, there is a profound difference between the method he sees in Kant, Bentham and Mill, and which he endorses, and the method as assumed and employed by Sidgwick and Parfit. According to him, the latter pair use common-sense morality in order to formulate, test and revise moral principles, which in turn may lead to revisions in common sense. Despite this latter sort of revision, in this method common-sense morality is in the driving seat and the main use to which reason is put is in sharpening and refining it. The aim is to achieve a set of principles that, when combined with facts of a particular case, are enough to give us clear and specific direction as to what we should do.

In contrast, the method that Wood favours gives an unquestionable and central role to some fundamental idea or principle. From first principles, and from reasoning about deep intuitions about the nature of morality itself, we establish some basic idea about morality. In the case of Kant, this is to identify morality with rationality, whilst for Bentham and Mill the link is with human happiness. The articulation of this basic moral idea sets the scene for everything that follows. It gives us the entire moral landscape and allows (more specific) moral reasoning and judgement to happen. Three other ideas are crucial. First, we are able to judge what we should do. But we do not infer directly from the fundamental idea or principle to any particular case. Instead, we have some mediating principles, principles that are more general than the particular case but are a more specific articulation of the general idea. Second, common-sense moral intuitions cannot be used to challenge the fundamental principle or idea. As I see it, Wood thinks of this idea as establishing the moral landscape in the first place. Third, this fundamental idea is linked to what is practical through some judgement and interpretation of that idea. This is contrasted with the Sidgwick–Parfit method, which seeks to discern a precise principle that tells us what to do once the (nonmoral) facts are established.

There are questions to raise about this. We might ask whether Wood is correct that the methodologies he contrasts can be found in Kant, Bentham, Mill and Sidgwick. I leave this question aside but agree with his broad characterization of Parfit. We might also ask for more detail about the contrast between 'precise principles' that when matched with facts deliver exact practical advice and the exercise of judgement in applying some general, fundamental moral vision. I am happy to accept that there is something to Wood's contrast, albeit something that requires sharpening.

Wood furthers many of these points about methodology by thinking about trolley problems. He is sceptical about how effective they are and how much they unjustifiably skew how we should reason morally. He lists a number of interrelated worries with them and the methodology behind them. Here are four.

First, we are led to think that the chief bearers of value are states of affairs, in a way familiar from discussions of consequentialism. Of course, we need to think how we act as well and not just consider death, injury and survival. But those possible end points are the driving force behind what we do. Other considerations, such as "circumstantial rights, claims and entitlements", which people have in real-life situations, are 'ignored or stipulated away'.[26] Second, in putting forward his support for the Formula of Humanity, Wood argues that trolley problems encourage us to think that "human lives have the sort of value that can be measured and reckoned up".[27] They may even encourage us to think that this is the chief subject matter of normative ethics.[28] Third, matters are set up so that we have to reach a determinate decision. Even if the correct moral reaction might be to question the set-up itself, this is not permitted. Lives are at stake and we must decide to do something.[29] Fourth, it is often stipulated what the morally relevant features are and that there are no others. From this it is assumed that the agent knows a great deal and can be confident of what will happen, in a way that is quite unrealistic. This matters because the intuitions drawn from such cases are therefore unreliable data: we go from intuitions about a suspect scenario to construct principles that are supposed to have some secure moral foundation, so that they can be of concrete help in real-life scenarios.

In summary, Wood gives us a significant distinction between two methodologies. But his criticism is not just that. In skewing everyday moral thought, Parfit encourages us to think that this methodology is the only game in town: this is just what moral thinking *is*.

I find Wood's approach refreshing and appealing. Yet Parfit, or anyone who endorses the methodology Wood dislikes, has a ready response to at least some of the details of the criticism. Once we have thought about this I will connect Wood to Wolf.

A response to Wood on behalf of Parfit

My partial defence of Parfit begins from something Wood says.

> There are some extreme and desperate situations in human life – such as war or anarchy, or sometimes pestilence, famine or natural disaster – in which it can look as if the only way to think rationally about them is simply to consider coldly and grimly the number of people, the amounts of benefit and harm, and the kinds of actions available to you that will produce the benefit and harm. But it is significant that we should think of such decisions as being made coldly and grimly, calculating consequences with a kind of economist's tunnel-vision while totally denying all of our human thought and feeling. For those are situations in which human beings have been deprived of humanizing social institutions (like those that should provide enough lifeboats . . .) that make it rationally possible *not* to look at matters in this way. I grant you that trolley problems might help you to think in a rational (if dehumanized) fashion about situations in which that is the only way left to think about them because the situations themselves have already been dehumanized. That is a powerful argument *against* using trolley problems in moral philosophy.

> We think of war as a morally unacceptable condition, in large part because in war it can indeed seem rational for people to think about their lives and the lives of others in truly monstrous ways. One of our primary tasks as human beings is to view things in better ways, and if necessary to make changes to the world (regulating the behaviour of doctors and trolley systems) so as to bring it about that there are other ways of viewing things rationally. If you take some part of human life (such as health-care delivery) which is not as inherently barbarous as war, and come to regard this as the only way to think about it . . . then that amounts to a voluntary decision on your part to turn health care, or even human life as a whole, into something horrible and inhuman, something like war, that ought never to exist.[30]

I think Wood overplays the analogy and the descriptions. War *is* monstrous and much of the decision-making in war is also monstrous. (I presume Wood has in mind decisions that involve where to place one's troops and resources so as to engage with the enemy, knowing full well that this will result in severe injury and death for 'us' and 'them'.[31]) But just because the reasoning in war is similar to the reasoning in health-care allocation does not mean that health-care allocation is monstrous, nor that any reasoning involved in it is monstrous. Nor is such reasoning morally reprehensible in some lesser way. Health-care administrators, and other officials charged with the organization and distribution of resources, have some hard choices to make, precisely because of the clash between seemingly unquenchable demand and the limited nature of those resources. Administrators and managers need to make sure that their decisions are sound, fair and transparent to others. Further, they need to make sure that how they reason can be adopted by others and at least serve as an initial basis for other, similar situations. One way in which to achieve all of this is to adopt the Sidgwick–Parfit methodology. We judge which features are relevant to our decision in this situation. We focus on these features. We make a judgement. We test that judgement by placing those features in a slightly changed situation. Does the same moral judgement seem acceptable? If so, why? If not, why not? By repeating this process can we garner more general moral principles that may serve to help us and many other people across many situations? And so on.

Further, although we may get a sense of how we should reason morally from our 'common sense', resource allocation is such a fraught business that some may think it is better to decide that much, if not everything, is up for grabs when we reason. That may include our initial moral intuitions. If these intuitions lead us to unacceptable or imperfect results, then we need to rethink them.

Nothing here seems to be morally terrible, let alone monstrous. It is reasoning motivated by the best of intentions: to make sure that medicines get to sick people, that roads get repaired in the correct order, that there are enough good schools and places for our children and so on. What may be morally regrettable and even terrible is that some people lose out: some children have to go further to schools than others; some ill people suffer and may even die because they cannot get the medicines and treatment they require. Although these are bad matters, this seems to be a direct function of the gulf that exists between demand and supply. Why is the methodology itself to be blamed?

Indeed, we should note that Wood's methodology will not be able to solve the issue, or, at least, cannot do so obviously. Talk of moral orientation and exercise of judgement seems all very well, as does an emphasis that we should make moral judgements humane. But in the end a judgement will be made where some people get their roads and school places and medicines, and some do not. Parfit, or his supporter, might reply that at least the supposedly suspect methodology is honest about this.

There are also some details of Wood's account that I find Parfit can question. In the previous section I listed four criticisms of trolley problems. The first was that people, including Parfit, are led to believe that the ultimate bearers of value are states of affairs, and this is fraught with philosophical difficulty. And, in the quotation just given, Wood talks of calculating consequences in some grim way. Further, we can imagine someone advancing the view that Parfit thinks of human lives as a mere resource, to be employed in the service of some ultimate best state of affairs. I do not think this is fair to Parfit. I do not detect an explicit argument or theme that states of affairs are the ultimate bearers of value and no thought that people are resources in some ultimate (and monstrous) way. True, he does talk of optimific results and the adoption of principles that will lead to the ideal state.[32] But this is far from the sort of consequentialism that Wood may have in mind. Parfit is thinking in terms of the best moral life and world, in the way that most moral thinkers think.

I mention all of this since it may detract from what is of real value in Wood's commentary. Think of the second and third points I listed when thinking about trolley problems.[33] Humans and human lives may not be a resource, to be used in the service of states of affairs, but they can still be measured and reckoned up, balanced against one another. Further – and I now emphasize a justificatory link – we can treat them in this way and must treat them in this way *because* we must reach a determinate decision in every problematic situation. We have to decide what to do, and so we must decide whether to save a life or significantly injure someone else against their will and then discern the principle that justifies our action and see how far it extends to other cases.

These points hit home and they return us – I hope, obviously – to Wolf.

Wolf and Wood

First, it is easy to see what support Wood gains from Wolf. We may feel awkward about Parfit's methodology and about trolley problems in part because Wolf is correct about the variety of what is of value and the fact that such value has a fundamentally incommensurate nature. We are asked to make determinate, clear decisions where we may also need to acknowledge the range of considerations that are left behind and further acknowledge those considerations and questions that sit outside traditional characterizations of trolley problems.

At this point we can easily return to my highlighting of §121. Wolf *and* Wood clearly do not get the impression from Parts Two and Three that Parfit is willing to allow some measure of imprecision and indeterminacy in moral thought. This again highlights the need for more detail and also shows us that the point I made with reference to Wolf's criticism applies to Wood. If Parfit had thought in a more detailed fashion about the phenomena of indeterminacy and imprecision, he may have been led to realize that value is complex and admits of incommensurability of a sort. That may have led him to recast and rethink the importance of trolley problems and his whole methodology. More factors than are typically listed in such problems may be important. One's view about how people should take normative ethical decisions and what their reasoning should be may have to change.

This, of course, exposes how Wood and Wolf are in tension. Whilst both may agree that there is a fundamental flaw in thinking there is a precise principle to take us from 'here to there' which leaves little or no residue, Wood still views value and what is of value from a certain perspective, namely a Kantian one. His general orientation will be different from Mill's, for example. I strongly suspect that Wolf will think this orientation is too narrow and does insufficient justice to the variety of life. Wood may be able to register support for the idea of value incommensurability, but he will not see as much that is of value, in as many ways, as Wolf may want.

Second, we can also see how Wolf can gain support from Wood. The Triple Theory in its present form does not work because there is at least one perspective, a particular Kantian view, that is missing from what Parfit has given us. But this is not just a matter of a quick fix. The deeper point that Wood shows us is that there is a fundamental disagreement to be had about normative ethical methodology. One's choice of methodology shows what one thinks is of value in practical reasoning simply because one presents a certain view as being constitutive of practical reasoning. One is giving a vision of the ethical life. (Again, this is the idea that Wood thinks a reader of OWM might think trolley-problem methodology is the only game in town.) So Parfit's methodology is presented or assumed to have not only philosophical value but also ethical value. It is an ethical claim that what we should be doing when we think ethically is primarily or exclusively justifying why people should perform certain actions and in that way motivating them accordingly. In contrast, I think that Wolf is arguing that registering and describing the various aspects of our moral lives is also of ethical value, even where (and perhaps because) such aspects are incommensurate with each other. Wood in part shows us this because he gives us a perspective where a different sort of methodology is seen as valuable, one where we do not try to offer precise practical guidance but instead try to articulate what is of value and how it is valuable, from within a perspective, and exercise judgement.

Again, there is some difference between Wood and Wolf. Wood is a Kantian, after all, and so what he regards as morally valuable and why it is so will be more limited than that offered by Wolf, I imagine. Plus he too is interested in guiding action. And it may be that he thinks of action guidance as the prime aim of morality. That said, these may be matters of emphasis for Wood: moral thinking should have as its main goal practical guidance, but whether it is its only goal is moot. And he may also be able to register support for value incommensurability in a way that Parfit cannot: the stress on, and worries about, the ideas of measuring and reckoning up suggests that. So, despite their differences, Wood and Wolf can still be seen closer to one another than either is to Parfit.

Conclusion

As I mentioned earlier when discussing Wolf, many of the ideas and themes mentioned here are intertwined and pulling them apart is somewhat artificial. But I hope that the overall challenge is clear. Are we content to jettison so much of what is part and parcel of three familiar normative ethical theories simply to provide guidance in a fairly simplified and unified way? (And is this *really* what Parfit is articulating? It is unclear.) The hope embodied by the Triple Theory is to give us moral progress: progress in thought and deed. Yet, in order to give us the sort of justification Parfit wants, something will be lost. And whilst there are some things that are lost which *deserve* to be lost, many other things do not. There are conflicting visions of the moral life that have to be lost mainly because we cannot imagine having a proper normative ethic that acknowledges and incorporates conflict. But why can't we? A moral vision that embraces conflict, and leaves room for value incommensurability, may itself be morally important.[34]

Notes

1. Some of their criticisms are echoed in Kitcher (2012).
2. OWM 2, p. 34. As I read him Parfit is not saying that the best versions of the three theories *happen* to converge on the same substantive principles. Revisions to these theories show that they have far more in common than is often thought, so it is no surprise that they converge as they do.
3. OWM 2, p. 35.
4. In case it is not obvious, I will not engage in Kantian scholarship here. Parfit thinks he has clear and good reason for reading Kant as he does, and then for adapting and improving on Kant. Putting aside what Kant himself may have meant, there is clearly a Kantian picture or pictures that is or are quite different from Parfit's.
5. OWM 2, pp. 39–40.
6. OWM 2, p. 41.
7. See also Schroeder (2011), who emphasizes Parfit's concern to show the possibility of moral progress.
8. OWM 2, pp. 46ff.
9. OWM 2, pp. 47–8. The two phrases quoted in the paragraph below are from p. 48.
10. OWM 2, pp. 147–52.
11. Apologies for the ugliness of this term.
12. OWM 2, p. 151.
13. I comment little on this idea, but this is what I take the Triple Theory to be, ultimately.
14. OWM 2, p. 35.
15. OWM 2, p. 53.
16. Here I leave aside some of the details of the recent discussion, such as how best to understand exactly the terms 'commensurable' and 'incommensurable', for example. For more on this whole issue see Chang (1997) and Hsieh (2013).
17. OWM 2, p. 554.
18. The following thoughts echo RP, pp. 146ff on the *mere addition paradox*.
19. OWM 2, p. 562.
20. For more on this phenomenon see Williams (1973), p. 179, and (1981).
21. I am grateful to an anonymous referee for pushing me on this point.
22. See Sen (1997), p. 746, and (2000), p. 486. For summary, see Hsieh §4.1.
23. For more on this general debate, see Anderson (1993) and (1997).
24. OWM 2, p. 35.
25. OWM 2, p. 155 (emphases original).
26. OWM 2, p. 70.
27. OWM 2, p. 68.
28. OWM 2, p. 77.

29 OWM 2, p. 72.
30 OWM 2, pp. 79–80.
31 I suspect that other decisions that are made in war and that are essential to it need not be monstrous, although they could be regrettable given the situational background. But I won't argue for that here.
32 For example, the argument in OWM 1, p. 408.
33 I ignore the fourth, that concerning the stipulation of the situation and the fact that the data are unreliable. It may be relevant to what I say, but I exclude it for reasons of space.
34 I am grateful to Sophie-Grace Chappell and Nicholas Smyth, both of whom read an earlier draft of this chapter, and to Alexandra Trofimov for the many conversations we have had about OWM and Parfit's methodology. I am also grateful to three anonymous referees for their comments.

References

Anderson, Elizabeth (1993) *Value in Ethics and Economics* (Cambridge, MA: Harvard University Press).

Anderson, Elizabeth (1997) 'Practical Reason and Incommensurable Goods', in *Incommensurability, Incomparability, and Practical Reason*, Ruth Chang (ed.) (Cambridge, MA: Harvard University Press, 1997), pp. 90–109.

Chang, Ruth (1997) (ed.) *Incommensurability, Incomparability, and Practical Reason* (Cambridge, MA: Harvard University Press).

Hsieh, Nien-hê (2013) 'Incommensurable Values', in the *Stanford Encyclopedia of Philosophy*, Edward N. Zalta (ed.): http://plato.stanford.edu/entries/value-incommensurable/.

Kitcher, Philip (2012) 'The Lure of the Peak', *New Republic*, 2 February: http://www.newrepublic.com/article/books/magazine/99529/on-what-matters-derek-parfit.

Parfit, Derek (1984) *Reasons and Persons* (Oxford: Oxford University Press).

Parfit, Derek (2011) *On What Matters* (Oxford: Oxford University Press), vols 1 and 2.

Schroeder, Mark (2011) 'Review of *On What Matters, Volumes 1 and 2*', *Notre Dame Philosophical Reviews*, 1 August: http://ndpr.nd.edu/news/25393-on-what-matters-volumes-1-and-2/.

Sen, Amartya (1997) 'Maximization and the Act of Choice', *Econometrica* 65, pp. 745–79.

Sen, Amartya (2000) 'Consequential Evaluation and Practical Reason', *Journal of Philosophy* 98, pp. 477–502.

Williams, Bernard (1973) 'Ethical Consistency' in his *Problems of the Self* (Cambridge: Cambridge University Press), pp. 166–86.

Williams, Bernard (1981) 'Conflicts of Values' in his *Moral Luck* (Cambridge: Cambridge University Press), pp. 71–82.

2

NORMATIVE NATURALISM AND NORMATIVE NIHILISM

Parfit's dilemma for naturalism

David Copp

The fundamental issue dividing normative naturalists and non-naturalists concerns the nature of normativity. Non-naturalists typically hold that the normativity of moral properties and facts sets them apart from natural properties and facts in an important and deep way. Because these properties and facts are normative, they are in a fundamentally different metaphysical category from garden-variety natural properties and facts such as meteorological, psychological, or economic ones. Naturalists deny this. They should agree that the normative and the *non-normative* are importantly different, but they deny that the normative and the *natural* are importantly different since they hold that normative properties and facts *are* natural. They contend that these properties and facts are similar in all metaphysically and epistemologically important respects to other natural properties and facts.

If Derek Parfit is correct, however, the naturalist's project is deeply misguided. Indeed, he makes the astonishing claim that normative naturalism is "close to nihilism."[1] If normative naturalism were true, he contends, "there would be no point in trying to answer such questions" as "what matters, which actions are right or wrong, and what we have reasons to want, and to do."[2] We philosophers who have worked in moral philosophy, trying to answer such questions, "would have wasted much of our lives" and "our only consolation would be that it didn't matter" since "nothing matters."[3] Parfit similarly contends that the truth of normative naturalism would "eliminate morality."[4] His most direct argument for this pessimistic view may be his so-called "Soft Naturalist's Dilemma." He holds that if normative naturalists are correct that there are no "irreducibly normative facts," then normativity is "an illusion."[5] I find this a surprising and puzzling view, and my goal in this chapter is to understand it and, I hope, to set it to rest. Properly understood, naturalism does not eliminate normativity. It aims to explain what normativity consists in.

Parfit presents his arguments against naturalism in his major work, *On What Matters*. I have discussed his arguments systematically in another place,[6] but I think that Parfit and many other non-naturalists may be driven to reject naturalism less by arguments than by the prior conviction that no natural fact *could* be normative. Their view is that normative naturalism is hopeless, not in detail, but in basic conception. They have the sense that it is simply impossible that any normative moral property such as wrongness could be identical to a natural property. Hence, Parfit suggests, just as "heat could not have turned out to be a cabbage," so normative naturalism could not possibly be true.[7] I aim to uncover the mistake behind this thought.

In the first section I introduce the Dilemma, but before I can begin to explore responses to it, I need to prepare the ground. Hence, in the second section, I explain some key details of the naturalist's view. In the third section I return to the Dilemma and discuss some preliminary responses. In the fourth section I propose a further response. Toward the end of this section I suggest that this response can be strengthened if we can make sense of the idea that motivation is in an interesting sense 'internal' to certain ways of thinking of normative properties. In the fifth section I introduce and explain my use of the term 'way of thinking,' or 'WOT,' and distinguish the idea of a WOT from the idea of a concept. In the sixth section I introduce the idea of an 'internal' WOT of a normative property. In concluding, I return to Parfit's Dilemma and explain how the account of internal normative WOTs can help to explain where Parfit goes wrong.

Perhaps the most interesting and novel idea in the chapter is the proposal that there are two normative ways of thinking of a normative property: the *ordinary* normative WOT and the *internal* normative WOT. Postulating the internal normative WOT helps to explain what underlies J.L. Mackie's argument from queerness against moral realism;[8] it helps to explain the persistence of the dispute between moral-judgment externalists and internalists; and it helps to explain John McDowell's view that virtuous people conceive of situations in a distinctive way.[9] I will not be able to discuss these claims here, unfortunately.[10] The important point is that postulating the internal normative WOT helps to explain the widespread resistance to normative naturalism, and it provides the naturalist with an additional response to Parfit's Dilemma.

The Soft Naturalist's Dilemma

Let me now explain Parfit's Soft Naturalist's Dilemma. Here and throughout the chapter I will follow Parfit in using a kind of utilitarian normative naturalism to illustrate normative naturalism. According to the utilitarian naturalist, wrongness, for example, is the property of failing to maximize the general welfare.[11]

As Parfit explains matters, the normative naturalist distinguishes between normative *concepts* and the natural *properties* to which these concepts refer and also between normative *propositions* and the natural *facts* (or states of affairs) in virtue of which such propositions are true when they are true. She therefore purports to explain how there can be true normative beliefs and propositions and to do so without postulating the existence of anything non-natural. According to the utilitarian naturalist, for example, since wrongness is the property of failing to maximize the general welfare, wrongness can be represented in two ways, by the normative concept *wrongness* and by the naturalistic concept *fails to maximize the general welfare*. On this view, moreover, a proposition to the effect that such and such is wrong is made true by the same natural state of affairs that makes it true that such and such fails to maximize the general welfare. This state of affairs can be represented in two ways, by the proposition that such and such is wrong and by the proposition that such and such fails to maximize the general welfare.

Parfit distinguishes between "Hard Naturalist" and "Soft Naturalist" positions.[12] A Hard Naturalist claims that we have no reason to use normative language in making normative claims. In principle, we could express all facts in purely naturalistic language. The moral terms could be removed from our language and the moral concepts could be removed from our thinking without any loss in expressive power. A Soft Naturalist claims that even though we could in principle express all facts in purely naturalistic language, we still have good reason to use normative language in making normative claims.

Parfit contends that Soft Naturalism faces a dilemma. According to normative naturalism, normative claims are intended to state facts. Given this, he thinks, a naturalist must say that there is reason to use normative language only if there are facts that cannot be expressed in naturalistic terms. Naturalism denies that there are such facts, and yet Soft Naturalism claims that there nevertheless is reason to continue to have normative concepts and to use normative sentences. This is incoherent. So a naturalist is committed to Hard Naturalism.[13] Hard Naturalism implies that normative claims are of no importance. Parfit contends, then, that "Naturalism is close to Nihilism."[14]

The idea seems to be this. Naturalism holds that there are normative propositions and normative concepts but there are only natural properties and natural states of affairs. Natural properties are the referents of the normative concepts, and natural states of affairs are the truth makers of normative propositions. But these properties and states of affairs can just as accurately be represented by non-normative natural concepts and propositions. Accordingly, the moral terms could be removed from our language and the moral concepts could be removed from our thinking without any cognitive loss. We have normative concepts, and we can use them in formulating normative propositions, but Parfit takes the naturalist to be committed to thinking we have no reason to do so. This is why normative naturalism is close to normative nihilism. We have no need for normative concepts since there are only natural properties and states of affairs.

Normative naturalism

To see clearly where Parfit's reasoning goes wrong, we need to be clear about the naturalist's position. In this section, then, I first explain the kind of 'reductive naturalism' that I will be assuming is at issue. Second, I discuss the implications of this view for the issue of whether there are any normative properties or facts. To properly address this question, third, I distinguish between 'worldly' and 'propositional' conceptions of facts. Fourth, I explain the 'fine-grained' criterion for the individuation of propositions that I will be assuming in this chapter. Finally, I explain why a naturalist should claim that there can be more than one concept of a normative property. All of this will help make sense of Parfit's Dilemma.

A: reductive naturalism. Naturalists and non-naturalists are normative realists who agree that there are normative properties. They agree there is such a thing as wrongness, for example. The characteristic thesis of moral naturalism is that moral properties are *natural* properties.[15] The *normative* naturalist claims, more generally, that *normative* properties are natural properties. This is the thesis Parfit and other non-naturalists want to deny.

Unfortunately, there is disagreement as to what is meant by a 'natural' property. That is, there is not an agreed criterion as to what distinguishes natural properties from putatively non-natural properties. For our purposes, we can take it that natural properties are those that are 'countenanced' in what we might characterize as 'a scientifically constrained view of what exists.'[16] I intend this characterization to allow a property to count as natural even if it is not *studied* in any science—examples might be the property of being a fountain pen and the property of being a Canadian 'looney' coin, which I count as natural properties—and to exclude only properties that would not be countenanced in a scientifically constrained view, such as the property of having a soul. Non-naturalists can agree with this characterization of natural properties. They hold that normative properties differ fundamentally from properties that would be countenanced in a scientifically constrained view of what exists.

To focus attention clearly on the issues, I am going to restrict attention to naturalist theories that are 'reductive.' Reductive naturalism aims to identify each normative property with a property that would be countenanced in a scientifically constrained view of what exists. To be more specific, reductive naturalism proposes that, for any normative property M-ness, there is a non-trivial and explanatorily and philosophically interesting truth of the form 'To be M is to be N,' where N is replaced by a term standing for a property that would be countenanced in a scientifically constrained view of what exists.[17] A reductive naturalist might of course aim, more realistically, to defend a philosophically interesting identity statement of this kind for at least *some* normative property.

Reductive naturalism is not committed to the further thesis that the crucial statements of the form 'To be M is to be N' are analytic or conceptual truths. This thesis would be difficult to defend since there seems to be a logical and conceptual gap between any description of a state of affairs in wholly naturalistic terms and any normative evaluation of it. For this reason, the most defensible form of normative naturalism is a kind of 'nonanalytic naturalism' that rejects the further thesis. In what follows I will be discussing nonanalytic reductive naturalism.

B: *normative properties*. If the naturalist holds that the property M-ness is identical to the natural property N-ness, she obviously is committed to holding either that this property is *not* normative or that it *is* normative. For instance, the utilitarian normative naturalist must contend either that the property wrongness—which she holds to be identical to the property of undermining the general welfare—is normative or that it is not normative. So far I have been writing as if the naturalist must contend that the properties at issue *are* normative. But Parfit may be thinking that since, for instance, the property of undermining the general welfare obviously is not normative, the utilitarian naturalist must admit that on her view wrongness also is *not* normative.

At issue is the second-order property of being normative. Intuitively, this property is possessed by a variety of properties, including wrongness, the property of being morally required, the property of being rationally required, and so on. Intuitively, as well, evaluative properties are normative, including the property a person can have of being virtuous and the property of being good. The naturalist has the choice of two strategies. There is the 'eliminativist' strategy of arguing that in fact no property is normative since all (putatively) normative properties are natural and no natural property is normative. And there is the 'bold' strategy of arguing that in fact some natural properties are normative since all normative properties are natural properties. To my mind, the best strategy is the bold one, the strategy of maintaining that the natural properties that are identical to properties such as wrongness are in fact normative properties. Some natural properties are normative. In what follows I will be discussing versions of nonanalytic reductive naturalism that take up this bold strategy.

To make good on the bold strategy, a naturalist would need to explain what it is for a property to be normative. Unless she can explain this, she would be hard pressed to explain how it could be that a natural property is normative. Note, however, that although a naturalist needs to explain what the *property* of being normative consists in, she has no need to hold that the *concept* of normativity is analyzable. Naturalists and non-naturalists can in principle agree that the *concept* is not analyzable, and, indeed, this seems plausible. If so, then we cannot reasonably demand an analysis of the concept, whether from naturalists or from non-naturalists. It might be possible, nevertheless, to provide an illuminating account of what normativity is or about what all normative considerations have in common, without providing an analysis.

In other work I have provided a naturalistic account of normativity that I call *pluralist-teleology*.[18] Obviously, I cannot attempt to argue for the theory here, or even to explain it in detail, but I can offer it to illustrate the kind of account that I believe a naturalist needs to provide in order to take up the bold strategy that I recommend.

According to pluralist-teleology, normative facts are grounded in facts about solutions to, or ways to ameliorate, certain generic problems faced by human beings in their ordinary lives. These are problems that we can better cope with when we subscribe to appropriate systems of norms than would otherwise be the case, so I call them *problems of normative governance*. A familiar example is the problem of *sociality*. People need to live in societies in order to meet many of their basic needs and to be in a position to achieve the things they value, but there are a variety of familiar causes of discord and conflict that can undermine cooperation and make a society less successful than it otherwise could be at enabling people to pursue what they value with a reasonable prospect of success. This is the problem of sociality. Unless it is mitigated in some way, members of the society are less able than would otherwise be the case to achieve what they value. Plainly, widespread subscription to a moral code can help to ameliorate the problem, provided that the code calls for people to be willing to cooperate and generally to avoid discord and conflict.[19] Of course, some moral codes would do better than others at ameliorating the situation. To simplify, say that the *ideal moral code* is the code with the currency that would do most to ameliorate the problem of sociality.[20] Pluralist-teleology says, in effect, that morality is the solution to the problem of equipping people to live comfortably and successfully together in societies.[21] According to pluralist-teleology, the normative truth in a given context, where a specific normative question has been raised, is, roughly, a function of the content of the system of norms with the currency that would do most to ameliorate the relevant problem of normative governance. Thus, for example, the moral truth depends on the content of the ideal moral code. Wrongness is the property (roughly) of being ruled out or prohibited by the ideal code.

A naturalist needs to provide some such account of normativity in order to sustain the bold strategy that I am recommending. It is also the case, however, that a non-naturalist needs to explain what it is for a property to be normative in order to explain why, in her view, it is not possible for a natural property to be normative. Non-naturalist theories typically hold, however, that normativity is unanalyzable, that normativity cannot be analyzed in non-normative terms. This places them in an awkward position. They claim that no natural property could be normative, but it is difficult to see how they could explain why this is so without providing an account of what normativity consists in.

To be sure, non-naturalists have attempted to give an account of what all normative considerations have in common. Parfit distinguishes four conceptions of normativity, and he contends that one of the four, the conception of normativity in the "reason-implying sense," is the philosophically most important.[22] This view has been called 'reasons-fundamentalism.'[23] It contends that all normative considerations have in common that they are suitably related to reasons. An alternative is 'ought-fundamentalism,' which contends that the mark of the normative is a suitable relation to claims about what ought to be done or believed or the like.[24] These approaches may be illuminating, but they do not explain what normativity *consists in*. They attempt, rather, to reduce all normative considerations to one fundamental kind of normative consideration. To see this, note that there are kinds of reason that presumably are not normative in the most interesting and important sense, perhaps including reasons of etiquette. To account for this, reasons-fundamentalism needs to be understood as

33

claiming to explain normativity in terms of reasons that are *normative*. This is not meant as an objection. I am, rather, pointing out that reasons-fundamentalism does not explain what it is for a reason to be normative. A non-naturalist might take the idea of the normative to be unanalyzable, but this approach will not help her to explain why she thinks it is not possible for a natural property to be normative.

Naturalists and non-naturalists take themselves to disagree as to whether a natural property could be normative in the philosophically most important sense. To see them as disagreeing rather than as talking at cross purposes, we need to suppose that they share a concept of normativity. They may show themselves to share a concept in their agreement about examples, such as the agreement that moral requirements are normative in the philosophically most important sense. Agreement about key examples may be enough to enable us to proceed.

C: two conceptions of facts. On a 'worldly' conception, *facts* are the *truth makers* of propositions; they explain the truth values of propositions; perhaps they are *states of affairs*. As I understand normative naturalism, it holds that normative propositions can be true in a robust sense, such that they are made true by some relevant worldly fact (or state of affairs).[25] There is a contrasting 'propositional' conception of facts, according to which a fact is simply a true proposition—taking propositions for our purposes here to be the bearers of truth value. In this chapter, unless I indicate otherwise, I will be using 'fact' in the worldly sense, to refer to states of affairs. But in some contexts the propositional conception will be at issue.

On the worldly conception of a fact, the naturalist claims that normative facts are natural facts. On the propositional conception, however, the naturalist can agree that normative facts are *not* natural facts. This may be confusing, but it is an important point. To explain it, I need to introduce the fine-grained criterion for individuating propositions.

D: a fine-grained criterion for the individuation of propositions. Even given that water is H_2O, the belief that water is H_2O seems clearly to be distinct from the belief that water is water. If beliefs are individuated by their propositional objects, then, since these are different beliefs, they must have different propositions as their objects. The proposition that water is H_2O must be distinct from the proposition that water is water. To make sense of this, we need a fine-grained criterion for the individuation of propositions. On Jeffrey King's approach, these propositions are distinguished from one another on the basis that they have different *structures*,[26] but there may be other fine-grained theories. We may, for example, think that propositions are structures of concepts and note that, even if water is H_2O, the *concept* of water is different from the *concept* of H_2O.[27] The important point for now is that we need a theory that allows us to distinguish the proposition that water is H_2O from the proposition that water is water.

On the propositional conception of facts, a fact is a true proposition, so a fine-grained criterion for individuating propositions commits us to a similar criterion for individuating facts. On such an approach, then, on the propositional conception of facts, the fact that water is H_2O is distinct from the fact that water is water. Such an account has important implications for normative naturalism. For, on a fine-grained account, a normative naturalist can claim, for example, that even on the assumption that wrongness is identical to the property of undermining the general welfare, the *proposition* that torture is wrong is distinct from the *proposition* that torture undermines the general welfare. Accordingly, on a propositional conception of facts, the naturalist can claim that the *fact* that torture is wrong is distinct from the *fact* that torture undermines the general welfare. This is not problematic. A naturalist must identify normative *properties* with natural *properties* and normative *states of affairs* with natural *states of affairs*. The utilitarian naturalist claims that wrongness is identical to the property of undermining the general welfare and that the state of affairs that torture is wrong is a natural state of affairs. Nevertheless, on the propositional account of facts, the fact that torture is wrong is distinct from the fact that torture fails to maximize the general welfare. If we view facts as true propositions, then even if a normative property M-ness is identical to the natural property N-ness, the naturalist may say that M-facts are distinct from N-facts.

E: *concepts of normative properties*. A naturalist needs to claim that there can be more than one concept or way of thinking of a normative property. On a fine-grained account of the individuation of propositions, we can make sense of the idea that, even if wrongness is identical to the property of undermining the general welfare, a person can believe that an action will undermine the general welfare without believing that it is wrong and vice versa. For on a plausible fine-grained account, the proposition that an action will undermine the general welfare is distinct from the proposition that this action is wrong even if, as the utilitarian naturalist holds, there is only the one property. Because these are distinct propositions, a person could have the one belief without having the other belief. This can be explained on the basis that the concept of wrongness is distinct from the concept of undermining the general welfare. Only the one property is at issue, but different concepts of it represent it in different ways. These different concepts would be involved in the different beliefs, for, plausibly, the propositions that are the objects of these beliefs are structures of concepts,[28] and these propositions involve different concepts.

Consider, then, a bold form of nonanalytic reductive normative naturalism according to which the normative property M-ness is identical to some natural property N-ness. Since M-ness is a normative property, if M-ness is identical to N-ness, it follows that N-ness is also normative. According to normative naturalism, then, importantly, there are *natural* properties and *natural* states of affairs that are *normative*. Moreover, the theory implies that the concept of M-ness and the concept of N-ness are both concepts of the one property, M-ness or N-ness. It also implies that the proposition that such and such is M and the proposition that such and such is N represent the same state of affairs or worldly fact. These propositions both would be made true by this worldly fact, viz. the natural state of affairs that such and such is N (or M).

Initial responses to the Soft Naturalist's Dilemma

Let me now return to Parfit's Soft Naturalist's Dilemma and discuss certain initial responses to it. Recall that Parfit is contending that "Naturalism is close to Nihilism" (368).[29] According to Parfit, the Soft Naturalist contends that, although we could in principle express all facts in purely naturalistic language, we still have good reason to use normative language in making normative claims. Parfit argues that this position is incoherent. His idea seems to be that, according to the normative naturalist, there are normative propositions and normative concepts but there are only natural properties and natural states of affairs. According to the naturalist, these properties and states of affairs can be represented just as accurately by non-normative natural concepts and propositions as by normative concepts and propositions. The naturalist therefore must agree, Parfit thinks, that the moral terms could be removed from our language and the moral concepts could be removed from our thinking without any cognitive loss. We can use normative concepts in formulating normative propositions, but Parfit takes the naturalist to be committed to thinking we have no need to do so in order to accurately represent the worldly facts. Naturalism is close to normative nihilism.

In an earlier paper, I responded to Parfit in the following way.[30] A naturalist can claim that our moral and other normative claims do more than merely communicate putative information about what facts there are. According to the realist-expressivism that I have proposed, a person who makes a normative assertion using normative language expresses both a belief and a relevant conative attitude.[31] For example, I claim, a person who asserts that torture is wrong asserts a normative moral proposition, but she also expresses commitment to a policy (or, roughly, a general intention) of opposing and avoiding wrong acts. This view can explain why we have reason to use normative language even if normative naturalism is true, for we may have reason to express attitudes of commitment to practical policies. We might also have pragmatic reasons to continue to use normative moral language since, I believe, the naturalistic truth conditions of moral claims are enormously complex and might never be known in detail. We might have good reason to continue to make moral claims and no reason to fret over stating them in naturalistic terms. Hence, I claimed, Soft Naturalism can be defended by invoking a combination of pragmatic concerns and expressive concerns.

It is not clear that this response does justice to Parfit's challenge. As for the pragmatic concern, on the naturalist's way of seeing things, there arguably is no need to use a normative term or concept to represent the complex naturalistic property N-ness that, according to the naturalist, is represented by a normative term 'M.' Instead, we could introduce a bit of stipulative naturalistic vocabulary. If we are uncertain what precisely is the natural property that is ascribed by the term "wrong," we could introduce the predicate 'N-wrong' and stipulate that it ascribes the natural property, whatever it is, that is identical to wrongness. Once we have done this, it would seem we would have no need to retain the normative concept of wrongness. We could then use the sentence 'Murder is N-wrong' to report the naturalistic fact of interest. As for the expressive concern, we could imagine introducing into our language a device that enabled us to add an expressive flourish to ordinary predicates.[32] Perhaps the number sign would be used to convey disapproval. Then instead of asserting "Murder is wrong," we could assert "Murder is N-wrong#." If our language and naturalistic conceptual repertoires were enhanced in these ways, Parfit could restate his objection. He could say in this case that there would be no function for the normative concepts to play. The moral terms could be removed from our language and the moral concepts could be removed from our thinking without any cognitive loss.

These responses to my pragmatic and expressive objections to Parfit's Dilemma seem unsuccessful. They do not show that we could do without the normative concepts, because they involve stipulation that employs normative concepts. The concept wrongness is used in defining the concept of N-wrongness.[33] So it remains the case that, for all Parfit has shown, we could not remove the normative concepts from our thinking without cognitive loss. And there are additional reasons to think this. To begin, let me point out two mistakes in Parfit's formulation of the Soft Naturalist's Dilemma.

First, as Parfit understands things, the naturalist holds that there are normative propositions and normative concepts but no normative properties or states of affairs. There is nothing normative in nature, and natural phenomena are the referents of the normative concepts and propositions. This is why, he thinks, normative naturalism is close to normative nihilism. Parfit here seems to be assuming that the naturalist will be an eliminativist, but there is the bold alternative that I outlined previously. If we take this approach, then, again using the utilitarian naturalist to illustrate the point, the naturalist holds that since wrongness is a normative property, and since wrongness is identical to the property of undermining the general welfare, it follows that the property of undermining the general welfare is also normative. Given this, moreover, a state of affairs that contains undermining the general welfare as a constituent, such as the state of affairs that torture undermines the general welfare, is also normative since, again, the property of undermining the general welfare is identical to the normative property of wrongness. According to normative naturalism, then, at least on the bold strategy, there are natural properties and states of affairs that are also normative. This is why, at bottom, this form of normative naturalism is far from normative nihilism.

Second, Parfit contends that a naturalist must allow that there is no reason to use normative language or to deploy normative concepts unless there are normative facts that cannot be expressed in non-normative terms. Parfit assumes that naturalists must deny that there are any such facts. As I have explained, however, there are two conceptions of facts, a worldly conception and a propositional conception. Parfit's assumption may be correct on a worldly conception but it is incorrect on a propositional conception. For if we assume a fine-grained account of the individuation of propositions, a naturalist can insist, for example, that the proposition that torture is wrong is distinct from the proposition that torture undermines the general welfare. And on the propositional conception of facts, she can therefore insist that the fact that torture is wrong is distinct from the fact that torture undermines the general welfare. She can insist that the reason to use normative language is that it enables us to assert propositions such as that torture is wrong, and the reason to deploy normative concepts is that these concepts enable us to have corresponding beliefs, such as the belief that torture is wrong.

Parfit should simply concede that if normative naturalism were true, at least as it is understood by those pursuing the bold strategy, there would be natural properties and states of affairs that are normative. This concession takes much of the steam out of his claim that normative naturalism is akin to nihilism.

Of course, non-naturalists deny that a natural property or state of affairs *could* be normative, but this is a different line of argument from the argument Parfit is pursuing with his Dilemma.[34] I will return to it below. I have conceded that the naturalist needs to provide an account of the nature of normativity in order to explain how it could be that a natural property is normative. Without such an account, it may seem glib simply to insist that, if naturalism is true, there are natural properties and states of affairs that are normative. But, as I have explained, my theory of pluralist-teleology is an attempt to provide an account of the nature of normativity. I refer the interested reader to papers where I have developed this theory more fully than I am able to here.[35]

Parfit should also concede that if naturalism is true, then there are propositions that we could not assert without using normative language and that we could not believe if we lacked normative concepts. But the naturalist maintains that the truth conditions for any such proposition are a natural state of affairs that could be described adequately without using normative language or concepts. Given this, it remains unclear what the point would be of asserting or believing these propositions. It may seem that if the naturalist is correct, there is no cognitive point to expressing these propositions or to believing them to be true since they are about states of affairs that could adequately be described in other ways. This is Parfit's view.

To respond adequately to this challenge, then, we need to explain the role the normative concepts play in our conceptual repertoire, such that they still have a significant function even if normative naturalism is true.

Further responses: the role of the normative concepts

What we need, then, is an account of the role of the normative concepts that explains what the cognitive loss would be if we lacked these concepts and why there would be such a loss even if naturalism is true, so that the properties represented by these concepts could also in principle be represented by non-normative naturalistic concepts. I have already laid the groundwork for this task. The naturalist can point to the different conceptual roles played by the normative and the naturalistic concepts of properties, such as wrongness, and the different roles played in our reasoning by the corresponding beliefs about wrongful actions. Let me explain.

First, if we did not have the normative concepts, we would be unable to have such beliefs as that torture is wrong. For even though, as we are assuming for present purposes, the property of undermining the general welfare *is* the property of wrongness, the proposition that torture undermines the general welfare is distinct from the proposition that torture is wrong. Obviously, a person could believe that torture undermines the general welfare without believing that torture is wrong. If we lacked the ordinary normative concept of wrongness we would be unable to have beliefs—such as the belief that torture is wrong—that represent the property in the way this concept does, as a violation of an authoritative standard. This would be a cognitive loss.

Second, if we did not have the normative concepts, we would not be in a position to make certain metaethical claims, such as that it is possible for a person to believe that torture undermines the general welfare without believing that torture is wrong. For in making this claim, I deploy the ordinary normative concept of wrongness. If we lacked this concept, we also would not be in a position to make (nor to deny) such claims as that the property of undermining the general welfare *is* the property of wrongness or that the proposition that some action will undermine the general welfare is distinct from the proposition that this action is wrong. Without this concept, we also would not be in a position to recognize that it does not follow logically from the fact that performing some action will undermine the general welfare that this action is morally wrong. These would also be cognitive losses.

Third, we need the normative terms and concepts to make sense of certain kinds of metaethical disagreement.[36] We have been assuming for present purposes that the property of undermining the general welfare *is* the property of wrongness, but, obviously, it is possible to disagree. I disagree, for instance, as does Parfit. A utilitarian naturalist recognizes, of course, that many people would reject her view that wrongness is identical to the property of undermining the general welfare. She wouldn't even be able to have this thought if she lacked the normative concept of wrongness, nor could we who disagree have the thought that captures the proposition about which we disagree. These would be cognitive losses.

Analogous points could be made regarding the thesis that to be water is to be H_2O. We could not even formulate this thesis if we lacked either the ordinary concept of water or the concept of H_2O. If we lacked either of these concepts, we would not be able to recognize the possibility of believing there is water in Donner Lake without believing there is H_2O in the lake. There would be a cognitive loss if we had only the concept of H_2O. There would be this loss even if to be water *is* to be H_2O.

There is a fourth point as well, but it assumes that a version of moral-judgment internalism is true. According to the internalist, it is a conceptual and a necessary truth that a person with a moral belief is motivated accordingly, at least to some degree. For example, according to the internalist, a person who believes that lying is wrong is motivated to avoid lying. It may indeed be thought that it is a necessary and conceptual truth that any normative belief—any belief couched with normative concepts—motivates the believer appropriately, at least to some degree. This would presumably be explained by a feature of the normative concepts. For if normative naturalism is true, then for any belief to the effect that something is M, where M expresses a normative concept, there is a corresponding belief one might have to the effect that the thing is N, where N expresses a naturalistic concept. According to normative-judgment internalism, the former belief would be motivating in a way that the naturalistic belief would not be, and this difference between the beliefs presumably is due to the difference between the normative and the naturalistic concepts. For instance, even if utilitarian naturalism is true, there is a difference between the belief that lying is wrong and the belief that lying undermines the general welfare. This difference is due to the difference between the concept of wrongness which figures in the one belief and the concept of undermining the general welfare. If normative-judgment internalism is true, the difference between the two concepts presumably would explain why it is a conceptual and necessary truth that the moral belief motivates the believer whereas it is not a conceptual and necessary truth that the naturalistic belief motivates the believer. Hence, plausibly, if normative-judgment internalism is true, the nature of normative concepts is such as to explain the immediacy of moral motivation for people who have moral or other normative beliefs.

I have argued against moral-judgment internalism in other work,[37] but my arguments leave it open that there are different ways of thinking of normative properties, such as wrongness, where some such ways of thinking bring motivation in their train. This is what I will go on to suggest in the remaining sections of the chapter. I will introduce the idea of the *internal* way of thinking (or WOT) of wrongness, where the internal WOT is such that, if one thinks of wrongness in *this* way, and if one believes that, say, lying is wrong, one will be motivated accordingly, at least to some degree. We can say that *internally* represented moral beliefs are motivating. This is a distinctive role for internal normative ways of thinking.

This leads to a fifth and final point, which also rests on the idea of an internal normative WOT. Parfit suggests that naturalists are making a mistake comparable to the mistake of thinking that heat is a cabbage.[38] The normative concepts constrain what a normative property could possibly be. The concepts leave open various possibilities, and we must decide among them on non-conceptual grounds, but "[m]any other possibilities are, however, conceptually excluded." Similarly, the concept of heat constrains what heat could possibly be. "[H]eat could not have turned out to be a cabbage, or a king ... given the meaning of these claims, they could not possibly be true." Similarly, moral naturalism and normative naturalism could not possibly be true, Parfit thinks.[39]

The argument turns on Parfit's claim that the normative concepts exclude the possibility that a normative property be natural. Notice that we could not even formulate this claim if we lacked the normative concepts. This was the second point I made about the role of the normative concepts in formulating metaethical claims. More importantly for present purposes, Parfit gives us no reason to accept his claim. The analogy of heat is no help. It is plausible that the concept of heat rules out the possibility that heat is a cabbage and it is plausible that the concept of wrongness rules out the possibility that wrongness is a horse. But the fact that the concept rules out *certain* possibilities gives us no reason to think that it rules out the possibility that wrongness is a natural property. I see no reason to suppose that naturalists are making a mistake comparable to the mistake of thinking that heat is a cabbage. I propose instead that *non-naturalists* may be making a mistake that can be explained by the role of the internal normative WOTs in their thinking. Here is an analogy. Certain lovers of cats may think of cats as intrinsically lovable. They might claim on this basis that no cat could be a mere animal since no mere animal is *intrinsically* lovable. The mistake that non-naturalists make, in thinking that no normative property could be a natural property, may be analogous to this mistake of these cat-lovers, as I will explain in the remaining sections of the chapter.

It is true that, on the naturalist's view, all the *worldly* facts are natural facts such as the fact that some action will undermine the general welfare. There is no extra or additional *worldly* normative fact such as the fact that this action will be wrong.[40] Hence, in believing that torture undermines the general welfare without believing that torture is wrong, and in having the naturalistic concept of wrongness without having the ordinary concept of wrongness, we would not be failing to represent some worldly fact or some property. For according to the naturalist, the worldly facts are only the natural facts and there are only the natural properties. Wrongness is not some property in addition to the property of undermining the general welfare. This is correct as far as it goes.

It is obvious, however, that there is room to debate whether wrongness is identical to the property of undermining the general welfare. If we lacked the ordinary normative concept of wrongness, we could not understand this debate. If we lacked this concept, there are truths we could not entertain, much less believe, such as the fact that torture is wrong. Moreover, if we lacked this concept, we could not have a policy of avoiding wrongdoing. Even if we saw how to avoid undermining the general welfare, we might not understand that this is how to avoid wrongdoing. These would be significant losses.

Concepts and ways of thinking

In this section of the chapter I will introduce a distinction between concepts and 'ways of thinking' of things. In the next section I will introduce a distinction between the *ordinary* way of thinking of wrongness and the *internal* way of thinking of wrongness.

The term 'concept' is a technical term that is used differently by different theorists in different areas of philosophy. For my purposes, rather than risk misunderstanding by stretching the term 'concept' to fit what I have in mind, it will be better to introduce a new term. It is for this reason that I will introduce the term 'way of thinking,' or 'WOT.' In this chapter I distinguish the idea of a WOT from standard philosophical ideas of concepts.

We can perhaps think of concepts as ways of thinking of their objects or as ways of representing their objects. For example, the ordinary concept of water is the concept of *the clear, potable liquid that flows through the rivers and falls from the sky as rain*. This is a way of thinking of water. A chemist presumably thinks of water as *the substance composed of H_2O molecules*. It is not clear whether we should say that the chemist has a different *concept* of water, but it is clear that she has a different *way of thinking* of water. Some ways of thinking of things would not be classified as concepts in standard philosophical discussions. For instance, a cat-lover who thinks of cats as intrinsically lovable thinks of them differently from a person who hates cats. They have different WOTs of cats, but it would be misleading in typical philosophical contexts to describe the cat-lover and the person who hates cats as having different *concepts* of a cat. Perhaps all concepts are WOTs, but not all WOTs would standardly be treated as concepts.

It is hard to see how one could plausibly deny that there can be different concepts and so different WOTs of one and the same thing. Parfit himself gives the examples of water and heat.[41] A body of liquid can have the property of being water, and there are two WOTs of this property, the ordinary, folk concept and the chemical WOT. Parfit says that these examples do not help the naturalist, for reasons I have discussed elsewhere,[42] but he does not deny that different concepts (or WOTs) can refer to the same property. The assumption that there can be different concepts of one and the same property is basic to the position of the nonanalytic reductive naturalist. For example, according to the kind of utilitarian moral naturalism I described, the concept *wrongness* and the concept of *the property of undermining the general welfare* are concepts of one and the same property.

In what follows, I will attempt to articulate how some of our WOTs represent their objects. In doing this, I summarize what I take to be basic truths or putative truths— *platitudes*—that characterize this way of thinking. In doing this, I do not claim to offer a philosophical *analysis*.[43] Compare, for example, the chemical WOT of water with the ordinary, folk concept. The chemical WOT represents water as *composed of H_2O molecules*. The ordinary WOT represents water as *the clear, potable liquid that flows through the rivers and falls from the sky as rain*. The associated platitudes vary in their epistemological and modal status. It is a necessary truth that water is H_2O, but it is *not* a necessary truth that water flows through the rivers. If someone denies that water is H_2O, what she says is not contradictory. As I use the term "WOT," then, there is no suggestion that a WOT can be analyzed in a way that gives necessary and sufficient conditions for something's instantiating it. Indeed, a WOT of a thing might *misrepresent* it. A stereotype is a WOT.

One view about concepts is that they are the meanings of words,[44] but as I use the term 'WOT,' there are WOTs that are not meanings. For example, the chemical WOT of water is not the meaning of the term 'water.' A person can use the English term 'water' to express her thoughts about water regardless of how she happens to be thinking of water at the time. The fact that there are two WOTs of water does not entail that the term 'water' is ambiguous.[45] There are several

WOTs of death: the WOT that young children typically have, the WOT that adults typically have, medical and biological WOTs, the vitalists' WOT, and a variety of religious WOTs. The term 'death' is not, however, multiply ambiguous. If one of these WOTs is the meaning of the term, I do not know which it is.

Another view about concepts is that they are constituents of beliefs.[46] It follows from this view that to accept a given proposition one must have the relevant concepts. Hence, for example, a person could not have thoughts about water unless she had the ordinary, folk concept of water. A Martian chemist who had only the chemical WOT of water could not have the belief that Donner Lake is full of water, although she could have the belief that it is full of H_2O molecules. Given this approach, the utilitarian naturalist can say, as I suggested before, that if we lacked the normative concept of wrongness, there are true propositions we would be unable to entertain or to believe. Among these is the proposition that torture is wrong.

Even if concepts are constituents of beliefs, however, there are WOTs that are not in the same way constituents of beliefs. A Christian and an atheist have different WOTs of death, but they can agree that John Lennon is dead. They can agree about this even if, at the time of their agreement, each is thinking of death in a different way. To be sure, if concepts are constituents of belief, the Christian and the atheist must each have the concept of death if they agree that John Lennon is dead. But even if they share this concept, they also have different WOTs of death. The example shows that the content of a person's beliefs is not determined by all of the ways in which she happens to be thinking of the objects of her belief at the time she has the belief.

Ordinary, folk concepts of things are associated with how we typically learn what these things are and with how we learn the meanings of predicates. For instance, people typically acquire the ordinary concept of death when they first have to deal with the fact that loved ones die and do not simply go away to another place. The Christian, the atheist, the biologist, and the vitalist presumably all have the ordinary concept of death, whatever that is, even though they also have different WOTs of death. These WOTs all seem to presuppose the ordinary concept since, to think of death in one of these ways is to have a thought about what *death* is. Similarly, people typically acquire the ordinary concept of water in the course of learning what water is. For we teach people what water is partly by teaching them the platitudes that characterize the ordinary, folk concept of water. This is the reason that the ordinary concept is the salient WOT of water for almost all people in most ordinary contexts. In what follows, I will use the term 'concept' to refer to the ordinary, folk WOTs of things that people typically acquire in learning what these things are.

Normative concepts and ways of thinking

I do not have a general account of what it is that makes a concept or a WOT normative. I am relying on our sharing a concept of normativity. On any plausible account, however, the ordinary concept of wrongness is a normative concept.

I suggest that the ordinary normative concept of wrongness can be characterized as the concept (roughly) of *the property of being a violation of an important, authoritative moral standard where blame is warranted, other things being equal, when a person violates such a standard*.[47] Of course, the concept of an authoritative moral standard is also normative, but it should be no surprise that a characterization of the normative concept of wrongness is normative. The nonanalytic naturalist agrees with the non-naturalist that normative concepts are not analyzable in non-normative terms, but she maintains that the properties picked out by the normative concepts are natural properties.

That is, the naturalist holds that if there is a property represented by the ordinary concept of wrongness, it is a natural property. To explicate the nature of this property, a normative naturalist presumably would need to provide a naturalistic account of authoritative moral standards. I have attempted to do this elsewhere with my theory of pluralist-teleology, which I sketched earlier in the chapter.[48] I say that the authoritative moral standards are, roughly, those with the currency in society that would enable the society to ameliorate the "problem of sociality."[49] Of course, I am not claiming that this is a conceptual truth or that a person with the ordinary concept of wrongness must have this view about the nature of authoritative standards. The normative concept of wrongness is simply the concept (inter alia) of being a violation of such a standard.

Recall, as I pointed out above, in the section "Further responses: the role of the normative concepts," that if normative-judgment internalism is true, the nature of normative concepts, plausibly, is such as to explain the immediacy of moral motivation for people who have normative beliefs. But even if normative-judgment internalism is *not* true, there may be a way of thinking of wrongness, for instance, such that, if one thinks of wrongness in *this* way, and if one believes that, say, lying is wrong, one will be motivated accordingly, at least to some degree. Call this the *internal* way of thinking of wrongness. This is the idea that I now wish to explain. I will distinguish between the ordinary normative concept of wrongness and the motivationally laden internal *way of thinking* of wrongness. As I will explain, an ordinary morally motivated person would typically have the internal WOT of wrongness, for she would be motivated to avoid wrongdoing, and she would think of wrongdoing in a way that is 'colored' by her motivation in a way I will explain.[50] Such a person would have the ordinary normative concept of wrongness, but, as we might say, she also would think of wrongness as normative *for her*.

Consider the difference between the way that a person who loves cats may think of cats and the way a person who is neutral in his feelings about cats presumably thinks of cats. Both have the ordinary concept of cats as *animals with the cat properties*, we might say. However, the cat-lover I have in mind thinks of cats as animals that are lovable *because* they have the cat properties. That is, she thinks of cats as *animals that deserve to be loved in the way that I love them because they have the cat properties*. The cat-lover is attracted to cats because of her love, and *in being attracted*, she thinks of them as *lovable*. Obviously, the cat-lover must have the ordinary concept of cats as well as the cat-lovers' WOT since she could not think of cats as lovable *because they have the cat properties* without having the ordinary concept of cats as animals with the cat properties. She thinks of the cats differently from the way the cat-neutral person does, but since both of them may have the ordinary concept of a cat, they may agree, for example, that there are many cats in the neighborhood.

Consider now the difference between the way that a Catholic presumably thinks of Catholics and the way that a bigot who describes Catholics as 'papists' presumably thinks of Catholics. The bigot perhaps thinks of a Catholic as (roughly) *a person who deserves to be held in contempt, in the way I hold Catholics in contempt, because they are Catholic*. Call this the *papist WOT*. To have this WOT, a bigot would need, of course, also to have the ordinary concept of a Catholic, because the papist WOT involves the ordinary concept. So a person with the papist WOT shares the ordinary concept of a Catholic with the rest of us and presumably can have ordinary beliefs about Catholics even if he thinks of Catholics as 'papists.' For example, a bigot may share with us the belief that there are many Catholics in Rome.

No analogy is perfect, of course, but I propose that we can understand the internal WOT of wrongness as relevantly similar to the cat-lovers' WOT of cats or the papist WOT.

Idealizing somewhat, we can think of the ordinary morally motivated person as having a policy of avoiding and opposing wrongdoing.[51] She may have other, conflicting policies and motivations, but she is motivated to some degree to avoid wrongdoing. My thought is, then, that an ordinary morally motivated person may have a way of thinking of wrongness that refers to her own policy of avoiding and opposing wrongdoing. Call this the *internal* WOT of wrongness. A person with this WOT thinks of wrongness as, roughly, *the property an action can have of deserving to be opposed and avoided, in the way my policy of opposing and avoiding wrong actions leads me to oppose and avoid such actions, because it is wrong, i.e. because it is a violation of an important authoritative moral standard*. This WOT represents wrongness in a way that is *colored* by a person's policy of avoiding and opposing wrongness. Her policy motivates her to oppose and avoid wrongdoing, and, *in being so motivated*, she thinks of wrongdoing as *to be avoided*.[52]

Note the following points about the two normative WOTs of wrongness. First, having the internal normative WOT presupposes having the ordinary normative WOT. For the internal WOT represents wrongness as the property (roughly) of being ruled out by my policy of avoiding and opposing *violations of authoritative moral standards* (and so on). One cannot have this WOT without having the idea of a violation of an authoritative moral standard (and so on), and this is the ordinary WOT of wrongness. Second, the ordinary normative WOT is the ordinary public concept of wrongness. It is the WOT that people ordinarily acquire in learning what wrongness is, for people learn what wrongness is in learning that there are certain standards, for the violation of which they will deserve blame, other things being equal. Third, we tend to assume that a psychologically normal person with the ordinary normative concept of wrongness also has the internal normative WOT. This is because we teach people to recognize wrongdoing as part of an endeavor to bring them to have a policy of avoiding wrongdoing. And a person with such a policy would normally think of wrongdoing as a violation of her policy.

When a person with the internal normative WOT of wrongdoing has an ordinary normative belief, such as the belief that lying is wrong, her belief involves the ordinary concept of wrongness, but presumably, in believing what she does, she also thinks of wrongness in the way that I have attempted to explain with my characterization of the internal WOT. In such cases I will say her belief is 'internally represented.' To clarify, the internally represented belief that lying is wrong is the ordinary belief that lying is wrong in a case where, in so believing, the believer thinks of wrongness as the property of *deserving to be opposed and avoided, in the way her policy of opposing and avoiding wrong actions leads her to oppose and avoid such actions, because they are violations of important authoritative moral standards*. So the internally represented belief is the ordinary familiar belief that lying is wrong in cases where this belief is colored by the internal WOT. (Similarly, a cat-lover may have the ordinary belief that there are cats in the neighborhood even if, in so believing, she thinks of cats as animals that are lovable because they have the cat properties.)

Internally represented beliefs have a characteristic bearing on the explanation and motivation of action. If I have the internally represented belief that lying is wrong, I am in a state of mind that, inter alia, represents me as having a policy of avoiding wrongdoing. That is, the state of mind of a person with an internally represented normative belief is first-personal in an important way. Recall here John Perry's point that first-personal beliefs, such as my belief that I am making a mess, can play a distinctive role in explaining action.[53] My point is related to Perry's, but it is a point about the way that beliefs can be represented rather than a point about their content. I am contending that a normative belief can explain action in the distinctive way that Perry had in mind if it is internally represented—if the believer thinks of the relevant normative property with the relevant internal normative WOT. For example, my state of mind in believing that lying is wrong, if I represent wrongness with the internal normative WOT, can help to explain my avoidance of lying in the distinctive way Perry had in mind.[54]

One might worry that if there are these different ways of thinking of wrongness, then the predicate 'wrong' is ambiguous. But there is more than one WOT of a cat, more than one WOT of water, and more than one WOT of death, and it does not follow from this that the terms 'cat,' 'water,' and 'death' are ambiguous. Similarly, the fact that there is more than one WOT of wrongness does not mean that 'wrong' is ambiguous. My view about WOTs of wrongness is a view about ways of representing or referring, in thought, to wrongness. It is not a view about the semantics of 'wrong.' And my view is compatible with the thesis that, in moral uses, the term 'wrong' makes exactly one contribution to the content of propositions expressed by sentences in which it appears.[55]

One might worry that, on my account, people who have different WOTs of wrongness might not be able to have the same beliefs about wrong action. They might be able neither to agree nor to disagree about wrong action. Perhaps a person with the ordinary normative WOT of wrongness would be at cross purposes with a person who has the internal normative WOT. Perhaps two people with the internal normative WOT would neither agree nor disagree with each other about wrong action since the internal WOT of each refers to *her own* policy of avoiding wrongdoing. To respond to this worry I need to explain how it is that people with different WOTs of wrongness can have the same beliefs about wrongdoing.

As I use the term 'way of thinking,' it is possible for people with different ways of thinking of a thing to entertain many of the same propositions about the thing. For example, people with different WOTs of water may share beliefs about water. Suppose that you have the chemical WOT of water but that I do not. This would not prevent us from agreeing that Donner Lake is full of water, provided that both of us have the ordinary concept of water. Similarly, in my view, an internally represented belief that lying is wrong has the same content as the ordinary belief that lying is wrong, even though the believer represents wrongness with the internal WOT. To see this, one must understand that a person with the internal normative WOT of wrongness must also have the ordinary normative WOT or concept of wrongness since the internal WOT presupposes the ordinary concept. It should be clear, then, on my view, that two people with the internal normative WOT would be able to agree or disagree about wrong action. They could share ordinary normative beliefs, such as the belief that lying is wrong, which, on a standard view about concepts, would have the ordinary normative concept of wrongness as a constituent. They might well share normative beliefs and agree or disagree with people who lack the internal normative WOT of wrongdoing, provided these people also have the ordinary normative concept of wrongdoing.[56]

Suppose that Abel has only the ordinary concept of wrongness and says that lying is not wrong, whereas Mabel, who represents wrongness with the internal WOT, says that lying is wrong. Mabel's belief is internally represented, yet, as I have explained, her belief is the ordinary belief that lying is wrong. So Abel and Mabel disagree. Suppose now that Gable also represents wrongness with the internal WOT and he says that lying is not wrong. Like Mabel, he must also have the ordinary concept of wrongdoing, and his belief is the ordinary belief that lying is not wrong. So he and Mabel disagree. In short, I think that my view does not run into difficulty explaining the phenomena of agreement and disagreement.[57]

It is now time to return to Parfit's Dilemma for Soft Naturalism. To respond satisfactorily to Parfit's challenge, I argued, the naturalist needs to explain why there would be a cognitive loss if we were to lose the normative concepts, even though, according to the naturalist, the normative concepts pick out properties that could also be picked out by naturalistic concepts. The naturalist needs to explain the different conceptual roles played by the normative concept of wrongness and the naturalistic concept of wrongness, and the different roles played in our reasoning by the corresponding beliefs about wrongful actions.

I made some progress with this project in the section "Further responses: the role of the normative concepts," above. In this present section I have added the new claim that there are internal normative ways of thinking of the normative properties, and that the nature of these WOTs is such that internally represented normative beliefs have a characteristic bearing on the explanation and motivation of action. This is a feature of internally represented beliefs that naturalistic beliefs do not have, not even if the naturalistic belief has the same truth conditions as the internally represented belief.

Furthermore, as I suggested above, the nature of the internal normative WOTs can go some way toward explaining why non-naturalists hold that no normative property could be a natural property. Certain lovers of cats may conceive of cats as intrinsically lovable, and this could lead them to claim that no cat could be a mere animal since no mere animal is *intrinsically* lovable. The mistake that non-naturalists make, in thinking that no normative property could be a natural property, may be analogous to the cat-lovers' mistake. A person with the internal WOTs has representations of goodness and rightness wherein their nature is to 'glow' and 'attract' and representations of badness and wrongness wherein their nature is to 'glower' and 'repel.' This apparent 'glowing' and 'glowering' is due to the fact that the internal normative WOTs relate the normative properties to one's own moral policies of seeking the good and the right and avoiding the bad and the wrong. To a person with the internal normative WOTs, however, this feature of the WOTs may seem to be a feature of the properties themselves. The normative properties themselves might seem to be *intrinsically* attractive or repellant. And this might in turn fuel an argument against moral naturalism, for one might think that no *natural* property is *intrinsically* attractive or repellant. The mistake here, of course, would be to confuse a feature of a concept with a feature of the property it represents.

Conclusion

Parfit thinks that normative naturalism is "close to nihilism."[58] Notice, however, that it would be an obvious mistake to think that the thesis that water is H$_2$O is close to nihilism about water. This is a thesis about what water is, not a theory that denies there is any such thing. In a similar way, the thesis that wrongness is a natural property is not close to nihilism about wrongness. It is a thesis about what wrongness is, not a theory that denies there is any such thing.

One reason Parfit thinks normative naturalism is close to nihilism is that he thinks naturalism implies that the normative concepts could be removed from our thinking without cognitive loss. In response, the naturalist can say that, *even if* the property wrongness is identical to a property N-wrongness, the proposition that torture is wrong is distinct from the proposition that torture is N-wrong. Hence, if we lacked the normative concept of wrongness, there are true propositions we would be unable to entertain or to believe, including the proposition that torture is wrong. This would be the case even if we understood all the natural facts. For if we lacked the normative concepts, we would not have the normative concept of wrongness. And in this case we could not have the thought that torturing people is wrong. There are true propositions that we would not even be capable of entertaining. Furthermore, as I explained, the internal normative ways of thinking of the normative properties play an important role in structuring beliefs that motivate moral action. They thereby figure in equipping us to ameliorate certain problems of normative governance that we face as human beings.[59] It should therefore be clear that normative naturalism does not imply that normative concepts could be removed from our thinking without any loss.

As we saw, Parfit contends that if normative naturalism were true, "there would be no point in trying to answer such questions" as "what matters, which actions are right or wrong, and what we have reasons to want, and to do" since, in that case, "nothing" would matter.[60] On the contrary, if normative naturalism is true, then there is some natural property, the property of 'N-mattering,' such that *to matter* is *to N-matter*. Clearly, it would not follow from this proposal that nothing matters. It is of course *compatible* with normative naturalism that nothing matters. The claim that nothing matters is also compatible with normative *non-naturalism*. But this pessimistic claim does not *follow* either from naturalism or from non-naturalism. Properly understood, naturalism does not eliminate the fact that it matters how we live our lives. It aims, rather, to explain what it is for this to matter.[61]

Notes

1. *OWM 2*, p. 267.
2. *OWM 2*, p. 367.
3. *OWM 2*, p. 367.
4. *OWM 2*, p. 304.
5. *OWM 2*, p. 267.
6. Copp (2012).
7. *OWM 2*, p. 325.
8. Mackie (1977), pp. 30–5.
9. McDowell (1978), p. 18.
10. Copp (in progress).
11. I do not endorse utilitarian naturalism. On my view, the property wrongness is, roughly, the property an action can have of failing to be in accord with the requirements of a system of standards, the currency of which in society would do most to ameliorate the 'problem of sociality.' See below for a brief explanation, and Copp (1995a, 2007, and 2009b).
12. *OWM 2*, pp. 364–77.
13. *OWM 2*, pp. 364–6.
14. *OWM 2*, p. 368.
15. Moore (1993), §§26 and 91. Realists need not be platonists about properties, but they reject a 'deflationary' conception of properties, according to which: for a thing to have a property is just for the thing to have some predicate be true of it. Let me say that a realist construes properties 'robustly.' One might suggest that properties are ways things can be *similar*; that is, things share a property just in case they are similar in some respect. Unfortunately, there are similar metaphysical debates about the nature

of similarities as there are about the nature of properties. A "robust" similarity is intended that does not merely consist in things being classified under a given predicate. I will here construe properties robustly. Parfit seems, however, to have a deflationary conception (OWM 2, p. 348).

16 For simplicity, I use 'property' to include relations.
17 Nicholas Sturgeon defends a 'non-reductive naturalism,' according to which, although moral properties are natural properties, there may be no true and *non-trivial* statement of the form 'To be M is to be N,' where M is replaced by a moral or other normative predicate and N is replaced by a term standing for a natural property. See Sturgeon (2006), pp. 98–9. (Of course, there is the *trivial* 'To be M is to be M,' where M is replaced by a moral predicate, for if naturalism is true, a moral predicate stands for a natural property.) Non-reductive naturalism of this kind needs to explain directly, without offering a reduction, how it is that a normative property such as moral wrongness would be countenanced in a scientifically constrained view of what exists.
18 Copp (2009b).
19 To *subscribe* to a norm in the sense I have in mind is to have a general intention to conform to it, and it is also to be disposed to experience a negative emotional response if one fails to conform.
20 I am simplifying here, ignoring some details and various complications that would need to be addressed in a full development of this view. I address some of the complications in Copp (1995a), pp. 199–200 and 213–45, and Copp (2007), pp. 25–6, 55–150, and 203–83.
21 For details, see Copp (2007), especially the introduction, and Copp (1995a).
22 OWM 2, pp. 267–9.
23 The term comes from Scanlon (2014). Scanlon uses the term in a slightly different way from how I do.
24 Gibbard (2012).
25 I shall be using 'true' in a 'robust' sense. There are also, of course, 'deflationary' accounts of the meaning of 'true.' See Beall and Glanzberg (2008).
26 King (1998, 2007).
27 Gibbard (2012), p. 27, provides such an account, although he calls the objects of belief *thoughts* rather than *propositions*. He would say that the thought that water is H_2O consists in a different structure of concepts from the thought that water is water.
28 Gibbard (2012), p. 27.
29 OWM2, p. 368.
30 Copp (2012).
31 Copp (2007), chapter 5, and Copp (2009a).
32 This is not my idea, but I am not sure where I got it from.
33 I am grateful to an anonymous referee for pressing me on this point.
34 With the Dilemma, Parfit aims to show that if normative naturalism is true, then a form of normative nihilism is true. With the other argument, non-naturalists aim to show that normative naturalism is not true.
35 See especially Copp (2009b).
36 I owe this point to a question asked by a graduate student—whose name I did not learn—when I presented my earlier paper on Parfit's arguments, Copp (2012), to the Department of Philosophy at Cornell University.
37 Copp (1995b).
38 OWM 2, p. 325.
39 OWM 2, p. 325.
40 As I explained, there is such a fact on the propositional conception of a fact as a true proposition.
41 OWM 2, p. 325.
42 OWM 2, p. 325. See Copp (2012).

43 Compare Michael Smith's discussion of the relation between the platitudes and conceptual analysis in Smith (1994), pp. 29–32.
44 Gibbard (2012), pp. 27 and 29–30.
45 The fact that there is more than one WOT of water is compatible with the view that the term 'water' makes exactly one contribution to the content of propositions expressed by sentences in which it appears. I believe that my views are compatible with a variety of theories about the semantics of predicates.
46 For example, Gibbard views 'thoughts' as structures of concepts. See Gibbard (2012), p. 27.
47 Compare Darwall (2006).
48 Copp (1995a, 2007, and 2009b).
49 Copp (2009b).
50 The term 'coloring' is from Gottlob Frege's discussion of pejoratives such as 'cur,' which he says is colored in a way that the corresponding neutral term, 'dog,' is not. See Frege (1979), pp. 140–1 and 197–8, and Frege (1984), pp. 161, 185, and 357. I do not intend to use the term in precisely the way that Frege did.
51 Here I am thinking of a policy as a general intention. See Bratman (2014), p. 20. So a person's policy of avoiding and opposing wrongdoing is, roughly, a general intention of avoiding and opposing violations of what is required by important authoritative moral standards.
52 I here use J.L. Mackie's words. See Mackie (1977), pp. 30–5. I am grateful to Peter Railton for helping me to think about how best to characterize the internal normative WOTs and for pointing out problems with earlier characterizations.
53 Perry (1979).
54 There is nothing here that is incompatible with a Humean belief/desire psychology. Strictly speaking, in such cases, the believer's policy or general intention motivates her, together with her beliefs. My belief that lying is wrong, when I represent wrongdoing as a violation of my policy of avoiding wrongdoing, helps to explain my avoidance of lying, because it relates wrongness to my policy of avoiding wrongdoing. This policy, together with my belief that lying is wrong, explains my avoidance of lying.
55 I here ignore a variety of complications that are irrelevant to the argument. For instance, 'wrong' can be used to mean 'false' or 'incorrect,' as in 'That newspaper's report was wrong,' and it can be used to mean 'morally ruled out,' as in 'What that person did was wrong.'
56 A person who has the internal normative WOT might also have beliefs of which this is a constituent. For instance, someone might believe that lying deserves to be opposed and avoided, in the way her policy of opposing and avoiding wrong actions leads her to oppose and avoid such actions, because it is a violation of an important authoritative moral standard. In this case she also would believe that lying is wrong—that it is a violation of an important authoritative moral standard. So such a person disagrees with someone who denies that lying is wrong.
57 Suppose that Fable disagrees with Mabel's belief, not that lying is a violation of an important authoritative moral standard, but that lying deserves to be opposed and avoided in the way her policy of opposing and avoiding wrong actions leads her to oppose and avoid such actions. Obviously, he could not express this disagreement by saying that lying is not wrong. So, again, there is no problem.
58 OWM 2, p. 267.
59 I explain this idea in Copp (2009b).
60 OWM 2, p. 367.
61 Versions of this chapter were presented to the Tenth Symposium on Ethics and Political Philosophy, Center for Ethics and Philosophy of Mind, Universidade Federal do Rio de Janeiro, Itatiaia National Park, Brazil, March, 2014; to the Rio-2015 Metaethics

Conference, January, 2015; and to the Department of Philosophy at York University, December, 2014. I am grateful to members of these audiences for helpful discussion and especially to Derek Parfit, Adam Sennet, Fabio Shecaira, and Teemu Toppinen for their detailed comments. In addition, I would like to express my gratitude to Christian Coons, Simon Kirchin, Nicholas Laskowski, David McNaughton, Wilson Mendonca, Claudia Passos, Peter Railton, Julia Telles de Menezes, Paul Teller, three anonymous referees, and the members of DaGERS, the Davis discussion group in ethics and related subjects, for helpful suggestions and comments.

References

Beall, J.C. and Glanzberg, Michael (2008) 'Where the Paths Meet: Remarks on Truth and Paradox', in *Truth and its Deformities*, *Midwest Studies in Philosophy* 32, P.A. French and H.K. Wettstein (eds), pp. 169–98.

Bratman, Michael (2014) *Shared Agency: A Planning Theory of Acting Together* (Oxford: Oxford University Press).

Copp, David (1995a) *Morality, Normativity, and Society* (New York: Oxford University Press).

Copp, David (1995b) 'Moral Obligation and Moral Motivation', in *On the Relevance of Metaethics: New Essays on Metaethics*, *Canadian Journal of Philosophy* supp. vol. 21, Kai Nielsen and Jocyelyne Couture (eds), pp. 187–219.

Copp, David (2007) *Morality in a Natural World* (Cambridge: Cambridge University Press).

Copp, David (2009a) 'Realist-Expressivism and Conventional Implicature', in *Oxford Studies in Meta-Ethics* vol. 4, Russ Shafer-Landau (ed.) (Oxford: Oxford University Press), pp. 167–202.

Copp, David (2009b) 'Toward a Pluralist and Teleological Theory of Normativity', *Philosophical Issues* 19, pp. 21–37.

Copp, David (2012) 'Normativity and Reasons: Five Arguments from Parfit against Normative Naturalism', in *Ethical Naturalism: Current Debates*, Susana Nuccetelli and Gary Seay (eds) (Cambridge: Cambridge University Press), pp. 24–57.

Copp, David (in progress) 'Normative Properties and Ways of Thinking'.

Darwall, Stephen (2006) *The Second-Person Standpoint: Morality, Respect, and Accountability* (Cambridge, MA: Harvard University Press).

Frege, Gottlob (1979) *Posthumous Writings*, Hans Hermes, Friedrich Kambartel, and Friedrich Kaulbach (eds) (Chicago: University of Chicago Press).

Frege, Gottlob (1984) *Collected Papers on Mathematics, Logic, and Philosophy*, Brian McGuinness (ed.) (Oxford: Blackwell).

Gibbard, Allan (2012) *Meaning and Normativity* (Oxford: Oxford University Press).

King, Jeffrey C. (1998) 'What is a Philosophical Analysis?', *Philosophical Studies* 90, pp. 155–79.

King, Jeffrey C. (2007) *The Nature and Structure of Content* (New York: Oxford University Press).

Mackie, J.L. (1977) *Ethics: Inventing Right and Wrong* (London: Penguin).

McDowell, John (1978) 'Are Moral Requirements Hypothetical Imperatives?', *Proceedings of the Aristotelian Society* supp. vol. 52, pp. 13–29.

Moore, G.E. (1993) *Principia Ethica*, Thomas Baldwin (ed.) (Cambridge: Cambridge University Press). Originally published in 1903.

Parfit, Derek (2011) *On What Matters* (Oxford: Oxford University Press), vols 1 and 2.
Perry, John (1979) 'The Problem of the Essential Indexical', *Noûs* 13, pp. 3–21.
Scanlon, T.M. (2014) *Being Realistic about Reasons* (Oxford: Oxford University Press).
Smith, Michael (1994) *The Moral Problem* (Oxford: Blackwell).
Sturgeon, Nicholas (2006) 'Ethical Naturalism', in *The Oxford Handbook of Ethical Theory*, David Copp (ed.) (New York: Oxford University Press), pp. 91–121.

3

ON WHAT IT IS TO MATTER

Julia Markovits

Derek Parfit's sweeping exploration of normativity in his book *On What Matters* (hereafter OWM) is predominantly a very welcome exercise in philosophical reconciliation. He is concerned to show that the leading and most plausible approaches to thinking about first-order normativity—about what we should do, and what matters—ultimately take us to more or less the same conclusion. As he evocatively describes it: though we may start from different places, and take different routes to the top, we (Kantians, Contractualists, Rule-Consequentialists) are all "climbing the same mountain, on different sides."[1] What looks to most philosophers like irresolvable disagreement is in fact illusory—we agree much more, Parfit thinks, and about more fundamental things, than we might think.

But the conciliatory tone of the book begins in Part Two. In Part One of the book, 'Reasons,' Parfit argues instead that a particular division is deeper than we might have thought. In fact, it seems to represent, for Parfit, the most fundamental and important divide in ethical theory. The division that concerns him is between 'object-given' reasons, or 'objective' theories of reasons, on the one hand, and 'subject-given' reasons, or 'desire-based,' or 'subjective' theories of reasons, on the other. Both kinds of theory are presented as theories of *practical normative reasons*. But how such reasons, on each kind of account, relate to both epistemic reasons and motivating reasons will also be of interest in what follows.

So what distinguishes objective theories of reasons from subjective ones? According to objective theories, Parfit tells us,

> there are certain facts that give us reasons both to have certain desires and aims, and to do whatever might achieve these aims. These reasons are given by facts about the *objects* of these desires or aims, or what we might want to try to achieve.[2]

According to subjective theories,

> our reasons for acting are all provided by, or depend upon, certain facts about what would fulfil or achieve our present desires or aims. Some of these theories appeal to our actual present desires or aims. Others appeal to the desires or aims that we would now have, or to the choices that we would now make, if we had carefully considered all of the relevant facts. Since these are all facts about *us*, we can call these reasons *subject-given*.[3]

Later on, Parfit discusses some variations on the subjectivist theme, including versions of Subjectivism that emphasize the desires and aims we would have after *procedurally rational* deliberation: deliberation that is fully imaginative, avoids wishful thinking, assesses probabilities correctly, and follows other purely procedural rules of reasoning.[4] Procedural rules, as I understand them, are rules that govern the relations between our cognitive states, desires, aims, and intentions, and how we move between them, as opposed to rules that tell us, directly, to have certain aims or make certain choices, regardless of their relation to what we care about or believe already. (A wide-scope norm of instrumental rationality, telling us to desire or aim at the known, necessary means to the ends we desire or aim at, is a paradigmatic example of a procedural rule.)

In contrast to his consensus-building project in the rest of the volume, Parfit's aim here is not to find common ground between the Objectivist and the Subjectivist, or reconcile these opposing sets of views, but rather to reject one of them. Subjectivism, Parfit tells us, has deeply implausible as well as deeply troubling consequences. It implies, Parfit argues, that we can have no reasons for desiring anything or having certain aims. If Subjectivists are right, then even the fact that some choice will ensure that we suffer agony in the future may not entail that we have a reason to avoid it, if our desires are sufficiently weird. On the objectivist picture, "goodness would give us reasons 'because it's out there, shining down'."[5] If, on the other hand, Subjectivism is true, Parfit laments, "we must make our choices in the dark."[6] Worse, since, according to Subjectivism, all our reasons depend on the desires we have no reason to have, Subjectivism entails a dark and nihilistic picture of the normative world, whether its proponents see it this way or not.

I will argue that the divide between subjective and objective theories may not be as deep or as fundamental as Parfit makes it seem. Subjectivism also has advantages Parfit does not consider. And while I will not be developing a full case for optimism here,[7] I will suggest that the Subjectivist has resources to resist the bleak conclusions about what is valuable and what we have reason to do to which Parfit fears her view commits her.

Parfit structures his attack on subjectivist theories in Part One like this: first, he explains the difference between objective and subjective theories of reasons and states his preference for the former; then, he offers a series of *debunking explanations* (ten of them!) to *explain away* the popularity of subjectivist views—to explain why so many otherwise dependable philosophers have been attracted to a view that is (he thinks) so deeply mistaken and unattractive; finally, he argues directly against the plausibility of Subjectivism, primarily on the grounds that it has unacceptable implications for what we have reason to do.

Conspicuously missing from Parfit's discussion is any extended consideration of the arguments *in favor of* Subjectivism. His discussion of Subjectivists' defenses of their view is confined to the short (three-page) final section of Chapter 4.[8] Parfit also spends very little time addressing worries for objectivist theories of reasons. He thinks that once we see how problematic the commitments and entailments of Subjectivism really are, and once we understand the sources of the illusion that the view holds some plausibility, we will no longer find ourselves in its sway.

Well, I do still find myself in Subjectivism's sway, despite (I think) sharing many of Parfit's philosophical instincts and hopes. So I hope, in what follows, to explain why. After briefly further exploring the distinction between Subjectivism and Objectivism, and trying to pinpoint what the disagreement between Subjectivists and Objectivists is a disagreement *about* (in my first section), I will set out (in the second section) Parfit's diagnosis of where, as a Subjectivist, I may have gone wrong: his *debunking* arguments. Some of these explanations for the appeal of Subjectivism, I will argue (in the third section), are less debunking than they seemed to Parfit. This discovery provides a way into supplying what was missing from Parfit's discussion: a sketch of some arguments *for* a subjectivist theory of reasons that Parfit does not consider and an account of what strikes Subjectivists as unsatisfactory about Parfit's preferred objectivist account of normativity. Finally, I hope to begin to address Parfit's worry that Subjectivism entails a bleak and nihilistic picture of the normative world.

Objectivism and Subjectivism

What is the dispute between Objectivists and Subjectivists a dispute about? As Parfit's discussion makes clear, the question may not have a unique answer.

Parfit distinguishes between 'substantive' and 'analytical' versions of Subjectivism. Analytical Subjectivists, Parfit tells us, are simply *reporting* that when they ascribe a "reason" to someone to do something, what *they mean* is that doing that thing will best fulfill that person's desires (corrected, perhaps, for lack of information or procedural error). They are in essence *stipulating* a definition for the term 'reason,' as they are using it. So if an analytical Subjectivist makes claims like 'A has a reason to ϕ only if ϕing would fulfill one of A's informed desires,' she is, Parfit says, asserting little more than a "concealed tautology," which everyone should accept, but which is trivial. "Analytical Subjectivists," Parfit says, "do not make substantive claims about what we have reason to do, or about what we should or ought to do."[9] The appearance of disagreement between analytical Subjectivists and Objectivists is, he says, a mere illusion.

But it is clear that when most Subjectivists and Objectivists disagree about reasons, they are not talking past each other in this way. And when Subjectivists make claims about the conditions of having a reason to do something, they aren't intending to simply *stipulate* a definition of their term 'reason.' Nor need Subjectivism be understood as a (non-stipulative) account of what our ordinary word 'reason' means, any more than the theory that water is bonded hydrogen and oxygen represented an attempt to explain what we mean by the term 'water.' Subjectivism (of the sort that interests me here) instead aims to provide an informative account of what property a certain property is identical to: in this case, the property of being a reason—a consideration that counts in favor of something. Subjectivism, in other words, addresses the *reference*, not the *sense*, of our term 'reason.'[10]

Subjectivism of this sort advances a thesis about *what normative reasons*, in a sense that is common to both parties to the dispute, *are*. Both Subjectivists and Objectivists agree, in other words, that reasons are considerations that count in favor of actions—that in some sense *justify* actions. What they disagree about is what is involved in some fact's counting in favor of an action.[11] Subjectivists think this counting-in-favor-of relation is grounded in or constituted by or depends in some way on facts about what people care about. Objectivists like Parfit deny this, and, in fact, deny (at least in Parfit's case) that there is anything further that can be said to explain what it is to count in favor of in this way.[12]

Some Subjectivists might instead defend a desire-based view as a first-order normative thesis about *what reasons there are*—what sorts of considerations count in favor of actions. They might defend the view that the fact that some end is desired is the most basic normative reason for someone to pursue it.[13] But the version of Subjectivism I have been describing is not a first-order normative thesis about *what reasons there are*—about what sorts of fact most fundamentally count in favor of acting. Instead, it makes a *meta*-normative claim about what the counting-in-favor-of relation itself comes to. According to this thesis, it is not the fact that some act will satisfy my idealized desires that counts in favor of my performing it. Rather, some *other* fact counts in favor of performing the action *because* my desires, suitably idealized, include a desire to which that fact is relevant, and *what it is* for a fact to count in favor of an action is for that fact to show how the action would help fulfill some idealized desire. So, to take an example of Parfit's, it is the fact that quitting smoking now will extend my life that counts in favor of quitting, but it does so *in virtue of* the fact that it shows how quitting would satisfy a desire I have, or would have if I were procedurally rational. (In this sense, the Subjectivist can agree with the Objectivist that our reasons are 'object-given'—they are provided by facts about the objects of our desires, or what we want to achieve.)[14]

To bring out the difference between Subjectivism understood as a *first-order normative thesis* about what counts in favor of our acting one way or another and Subjectivism understood as a *meta-normative thesis* about the nature of the counting-in-favor-of relation, it helps to note that philosophers who agree on the truth of Subjectivism often disagree substantially about the first-order question of what reasons there are. For example, both Kant and Mill sound, at times, like Subjectivists about reasons: both seem to take the possibility of categorical or universal practical reasons to depend on the existence of a desire or end all people (or at least all procedurally rational people) share. But they have very different views, of course, about what that end is (Kant thinks it is rational nature, Mill happiness) and correspondingly different views about what we have reason to do.[15]

So agreement on the meta-normative question of what it is for something to *be* a reason doesn't secure agreement on what reasons we have. For example, a Millian might allow that the fact that lying will promote the greater happiness is, in a particular case, a sufficient reason to lie to someone, whereas a Kantian might say that the fact that lying prevents us from treating the person we lie to as an end in herself, in the sense that she cannot share the aim of our action with us, gives us sufficient reason *not* to lie, even to promote the greater good. But Mill and Kant might agree on what it is in virtue of which either fact gets to count as a reason, if it does: it counts as a reason because it shows how some action (or inaction) promotes or respects the value of some end we all have, or would have if we were procedurally rational.

Similarly, when Objectivists like Parfit and Scanlon agree that nothing further useful can be said about *what reasons are*—that the notion is basic—they are not agreeing that we cannot make any further general, informative claim about *what reasons there are*. Indeed, much of Parts Two and Three of OWM is devoted to exploring and defending the plausibility of some such further claims. And just as the agreements between Kant and Mill, and between Scanlon and Parfit, are not best characterized as substantive first-order agreement about what reasons we have, the *dis*agreement between Subjectivists and Objectivists is not really a substantive first-order *dis*agreement about what reasons we have.

But this is not to say that that disagreement cannot have important implications for that first-order question: indeed, the case we have been looking at shows that it can, because both Kant and Mill arrive at their first-order conclusions about *what reasons there are* on the back of their meta-normative arguments about *what reasons are*. And this, in my view, makes the dispute between Subjectivists and Objectivists much more interesting than it otherwise would be. Parfit agrees. It is because he thinks Subjectivism has important (and, he thinks, depressing) implications for what matters—for what we have reason to do—that he dedicates Part One of his book to rejecting the view.[16]

So the primary disagreement between Subjectivists and Objectivists is not about *what matters* but rather about *what it* is for something to matter. According to the Subjectivist, things *matter*, ultimately, *because they matter to us*, when we're reasoning well; sentient beings—beings to whom things matter—in this way introduce reasons into the world by caring. Why is it bad for people to die early of disease or war? Because this is something people very much want to avoid! According to the Objectivist, by contrast, things *matter to us*, when we are reasoning well, *because they matter*. People very much want to avoid an early and painful death because such a death is a very bad thing!

This is, I think, the fundamental dispute between Subjectivists and Objectivists. Put this way, it seems to me that both views have significant intuitive appeal. Which is just as it should be for such a longstanding and entrenched philosophical dispute.

The debunking arguments

Parfit is convinced that any intuitive appeal that Subjectivism seems to have is illusory. And he has a lot to say about *why* we are subject to the illusion. In Chapter 3, §9 of OWM, Parfit asks himself why so many people accept subjective theories: "How could all these people be so mistaken?" What follows are a series of *debunking* explanations of the appeal of Subjectivism—explanations of why people believe subjectivist theses that at the same time reveal such beliefs to be mistaken. (Parfit, in fact, counts off *ten* such diagnoses, some of which I will lump together in my discussion. To make it easier to keep track of how my comments track Parfit's explanations for those who'd like to do so, I've indicated by means of parenthetical numbering which of his explanations my comments address. I will follow the numbering Parfit gives in the text, but I won't always follow his order of exposition.)

First, Parfit points out that even if Objectivism is true, we should expect our reasons to (loosely) correspond to our desires, since we often desire what is independently worth achieving (1). For example, we often desire what is pleasant or enjoyable and desire to avoid what is painful or unpleasant. In this case, it is not our desires, but rather the fact that an experience would be enjoyable, or painful, that gives us reasons to pursue or avoid it (8). We are especially likely to desire what is independently worth achieving once we realize that it is worth achieving, since this very realization can give rise to the desire (2). When our desires track our reasons in this way, we may mistake conjunction for causation and arrive at the conclusion that the desires *generate* the reasons. In fact, Parfit thinks, often the opposite is true: it is the reasons that generate the desires.

Then there is the possibility, Parfit says, that Subjectivists are mixing up *motivating* reasons (which *are* desire-based) with *normative* reasons (which are not) (4). Or perhaps they are mixing up facts about what we have *reason* to do with facts about what we *ought rationally* to do: Parfit allows that it may be true that when some action would best achieve our aims, we *ought rationally* take it; but, he says, it doesn't follow that we *have reason* to take that action, if we have no reason to have the desire in the first place. In this respect, Parfit classes misguided desires together with false beliefs about what will fulfill those desires: both, he says, can make it *rational* for us to do something we have *no reason* to do (7).

What is more, Parfit notes, there are a number of ways in which our desires might give us *derivative* reasons—reasons that derive from more fundamental reasons that are not themselves desire-dependent—even if Objectivism about reasons is correct (3, 5, possibly 6,[17] 10). For example, Parfit says, some views of well-being—desire-fulfillment views—entail that the satisfaction of our desires is in itself good for us. If this is true, he claims, then we will have *value-based* reasons to fulfill our desires that derive from the value-based, desire-independent reason we have to promote our well-being. These value-based reasons to promote our well-being are easily mistaken, Parfit thinks, for desire-based reasons, if we accept a desire-fulfillment theory of well-being (3).

And even if we reject desire-based views of well-being, we may think we have reason to help fulfill *other* people's desires; but these reflect the reasons we have to respect others' autonomy and avoid paternalism. *These* reasons are not themselves desire-based (although fulfilling them may constitutively involve fulfilling other people's desires)—we have these reasons, if we have them, Parfit presumably thinks, regardless of what we, or others, desire (6).[18] Those who embrace Subjectivism on such anti-paternalistic grounds seem to be making the same mistake as the many people who embrace what Bernard Williams once called "vulgar moral relativism"[19] as a metaethical view on anti-imperialistic grounds. The reasons for tolerance and respect for autonomy such instincts recognize themselves have a force that is non-relative and non-desire-based.

And, finally, there are a number of ways in which our desires might affect our reasons because what we have reason to do *causally* depends on our desires. For example, the fact that we have some desire might cause us to feel pleasure or relief if that desire is satisfied, or frustration, discomfort, or distraction if it is not satisfied (Parfit points, by way of illustration, to the familiar irritation of not being able to recall some trivial fact). Since, Parfit thinks, we have desire-independent reasons to pursue pleasure and avoid discomfort and distraction, both for their own sake, and for the sake of our effectiveness in pursuing other valuable ends, we have reasons to fulfill such desires. But these reasons, again, derive from those desire-independent reasons. For similar reasons, we have derivative desire-dependent reasons to pursue those independently valuable aims that we desire to achieve, since we will probably be more effective in achieving them than we would be if we tried to achieve similarly valuable aims we did not desire (8, 10).

Perhaps, Parfit suggests, these many ways in which what we desire can shape what we have reason to do have misled people into thinking that our desires are the fundamental source of our reasons—that *what it is* to have a reason to do something is for it to fulfill one of our desires. But this, Parfit says, is merely an illusion: we have each of these desire-based reasons only because we have a more fundamental reason that is desire-independent: a reason to promote well-being (3), respect autonomy, avoid paternalism (6), provide pleasure, relieve frustration, or advance our pursuit of other goals whose value does not depend on our desires (5, 8, 10).

Does the fact, often emphasized by Parfit, that we have reason to do what we would like or enjoy, and reason to avoid what we would dislike or find unpleasant, entail that we have desire-based reasons? After all, liking or disliking a sensation or experience seems to be something *we*, the *subjects*, bring to the experience. Likability and pleasure are not, in general, out there in the world, independent of our subjective responses to things. Surely it is the fact that I like cilantro—that I want to eat it—that gives me reason to eat it; it is nothing about the cilantro itself. If I didn't like cilantro, as many people don't, I would have no such reason.

Parfit concedes the point, but turns it, he thinks, to his advantage: it is indeed true, he says, that our likings and dislikings can give us reasons to pursue certain experiences. But this does not show this important class of reasons to be desire-based, because likings and dislikings are not, Parfit argues, desires. To like or dislike an experience—to enjoy something or find it unpleasant—is not the same as wanting to have that experience or wanting to avoid it. The reasons our likes and dislikes generate, Parfit says, are *hedonic*, not desire-based. Of course, most of us *do* desire to have experiences we like and to avoid those we dislike. These are "meta-hedonic desires."[20] Subjectivists have, once again, according to Parfit, mistaken conjunction for causation and been misled by the frequent conjunction of hedonic reasons with meta-hedonic desires into thinking such reasons are desire-based (9).

Un-debunking Subjectivism

So Parfit has a *lot* to say about the mistakes that lead to an acceptance of Subjectivism. As I have noted, he says very little about the arguments Subjectivists offer in favor of their view. But I think that many of the 'mistakes' Parfit attributes to Subjectivists in fact reveal plausible grounds, in the vicinity of those mistakes, for embracing a subjectivist view of normativity. My goal now will be to defuse Parfit's debunking arguments and, along the way, to highlight these arguments *for* Subjectivism.

Is the Subjectivist mistaking conjunction for causation (1, 2, 8)? Let's begin with Parfit's first suggestion: that Subjectivists are mistaking the frequent conjunction of desires to pursue some aim with *reasons* to pursue that aim for a causal or grounding or explanatory relation from those desires to those reasons. If anything, Parfit says, the causal relation runs in the other direction: desire-independent value explains our desires.

Of course, given the frequent conjunction of what we desire and what we have reason to pursue, Subjectivists might offer a similar debunking explanation of Objectivism, as Hume famously did. "Tis a common observation," he noted in a different context,

> that the mind has a great propensity to spread itself on external objects, and to conjoin with them any internal impressions, which they occasion, and which always make their appearance at the same time that these objects discover themselves to the senses.[21]

This conjunction, a Subjectivist might insist, can lead us to mistake what is contributed by the mind for something contributed by the world, just as Parfit fears we might be making the opposite mistake. We project our desire for something onto that thing and come to see it as good independently of our desire.

We might even, noticing the pattern of conjunction, come to see it as *causing* our desire—as fixing our standard of taste. When A and B always and instantaneously appear together, it can, as Parfit notes, be hard to tell whether A causes B or B causes A. The possibility of such an error provides some indirect support for Subjectivism, by allowing the Subjectivist to explain away the contrary impression: though value appears to be something we discover in, rather than contribute to, the world, this appearance is merely that—an appearance.

Of course, if Parfit is right, then Objectivists can avail themselves of a nearly symmetrical debunking explanation. So where does this leave the debate between the two views? It seems to me to leave Subjectivism slightly ahead, although defeasibly so. Subjectivists, after all, can straightforwardly explain the conjunction between desire and the appearance of value: their view predicts it. What it is for something to have value, on the subjectivist view, is for it in some way to fulfill or express our desires or aims. Objectivists, on the other hand, owe us an explanation of *why* desire-independent value appears (so often, at least) to coincide with what we desire.

It may well be possible to explain this. Perhaps, as Parfit suggests, our desires often align with what we have desire-independent reason to pursue because we are good at recognizing such reasons, and that recognition generates the desire to act accordingly. But this, of course, pushes the question down the road: why think we're good at recognizing reasons? How do we recognize reasons? These questions become especially difficult to answer if we accept that reasons are object-given, mind-independent, and irreducibly normative. This is not to say, of course, that these questions cannot be answered. Parfit begins to address them in Volume 2 of OWM.[22] But the difficulty they present seems to me sufficient to give Subjectivism a defeasible advantage over Objectivism when it comes to explaining correspondence between what we desire and what we have reason to do.

Is the Subjectivist mistaking motivating for normative reasons (4)? Now consider Parfit's suggestion that philosophers have been misled into accepting Subjectivism because they are confusing motivating reasons (which are desire-based) with normative ones (which are not). Though Parfit is right that Subjectivists sometimes confusingly conflate normative reasons talk and motivating reasons talk, it seem clear to me that this is a *symptom* rather than a *cause* of their belief in Subjectivism. Their *acceptance* of Subjectivism reflects not a conflation of normative and motivating reasons but instead (at least in many cases) a prior, independent theoretical commitment to a close conceptual link between normative and motivating reasons.

Indeed, our concept of each kind of reason may constrain what counts as a plausible candidate for the other. Let's look first at the concept of a motivating reason. Motivating reasons are facts that explain why we do what we do; but our motivating reason is not picked out by just any such explanation. Some explanations are *merely* causal, as when we explain someone's snapping at someone by reference to her lack of sleep. Lack of sleep is not what *motivated* her to snap (unless, of course, she is snapping at someone for keeping her up at night). As Kieran Setiya has put it, "[m]otivation is distinguished from mere causation in being the expression of [a capacity to respond to normative reasons], though this expression may be flawed."[23] Motivating reasons, in other words, are considerations that move us through the exercise (flawed though it may be) of our rational capacities.

How about normative reasons? They are, many philosophers have suggested, considerations that move us when we are exercising these capacities *well*. If so, then normative reasons must be capable of *explaining* action. Similarly, Bernard Williams famously insists that

> It must be a mistake to simply separate explanatory and normative reasons. If it is true that A has a reason to φ, then it must be possible that he should φ for that reason; and if he does act for that reason, then that reason will be the explanation of his acting.[24]

The thought seems natural enough: normative reasons (both practical and epistemic) are considerations that feature in good reasoning (practical and epistemic). And a good number of other considerations support it. Surely, we *ought* to be motivated by any reason that applies to us—indeed, we ought to be so motivated when and because we are rational. Since *ought* implies *can*, it must follow that we *can* be motivated by any reason that applies to us, when we are rational. This thought becomes all the more forceful if we accept the very plausible claim that *virtue* is a matter of motivational responsiveness to practical reasons. For if we accept that claim but deny that we ought always to be responsive to our reasons, then we are denying that we ought always to act virtuously.

The power of reasons to motivate rational agents might also help explain another fact that often comes up in the literature on Subjectivism about reasons: that rational agents are reliably motivated to act as they judge they have reason to act. If considerations that provide reasons themselves have the power to motivate rational agents, this fact is neatly explained: rational agents are motivated to act by their judgment that they have reason to act because rational agents' judgments about their reasons are true and are the discovery of facts that themselves have the power to motivate those agents when they are rational.

The explanatory constraint on normative reasons—the thesis that normative reasons must be capable of motivating us—forms a premise in an argument for Subjectivism, a version of which Parfit briefly considers. Here's the argument as Parfit presents it:

(1) For us to have a reason to do something, it must be true that we *could* do it.

(2) We couldn't do something if it is true that, even after ideal deliberation, we would not want to do this thing or would not be motivated to do it.

Therefore

> For us to have a reason to do something, it must be true that after such deliberation, we *would* be motivated to do this thing.[25]

Parfit rejects the second step of this argument: in the sense of "can" at work in the *has-reason*-implies-*can* principle expressed by the first premise, he says, it's simply not true that in order for us to *be able* to do something, we must *want* to do that thing.

This might be debated. *Ought*-implies-*can* principles are plausibly interpreted as concerned with *psychological* possibility: the issue is whether an agent, burdened, at least at the outset, with his actual psychological profile—his actual desires and aims—might be motivated to act in accordance with his reason, and the question of how much those antecedent desires and aims constrain what he can be motivated to do is surely an open one.

But the argument Parfit considers is in any case not the version of this sort of argument I take Subjectivists to be making. That argument begins, not from the principle Parfit considers, but instead from the *explanatory constraint* on what counts as a normative reason:

> (1*) For a consideration to be a reason for us to do something, it must be true that we could be *rationally motivated* to do it for that reason—by that very consideration.

This premise, I've argued, also gets some support from an ought-implies-can principle, one that appeals to the thought that we not only ought to do as we have reason to do, but we ought to do for the right reason—that is, *for that very reason*, and in rational response to that reason. The argument continues:

> (2*) A consideration can rationally motivate us to do something only if it is relevantly connected to our antecedent desires and aims—that is, only if it *would* motivate us to do that thing if we were to deliberate in a procedurally ideal way from those antecedent desires and aims.

Therefore

> A consideration can be a reason for us to do something only if it would motivate us to do that thing if we were to deliberate in a procedurally ideal way from our antecedent desires and aims.

In other words, our reasons depend on the desires and motivations we have, or would have after procedurally ideal deliberation, as the Subjectivist claims.

The second premise of this argument—2*—looks quite different from the second premise of the simpler argument Parfit considers and rejects. That premise concerned the conditions under which it was possible for us to do as we have reason to do. This new premise instead concerns the conditions of *rational motivation*—the conditions under which we can properly be said to have arrived at a new motivation *through a process of reasoning*. Parfit may be right that, in the relevant sense of possibility, it is possible for us to act as we have reason to act even if we don't want to and don't have any desires that could, through procedurally ideal deliberation, give rise to such a desire. What 2* disputes is that we could, in such a case, be motivated to come to perform that action *for the reason we have to perform it, via a process of rational deliberation.*

So the subjectivist argument relies, first, on a claim about the nature of reasons—that reasons are facts that motivate us when we're deliberating rationally—and, second, on a claim about rational deliberation—that no process of rational deliberation could produce in someone a new motivation except by taking her existing motivations as a starting point. Both these claims, of course, can be and have been questioned. The second, characteristically Humean claim, has long been the subject of heated debate. The first (the explanatory constraint) may also be vulnerable to counterexamples.[26] But both claims have significant plausibility, and much can be said in their defense. Far from betraying a *confusion* between motivating and justifying reasons, and so providing a *debunking* explanation of the belief in Subjectivism, the appeal to the conceptual relation between normative and motivating reasons offers meaningful support for the subjectivist position and stands in need of a more elaborate objectivist response than the one Parfit offers.

Is the Subjectivist mistaking what is rationally required of us for what we have reason to do (7)? Parfit next suggests that while our desires do not, in any fundamental way, determine what we have *reason* to do, they may determine what it is *rational* for us to do. In this way, he says, they resemble beliefs, which may make it rational for me to take some action even if those beliefs are false. If running from the snake will make it attack me, I have no reason to run; but if I believe my life depends on my running, it may be rational for me to run nonetheless. Similarly, Parfit says, my desires do not give me reasons but may make it rational for me to do what it takes to fulfill them. The Subjectivist, he proposes, may be mistaking facts about what it is rational for me to do, which *do* reflect my desires, with facts about what I have *reason* to do, which do not.

Does the analogy between belief and desire on which Parfit's suggestion depends withstand scrutiny? Our beliefs can of course fail to reflect the way the world actually is. They can do this even if they are rationally held: even beliefs that are properly responsive to evidence can be false, since evidence can be misleading or missing altogether. So there is a possible gap between justification and truth. Parfit reserves the term 'reason' for what have sometimes (confusingly, in the present context) been called *objective* reasons. So reasons, in Parfit's view, are fixed by the truth, not by our evidence—by the way the world actually is, not by how it appears to us to be. This opens up the door to the possibility Parfit imagines: that we may have reason to do something we could not rationally do (because we lack evidence of our reasons) and may be rationally required to do what we have no reason to do (because the evidence misleadingly points to our having such reasons).

But Parfit's argument suggests there can be a similar gap between what it is rational for us to do and what we have reason to do, even when we have no such false beliefs—a gap generated not by misleading evidence but by *misguided aims.*

Just as there may be a split between what we believe (even when we are reasoning well) and what is *true*, there is room for a split between what matters to us (even when we are well-informed and procedurally rational) and what really matters. This gap too, Parfit says, can make it rational for us to act in ways in which we have no reason to act, confusing the Subjectivist into thinking we do have such reasons.

The Subjectivist, however, sees an important *dis*analogy between the case of beliefs and the case of desires. Our beliefs, even when we are fully procedurally rational, play no (non-trivial) role in determining the way the world is. But if Subjectivism is true, then the same is not true of our desires and aims. If Subjectivism is true, then what *makes* some goal valuable—one that we have reason to pursue—*is* that it stands in the right relation to what already matters to us. What we care about, in other words, *does* play a non-trivial role in determining what matters and what we have reason to do.

Our system of belief formation exhibits what John Rawls might call a kind of *imperfect procedural justification*:[27] even if we execute the epistemic procedure perfectly—forming our beliefs in accord with what our evidence supports—we may still fail to believe what is (belief-independently) true (and so, in that objective sense, fail to believe in accord with our reasons). But Subjectivists take good practical reasoning to exhibit what Rawls called *pure procedural justification*: reasoning well from her antecedent desires will make a person more likely to respond appropriately to her reasons, because a person's reasons are determined by what matters to her when she is reasoning well. So the close connection the Subjectivist recognizes between what we have reason to do and what it is rational for us to do does not reflect confusion but rather (once again) reflects a prior, independent theoretical commitment to the thesis that desires play a role in determining what matters, in contrast to beliefs, which do *not* play a role in determining what is true.

There is a further worry about Parfit's diagnosis here. On many prominent theories of epistemic *justification*—most notably coherentist theories—our beliefs *do* play a role in determining what we are *justified* in believing, even though they do not play a role in determining the truth. So even if we accept Parfit's close analogy between beliefs and desires, and allow that what matters is largely independent of what we care about, just as what is true is largely independent of what we believe, Parfit's analogy also suggests that *what we're justified* in caring about may be significantly determined by our desires. (In fact, I will suggest in a moment that a kind of coherentism about justification looks particularly plausible in the practical case.)

If that is right, then it seems that Parfit is conceding quite a bit when he appeals to the desire/belief analogy and allows that our desires, like our beliefs, can determine what it is rational for us to do. He seems to be conceding, for example, that someone who acts on desires Parfit considers reprehensible may nonetheless be justified—perhaps even morally justified—in acting as she does. Compare the way in which false beliefs that are rationally arrived at can make it morally justifiable—even morally obligatory—for us to take some unfortunate action—such as giving a child medication, at the recommendation of a generally reliable doctor, to which she is actually allergic. So Parfit's desire/belief analogy seems to imply that not only what it is rational for us to do but also what we are morally obligated to do depends on what we desire. (The same may hold even for his imagined future-agony-indifferent agents.) Once he has conceded that much, it is unclear to me that simply embracing Subjectivism in its entirety would be that much more costly with respect to our intuitions.

Is the Subjectivist confusing a value-based reason to respect others' autonomy and avoid paternalism for a desire-based reason to not interfere with, or help promote, the aims of others? Parfit says that this explains why many people accept Subjectivism: out of democratic or liberal or libertarian instincts—a belief that we ought not to tell others what to do. The claim that we should force people against their will to do what we think is best for them would be illiberal and paternalistic, but it is in no way entailed by Objectivism about reasons. On the contrary, Parfit might say, the anti-paternalist claim—that we have reason not to interfere with the choices of others, even for their own good—is itself a claim about object-given reasons—reasons that we have regardless of what we desire.

Parfit is certainly right that Objectivism does not entail any kind of paternalism. Objectivism is entirely compatible with the view that we have reason to respect the autonomy of others. But the characteristic Subjectivist worry is not that Objectivism has implausible first-order moral implications—that it tells us to impose our value system on others, say—but rather that it takes an implausible stance on the relationship between what matters and what matters *to us*. The worry is not so much about *tyranny* as it is about *alienation*. Peter Railton has made a point like this as part of a defense of a desire-based account of an agent's *good*: "it would be an intolerably alienated conception of someone's good," he writes, "to imagine that it may fail in any way to engage him."[28] It is appealing to think something similar must be true of our reasons more generally. As Williams and others have argued, it may be a limiting condition on our moral obligations that they somehow reflect what *drives* us.[29] This goes for our reasons to respect autonomy as well: the importance of respecting autonomy, according to Subjectivists, derives from the importance autonomy has *for us*.

Here is a more general way of bringing out the intuition: recall the fundamental subjectivist commitment that *things matter* because they *matter to us*. We, in this way, introduce reasons into the world. A world with no sentient beings in it, even a world with conscious life, but in which no creature had any desires at all, would be a world without reasons.[30] Objectivism fails to do justice to this sense in which our reasons are *ours*.

Is the Subjectivist mistaking merely derivative desire-based reasons, or value-based reasons to fulfill our desires, for fundamentally desire-based reasons? There are many ways, Parfit allows, in which our desires may affect what we have reason to do, and these reasons can then appear to be desire-based. This, he hypothesizes, has contributed significantly to the acceptance of Subjectivism. But, he says, the appearance is an illusion: any reason we have to do something because it fulfills our desires derives from a reason to act that is not desire-based—a reason to promote well-being, on a desire-fulfillment view of well-being, or provide pleasure, or relieve frustration, or advance our pursuit of other goals whose value does not depend on our desires.

Let's begin by considering desire-fulfillment views of well-being. According to such views, the fulfillment of our present desires is in itself good for us. Parfit says that it follows from these views that we have *value-based, object-given* reasons to fulfill our desires rather than *desire-based, subject-given* reasons to do as we desire. But it is very unclear what this difference comes to. Let's say someone has an informed desire to become a dentist. According to the desire-fulfillment view, becoming a dentist will increase her well-being. If this is right, Parfit says, she will have a value-based reason to become a dentist, because doing so will promote her well-being, which she has value-based reasons to do. But even on this picture, becoming a dentist is valuable—is something she has reason to do—in virtue of the fact that she desires it—and not because fulfilling her desires is, in this case, a means to doing something else she has reason to do regardless of her desires. The fulfillment of her desire has value regardless of whether it has any further beneficial effects, such as promoting her happiness. Defenders of a desire-fulfillment view of well-being have already embraced the subjectivist thought that things matter *for* us, ultimately, because they matter *to* us. So there is something odd about accepting such a view of well-being while rejecting Subjectivism.

Perhaps the difference between the Objectivist Desire-Fulfillment Theory's account of reasons to fulfill our desires and Subjectivism's account of these reasons is that the former is a substantive first-order normative theory, whereas the latter is a meta-normative theory. Objectivist Desire-Fulfillment Theory makes the first-order normative claim that I have a reason to φ if φing fulfills my desires, and that reason is provided by the fact that it fulfills my desires. Subjectivism makes the meta-level claim that *what it is* for me to have a reason to φ is for φing to fulfill my desire. If this is where the difference lies, the dividing line between Objectivism and Subjectivism has now gotten very fine indeed, at least with respect to our reasons to fulfill our desires.[31] And it is far from clear that Desire-Fulfillment Objectivism lies on the intuitively favored side of that line.[32] But it is, in any case, unclear why anyone would accept the substantive normative claim in question if she didn't accept the meta-normative claim.

There are, of course, as Parfit points out, lots of other reasons to fulfill desires. For example, fulfilling people's desires tends to promote their happiness and decrease their levels of frustration and unhappiness. People like getting what they want! To embrace this reason to promote desires is, of course, to move away from a desire-fulfillment theory towards a more hedonistic conception of well-being. The very plausible thought that hedonism captures at least a significant component of what matters is, Parfit argues, perhaps the main reason why people find the Subjectivist account of reasons attractive. After all, it seems that many, if not most, of the things that bring us pleasure do so in virtue of the attitudes we bring to them: there's nothing in itself good about the taste of olives or bad about the taste of truffles. But eating olives plausibly contributes to my well-being and eating truffles detracts from it, because *I enjoy* the taste of olives and *I detest* the taste of truffles. If I preferred the truffles to the olives, as many do, things would be different.

Nor is there a distinctive sensation—pleasure—that we can point to as the desire-independent locus of value in my eating olives. Parfit himself made that point forcefully in *Reasons and Persons*. He wrote:

> *Narrow Hedonists* assume, falsely, that pleasure and pain are two distinctive kinds of experience. Compare pleasures of satisfying an intense thirst or lust, listening to music, solving an intellectual problem, reading a tragedy, and knowing that one's child is happy. These various experiences do not contain any distinctive common quality.[33]

So what, then, are pleasure and pain? What is it that gives me reason to eat olives and avoid truffles? In *Reasons and Persons*, Parfit told us:

> What pains and pleasures have in common are their relations to our desires. On the use of 'pain' which has rational and moral significance, all pains are when experienced unwanted, and a pain is worse or greater the more it is unwanted. Similarly, all pleasures are when experienced wanted, and they are better or greater the more they are wanted. . . . On this view, one of two experiences is more pleasant if it is preferred.[34]

What makes some experience worth pursuing, on this view, is its relation to our desires.[35] But if this is right, then we seem to be back where we were: at least many of our reasons for acting are desire-based, after all.

Parfit, as we have seen, has since changed his view. He no longer thinks that what makes the pursuit of 'pleasurable' experiences worthwhile is that they are desired. Rather, what is distinctive about pleasurable experiences is that we *like* them; what is distinctive about painful or frustrating ones is that we *dislike* them. Hedonic likings and dislikings, Parfit argues, are not themselves desires. But they are easily mistaken for 'meta-hedonic desires.' This is because likings are, like desires, attitudes we bring to the world, and because they are almost always accompanied by desires: we almost always do desire to have experiences we like and avoid those we dislike.

A number of Parfit's debunking arguments depend on this distinction between hedonic likings and desires. Given its importance to his arguments, he defends it vigorously. He points to a number of factors distinguishing hedonic likings from meta-hedonic desires:

(1) Desires have fulfillment-conditions. Likings and dislikings cannot be fulfilled;

(2) unlike desires, which can be about the future, or the possible, likings and dislikings aim only at the present; and

(3) meta-hedonic desires are responses to reasons, but likings and dislikings are not.

It is *likings and dislikings*, Parfit says, not desires, that generate reasons for action.

But Parfit's rejection of the claim that hedonic reasons are desire-based by appeal to the distinction between hedonic likings and desires is unconvincing. All three factors above are, to begin with, entirely compatible with his earlier suggestion, in *Reasons and Persons*, that pleasures are experiences we desire and pains are experiences we desire to avoid. 'Liking' might simply be our name for a particular kind of fulfilled desire: the attitude of approval we take towards an experience we are currently undergoing, that we desire to be undergoing for the sake of what it is like to undergo it. 'Disliking' might be our name for a particular kind of unfulfilled desire: the attitude of disapproval we take towards an experience we are currently undergoing, that we desire to avoid, again, for non-instrumental reasons.[36] In that case, hedonic reasons would be as desire-dependent as we thought.[37]

Parfit suggests that while likings and dislikings can have *causes*, we do not like or dislike for *reasons*. So, for example, a bout of stomach flu after a fancy Italian dinner might cause me to dislike the taste of truffles for years; but it doesn't *give me a reason*—even a *motivating* reason—to dislike truffles. (Remember that motivating reasons, unlike mere causes, move us through the exercise—however flawed—of our rational capacities.) Nor would my dislike of truffles, so caused, be *irrational*. In this respect, Parfit thinks, the attitudes that ground hedonic reasons resemble hunger, thirst, and lust; and they are importantly unlike desires, since desires are, he thinks, things we can be called on to defend. But I am struck, in fact, by the opposite impression: likings are, in this respect, much more like other desires than like appetites such as hunger, or reactive mere sensations like physical pain. After all, we do, it appears, often have motivating reasons for liking or disliking something—we can say what it is we like or dislike about it.[38] We can even (with imperfect success) be persuaded to like something or to dislike it. By contrast, while I can offer a causal explanation for my thirst, or my pain, I have no motivating reason to feel thirst or pain. And you cannot persuade me to feel thirst or pain (though perhaps you can cause me to feel either by drawing enough attention to the issue).

Parfit, confessing a dislike of the feel of velvet, the sound of buzzing houseflies, and the effect of most overhead lights, insists plausibly that "[t]he oddness of these dislikes does not make [him] less than fully rational."[39] That is true. But that, of course, is exactly what Subjectivism predicts, if indeed these dislikes represent Parfit's desires, as I have argued. According to Subjectivism, if we are rational relative to our desires (deliberating well and not subject to misinformation), then we are rational, all things considered; and, what is more, we have good reason to fulfill these desires. It's the Objectivist, again, who is left with something to explain: if Parfit's dislikes represent desires (as I have argued), and if (as he thinks) there is reason for him to fulfill those desires only if they are themselves supported by desire-independent reasons, why think he has any reason to avoid velvet, or buzzing flies, or bleak overhead lighting?

The difficulty Objectivists have in explaining away the apparent role of our desires in grounding hedonic reasons—reasons to bring about pleasure and avoid pain—may seem to support only a *partial* Subjectivism about reasons: a Subjectivism about reasons of *taste*, perhaps. But once an Objectivist has conceded that Subjectivism is true of such reasons, there is some pressure on him to accept a more comprehensive subjectivist account of reasons. For there seems to be no good reason for thinking that occurrent desires for current experiences ground reasons, but, say, prospective desires do not.[40]

I have argued that each of Parfit's attempts to debunk belief in Subjectivism instead lends meaningful, though defeasible, support to the theory. Subjectivists are not mistaking the frequent conjunction of desire and reasons for causation; they are, in fact, better placed than Objectivists to explain the apparent conjunction of what we desire with what we have reason to do. Subjectivists are not mistaking motivating for normative reasons; instead, their independent theoretical commitment to a conceptual link between the two sorts of reason lends further support to their view. Subjectivists are not confusedly rejecting Objectivism as entailing a tyrannical moral theory; instead, they reject its conception of the good as implausibly alienating, since it entails that what matters *for* us is in no way constrained by what matters *to* us. And if Objectivists embrace, instead, a conception of our good that is more beholden to our desires, such as desire-fulfillment or a preference-hedonist view, Objectivism begins to look suspiciously like a less well-motivated version of Subjectivism.

If Subjectivism is true, what matters?

What if I am right? What follows if Subjectivism is true? Parfit argues that the truth of Subjectivism would be devastating to our normative intuitions. Subjectivism, he says, is compatible with the most absurd normative conclusions: for example, that the fact that some choice would prevent future agony for the agent may be no reason at all to take it. After all, Subjectivism relativizes our reasons to our desires, suitably idealized. And no process of merely procedural idealization, Parfit maintains, could ensure that we all have reason to avoid agony, regardless of what we care about going in. If we simply have no concern for our own future suffering (and, Parfit says, we can easily imagine someone who has no such concern), we may have no desire that could ground a reason to prevent it.[41]

But things are even bleaker than this: if we accept Subjectivism, Parfit argues, *then nothing matters*. For how could something come to matter simply in virtue of fulfilling a desire we have no reason to have?

Parfit's nihilistic foreboding is unequivocal when he's discussing *reductive-naturalist* versions of Subjectivism: accounts of reasons that equate normative-reasons facts with purely psychological facts about our motivational dispositions. (I am inclined to agree with him about such theories.) Parfit allows that a non-naturalist Subjectivist's conception of a reason, according to which our reasons reflect the ends and desires we would have after procedurally rational deliberation, is normative. Employing that conception may, Parfit says, allow us to make genuinely normative claims "about which ways of deliberating are procedurally rational, and in other ways ideal." But it is, he insists, "not relevantly normative." It would not allow us to make any genuinely normative claims "about reasons, or about what we should or ought to choose, or to do."[42]

Parfit thinks this because he cannot see how the kind of *merely relational* constraints the procedural standard of rationality imposes could generate genuine reasons for action: considerations that count in favor of some specific course of action. The procedural standard of rationality can only proclaim us rational or irrational *relative to* the desires, aims, or ends that we have. Objectivists think that some of these desires and aims are ones we have good reason to have, and that any reasons to fulfill those desires derive from the reasons we have to have them in the first place. But if Subjectivism is true, Parfit thinks, then "we have no such reasons to have our aims."[43] So "subjective theories," Parfit says, "are built on sand."[44] In other words: garbage in, garbage out.

Parfit seems to be assuming here that procedural reasoning runs only in one direction, from our desires and aims to the actions that would achieve those aims: that it is, essentially, purely instrumental. But that is a mistake. As Kant realized, procedural norms of coherence can put pressure on us not just to adopt the means to our willed ends but also to identify more fundamental ends—ends which bring unity and coherence to our set of desires. Imagine a person who, when asked why he flosses regularly, responds that he does it for its own sake. And imagine that he gives a similar response when we ask him why he does all the other things he does. Such a person's value commitments would strike us as totally bizarre, in large part because of their total lack of internal coherence. There is just something arbitrary and dogmatic about valuing many such unrelated, unsystematic, contingently chosen ends, without some more fundamental explanation for why they matter. Compare the epistemic case: imagine a person who, when asked why she believes each of the things she believes, responds, "I just *do*." Rational people's sets of beliefs are not so piecemeal and disconnected; their beliefs cohere and support each other. Justification may have to bottom out somewhere; but it had better not bottom out in *too* many unrelated articles of faith—especially not articles of faith about which there is irresolvable disagreement between otherwise rational agents. As Michael Smith has argued,

> we may properly regard the unity of a set of desires as a virtue; a virtue that in turn makes for the rationality of the set as a whole. For exhibiting unity is partially constitutive of having a systematically justified, and

so rationally preferable, set of desires, just as exhibiting unity is partially constitutive of having a systematically justified, and so rationally preferable, set of beliefs.[45]

So Subjectivism does not entail that we can have no reasons for our desires, and so no reasons to do anything to fulfill those desires. Desires are candidates for the same sort of justification *coherentists about justification* take beliefs to have: desires are justified when they are part of a coherent web of desire. In fact, as I've argued elsewhere,[46] coherentism about the justification of desires and aims is in two respects on firmer footing than coherentism about the justification of beliefs. First, there are plausible sources of non-doxastic justification for beliefs (sensory perception) and plausible candidates for *basic* beliefs—beliefs (such as beliefs about our own experiential states, or perhaps simple beliefs about the world that we are experiencing) that are not justified in virtue of their relation to our other beliefs but are instead self-justifying or justified directly by experience. But there is no obvious analog to these in the practical case.[47] Nor is there consensus among philosophers on a reliable means of directly forming simple, uncontroversial, unlikely-to-be-mistaken aims and intentions. Second, if the Subjectivist account of normativity is the right one, then coherentism about the justification of desire avoids one major worry faced by coherentist models of epistemic justification: the possibility that a fully coherent set of beliefs may nonetheless come completely untethered from the truth—from the way the world actually is. There is room for such systematic error in the epistemic case because our beliefs play no (non-trivial) role in determining the way the world is. But, as I noted earlier,[48] if Subjectivism is right, then there is no analogous possibility that our aims and desires depart radically from what we have reason to desire, because our desires *do* play a non-trivial role in determining what matters.

Subjectivism nonetheless inherits a different worry faced by coherentist theories of epistemic justification—what has sometimes been called the *alternative systems objection*: for each coherent system of beliefs or desires there exist, conceivably, other systems that are equally coherent yet incompatible with the first. If coherence is sufficient for justification, then, it seems, all these incompatible systems will be justified.[49] And if the input beliefs and desires are weird enough, we will end up having to recognize some very dubious reasons-claims, such as the claim that Parfit's imagined future-agony-indifferent man has no reason to avoid such agony.[50]

Such possibilities lead Parfit to doubt whether the mere coherence, or systematic unity, of a set of desires is enough to secure its rationality. He observes:

> Consider ... Smith's claim that we can be rationally required to have a more unified set of desires. Mere unity is not a merit. Our desires would be more unified if we were monomaniacs, who cared about only one thing. But if you cared about truth, beauty, and the future of mankind,

and I cared only about my stamp collection, your less unified set of desires would not be, as Smith's claim seems to imply, less rational than mine.[51]

Parfit's point illustrates that not every kind of unity of ends is, intuitively, equally rational. This is because reasons-judgments lay claim to a validity that is *non-parochial*. If I claim that I have genuine reason to pursue and protect and respect and promote my aims, then I am claiming more for my ends than just that they are *what I'm after*. In this way, my aims resemble my beliefs: if I take my beliefs to be rational, then I take them to be justifiable in a way that *others* should be able to recognize; I am not merely saying they are what I happen to think.

Michael Smith agrees. He writes:

> Part of the task of coming up with a maximally coherent and unified set of desires is coming up with a set that would be converged upon by rational creatures who too are trying to come up with a maximally coherent and unified set of desires; each rational creature is to keep an eye out to her fellows, and to treat as an aberration to be explained, any divergence between the sets of desires they come up with through the process of systematic justification.[52]

Smith thinks that this aim of convergence with others is part of our ordinary concept of a reason, which, he argues, is *non-relative*. He doesn't claim to have shown that such convergence is possible and so doesn't take himself to have established that there *are* any reasons in this non-relative sense. But it is worth noting that there are, of course, much better candidates for sources of interpersonal systematic justifiability than stamp-collecting. And it is worth reminding ourselves that both Kant and Mill were, in this respect, *optimistic* Subjectivists. Kant thought the value of humanity could serve as a source of non-parochial systematic justification for our aims, and so could serve as an end we all should embrace, on pain of procedural irrationality. Mill thought the same role could be played by pleasure. Much work, of course, would need to be done to see if either argument can be made to work. But the possibility remains tantalizingly open.[53]

Conclusion

So long as it does remain open, Parfit has himself shown us the most important reason to explore it. Near the close of Volume 1 he writes:

> Of our reasons for doubting that there are moral truths, one of the strongest is provided by some kinds of moral disagreement. . . . If we and others hold conflicting views, and we have no reason to believe that *we* are the people who are more likely to be right, that should at least make us doubt our view. It may also give us reasons to doubt that any of us could be right.[54]

He concludes, more optimistically:

> It has been widely believed that there are such deep disagreements between Kantians, Contractualists, and Consequentialists. That, I have argued, is not true. These people are climbing the same mountain on different sides.[55]

But the consensus Parfit finds in Part Three of OWM depends very heavily on prior assumptions about what it is substantively rational for us to do. Parfit's claims about the standards of substantive rationality are hardly less controversial than the claims about right and wrong he uses them to reconcile.

The greatest appeal of the subjectivist project is the possibility of doing better than this. If that project succeeds—if we can, through a collective search for systematic justifiability, identify goals we all have desire-based reasons to share—then what appeared to be a weakness of the subjectivist account of reasons may turn out to be its greatest strength. One of the appealing features of the subjectivist analysis of reasons is that it offers us something non-question-begging to say in defense of our reasons-ascriptions. The procedural standard of rationality to which Subjectivism appeals, though not exactly uncontroversial, may nonetheless be one that someone who disagrees with the subjectivist at the outset about what her *reasons* are might agree on. So it can serve as a kind of "Archimedean point" (to borrow a phrase from Bernard Williams) against which we might brace ourselves in disputes about reasons. (Objectivists like Parfit, by contrast, if they want to appeal to a supposedly shared standard of rationality to settle disagreements about reasons, must appeal to a substantive standard—one that simply incorporates, as a *rational requirement*, the need to respond to the very reason whose existence their interlocutor disputes. If she disputes the existence of the reason, she will also dispute the existence of the corresponding rational requirement.) What's more, the Subjectivist defends her claims about what someone has reason to do by appealing to that person's own commitments.

Moral philosophers have long been concerned about how to respond to the *amoralist*—the person who recognizes what morality requires of him but wonders *why he should do* what morality requires. The *moral ought*, this amoralist might concede, is certainly *about* him—it *refers to* him. But it does not follow merely from this that it has a *proper, normative hold on him* (whatever that comes to), any more than the fact that the dictates of some old-fashioned religion—a religion that in no way reflects what I care about—refer to me entails that I have any *real reason* to comply with them. Because subjectivist accounts of reasons ground reasons in facts about our desires, broadly understood, a subjectivist defense of moral reasons may allow us to provide a more satisfying answer to the amoralist: an answer that appeals to his own concerns and to a standard of reasoning that he *must*, as a rational agent, recognize as authoritative.

The hope for such an answer may be more than mere wishful thinking: it could be that, as Parfit partly recognized, the possibility of moral reasons depends on our being able to offer it. Because it may be a constraint on what counts as a moral theory, we may be able to justify its principles to those they claim to bind.[56]

Notes

1. OWM 1, p. 419.
2. OWM 1, p. 45.
3. OWM 1, p. 45.
4. OWM 1, p. 62.
5. Here Parfit is quoting Korsgaard (1996), p. 278.
6. OWM 1, p. 46.
7. I do so in Markovits (2014).
8. To be fair, one prominent motivation for embracing Subjectivism has been the aim of finding an account of reasons that is naturalistically respectable, and Parfit spends considerable time addressing naturalistic hopes more generally in OWM 2. Because I am not drawn to naturalist theories of normativity, for some of the reasons Parfit outlines, I will not be focusing on those arguments here. (I will return to this issue briefly in the fourth section, 'If Subjectivism is true, what matters?'.)
9. OWM 1, p. 72.
10. Parfit might be right that the *meaning* of his term 'reason' cannot be totally hidden from him (as it would be, he says, if Subjectivism proved true). But history (the case of water, among others) has taught us that the *fundamental nature* of the things our terms pick out can be hidden from us.

    Parfit might resist the analogy to the chemical analysis of water. He might reply that the pre-theoretical concept *water* had "an *explicit gap* that [was] *waiting to be filled*," and so was, in a sense, crying out for further analysis: that even our pre-theoretical concept of water was of *some substance—whatever it is—*that runs in our streams and fills our lakes and oceans and falls from the sky and is odorless, colorless, and potable, etc. *Reason*, he might say, is not 'gappy' in this way. Parfit makes precisely this move in rejecting reductive naturalist utilitarian accounts of *rightness*; rightness, he says, is not gappy in the way that our pre-theoretical concept of *heat* left a gap—that property, *whatever it is*, that causes water to boil and certain sensations in us, etc.—before scientists discovered it to be molecular kinetic energy (OWM 2, pp. 301–2). But I am much less confident than Parfit seems to be in our ability to recognize which of our concepts are or are not gappy—candidates for further reduction or analysis. It is not at all clear to me, for example, that *heat* would have struck me, pre-theoretically, as gappy.

    Can non-empirical analyses be surprising in the way that empirical analyses like chemical analysis can be? I think the arguments and advances in the philosophical debate about the proper analysis of *knowledge* suggests that they can. (I don't mean to suggest, however, that what we mean by our terms places no constraints on what counts as a viable analysis of a concept. I am, for example, sympathetic to Parfit's view that some proposed reductive analyses, such as naturalistic reductions of normative concepts, threaten to eliminate their objects.)
11. But see Manne (2014) for a defense of the claim that there may be multiple common and useful senses of the term 'reason,' at least one of which is distinctively subjectivist. Manne thinks that the general idea of a consideration counting in favor of an action may be broader than the distinctively subjectivist concept of a reason but argues that general idea elides some important distinctions.

12 Parfit approvingly cites Scanlon's claim that the idea of a normative reason—a consideration counting in favor of something—is primitive:

> Any attempt to explain what it is to be a reason for something seems to me to lead back to the same idea: a consideration that counts in favour of it. "Counts in favour how?" one might ask. "By providing a reason for it" seems to be the only answer.
>
> (Scanlon 1998, p. 17)

But as Ruth Chang points out (in Chang (2013), p. 167, n. 6), not all objectivists deny that more can be said here: for example, some objectivists might think facts about what is *valuable* can explain facts about reasons or considerations that count in favor of actions. Since Parfit (like Scanlon) ultimately wants to explain facts about value in terms of facts about reasons, he would reject this further explanation of reasons-facts as well.

13 I believe Sharon Street argues for a view like this. See Street (forthcoming).
14 For further discussion of the distinction between the normative and meta-normative questions we might ask about our reasons, see Chang (2013).
15 See Kant (1997) and Mill (1979), especially p. 34. For a more sustained attempt to read Kant and Mill along these subjectivist lines, some worries about their arguments, as well as the development of an alternative subjectivist defense of categorical reasons, see Markovits (2014, especially chapters 4 and 5).
16 To be precise, Parfit allows that there may be widespread agreement in practice between Subjectivists and Objectivists about what we have reason to do and about what matters. But, Parfit thinks, this agreement is largely contingent. It reflects the fact that most people, especially when informed and procedurally rational, in fact have desires which line up with what they have desire-independent, object-given reasons to do. So what they have object-given reasons to do will, to a significant extent, correspond with what will fulfill those desires. (This, Parfit says, is just what we should expect if Objectivism is true, assuming we are not terrible at picking up on what matters.) The most dramatic cases of divergence between the substantive reasons-claims made by the two kinds of theory will be hypothetical ones, involving imaginary people with bizarre desires. Such imaginary people feature prominently in Parfit's arguments against Subjectivism.
17 Parfit actually calls the reason to fulfill desires he discusses in his sixth debunking explanation a *non-derivative* desire-based reason, but it seems to me to be derivative in Parfit's sense, as I explain below.
18 As noted above (n. 17), Parfit does not class this as a derivative desire-based reason, perhaps because fulfilling others' desires is constitutive of respecting their autonomy.
19 Williams (1993), pp. 20–1.
20 OWM 1, pp. 52–6.
21 Hume (1978), p. 167. The context here, of course, is Hume's discussion of causation.
22 See especially Chapters 32–4 of OWM 2.
23 Setiya (2012), p. 17. Setiya is here interpreting Thomas Nagel's argument in Nagel (1970).
24 Williams (1995), pp. 38–9.
25 OWM 1, pp. 107–8.
26 I argue against the first premise of this argument in Markovits (2011b), revised as chapter 2 in Markovits (2014).
27 Rawls (1971), p. 86.
28 Railton (1986), p. 9.

29 As Williams puts it,

> [t]here can come a point at which it is quite unreasonable for a man to give up, in the name of the impartial good ordering of the world of moral agents, something which is a condition of his having any interest in being around in the world at all.
> (Williams 1981, p. 14)

30 It may seem that an Objectivist could accommodate this intuition if he accepts that all reasons are welfare-based as well as a hedonist or desire-fulfillment view of well-being. I explain in a moment why I think desire-fulfillment views and the recognition of hedonistic reasons in fact push us towards accepting Subjectivism.

31 The Objectivist Desire-Fulfillment Theorist needn't think that desire-based reasons are *all* the reasons there are.

32 Here is one difference between Objectivist Desire-Fulfillment Theory and Subjectivism, a difference that seems to me to favor the latter view: according to Objectivist Desire-Fulfillment Theory, it seems we have reason to satisfy our desires *de dicto* not *de re*. On this view, we have no more reason to satisfy our unfulfilled desires than to change them to desires that are more easily fulfilled: both would lead to the same increase in well-being. But the version of substantive Subjectivism I have been considering entails that we have reasons to satisfy our (rational, informed) desires *de re*; on this view, we have reason to relieve unfulfilled desires by changing them only if we have a higher-order desire not to have hard-to-fulfill desires. According to Subjectivism, we may have no particular reason to develop easy-to-satisfy desires. (Thanks to Daniel Greco for this point.)

33 *RP*, p. 493.

34 *RP*, p. 493.

35 In defending this claim, Parfit was following one of his "two masters" (see Parfit's wonderful preface to OWM 1, p. xxxiii.), Sidgwick, who wrote:

> when I reflect on the notion of pleasure,—using the term in the comprehensive sense which I have adopted, to include the most refined and subtle intellectual and emotional gratifications, no less than the coarser and more definite sensual enjoyments,—the only common quality that I can find in the feelings so designated seems to be that relation to desire and volition expressed by the general term "desirable".... I propose therefore to define Pleasure ... as a feeling which, when experienced by intelligent beings, is at least implicitly apprehended as desirable or—in cases of comparison—pleasurable.
> (Sidgwick 1981, p. 127)

36 Is it clear that likings and dislikings are only for the present? I can like an experience I am not currently undergoing and do not desire to be undergoing. I can also dislike a sensation I am not currently undergoing. But these future- or past-oriented desires do not count as pleasures or displeasures.

37 It is no objection to this view that we might sometimes desire not to have experiences we like or to have experiences we dislike (as when we wish to punish ourselves). There is no contradiction in both desiring that you have an experience and desiring that you not have it. It is, after all, perfectly possible to have conflicting desires. You might, for example, desire, all things considered, for the sake of punishing yourself, that you not have an experience that you *pro tanto* desire to have, for the sake of what it is like to have it.

38 Note that saying what you like about something is not the same as saying what causes you to like it. In Shakespeare's *A Midsummer Night's Dream*, it is Oberon's love

potion that causes Titania to fall in love with Bottom. But she tells us what she loves about him:

> Mine ear is much enamoured of thy note;
> So is mine eye enthrallèd to thy shape;
> And thy fair virtue's force perforce doth move me
> On the first view to say, to swear, I love thee.
> (*A Midsummer Night's Dream*, Act III, Scene i)

Titania is not mistaken in what she loves about Bottom, though she is ignorant of what causes her to love these things about him (Shakespeare (2005), p. 411).

39   OWM 1, p. 53.
40   Scanlon is one Objectivist who acknowledges this point. His worry about the arbitrariness of acknowledging that occurrent desires are reason-generating but insisting that prospective desires are not leads him to reject Subjectivism about reasons of taste. See Scanlon (2002), pp. 339–40. He embraces instead the kind of phenomenology-based account of our reasons to pursue what gives us pleasure that Parfit rejects in *RP*. For more arguments that phenomenology-based accounts are unpromising, and that Subjectivism is true at least for reasons of taste, see Copp and Sobel (2001) and Sobel (2005).

As Sobel points out, the Subjectivist nonetheless has a ready explanation for why our desires seem particularly normatively authoritative when it comes to matters of taste or pleasures and pains: most Subjectivists think only informed desires ground reasons, and it is in mere matters of taste, and matters of pleasure and pain, that the possibility of misinformed desires seems particularly remote. See Sobel (2005), pp. 447–8.

41   OWM 1, pp. 73–82.
42   OWM 2, pp. 285–8.
43   OWM 1, p. 46.
44   OWM 1, p. 91.
45   Smith (1994, p. 159) compares his account of this process of acquiring unifying desires through deliberation to Rawls' account of *reflective equilibrium* as a method for acquiring beliefs in a general principle given a particular set of specific beliefs.
46   For a much more detailed exploration of the analogy between Subjectivism and coherentist models of epistemic justification, and for an argument that the analogy supports Subjectivism about practical reasons, see Markovits (2011a), revised as chapter 3 in Markovits (2014).
47   That is, there are no aims that are uncontroversial, largely immune to erroneous adoption, and therefore not the kinds of things we feel people must offer further justification for caring about, beyond telling us they care about them. There are some ends, of course, that many of us share, and which are so widely understood that it might not occur to us to ask for or require further justification once they are appealed to (the well-being of our children, maybe, or pleasure). But this case is different—here, we don't feel the need to ask for further justification to believe the ends are supported by genuine reasons, because we share the ends (or very similar ones) at the outset. In the case of some beliefs supported by sense-experience, by contrast, the sincere avowal of the belief is itself enough to persuade someone of its justification, even if that person did not share the belief at the outset: even if I do not think that, say, hiccups can hurt, if someone says they do, then, unless I think they are being insincere, that is enough to convince me.
48   See the section "*Un*-debunking Subjectivism," above, and the discussion of the relationship between what we have reason to do and what it is rational for us to do.
49   Olsson (2013).
50   The significance of such hypothetical cases is debatable. Parfit argues that since Objectivism and Subjectivism will largely agree about what we have reason to do in real-life

cases, because people tend to desire what they have desire-independent reason to do, hypothetical cases about which they disagree become decisive. They must determine which view is more plausible on the whole (OWM 1, p. 77). But this is too strong a claim: implausible verdicts about hypothetical cases may be offset, to a certain extent, by other virtues of a theory, such as explanatory power. And we may feel that our intuitive judgments about far-fetched hypothetical cases cannot be trusted.

For a sustained effort to make the initially counter-intuitive verdicts Subjectivism seems to issue about some hypothetical cases seem more palatable, through an meticulous attempt at imagining such cases in detail, see Street (2009).

51 OWM 1, p. 80.
52 Smith (1995), p. 118.
53 I undertake an extended defense of the Kantian tack in Markovits (2014).
54 OWM 1, pp. 418–9.
55 OWM 1, p. 419.
56 I owe thanks to Stephen Kearns, Leonard Katz, Geoffrey Sayre-McCord, David Sobel, Steven Woodworth, and an anonymous referee for Routledge, as well as the members of the audiences at numerous presentations of this chapter as a talk (only some of whose helpful suggestions I have been able to acknowledge by name, above), for valuable feedback.

References

Chang, Ruth (2013) 'Grounding Practical Normativity: Going Hybrid', *Philosophical Studies* 164, pp. 163–87.
Copp, David and Sobel, David (2001) 'Desires, Motives, and Reasons: Scanlon's Rationalistic Moral Psychology', *Social Theory and Practice* 28, pp. 243–76.
Hume, David (1978/1740) *A Treatise of Human Nature*, L.A. Selby-Bigge and P.H. Nidditch (eds) (Oxford: Oxford University Press).
Kant, Immanuel (1997/1785) *Groundwork of the Metaphysics of Morals*, Mary J. Gregor (trans.) (Cambridge: Cambridge University Press).
Korsgaard, Christine (1996) *Creating the Kingdom of Ends* (Cambridge: Cambridge University Press).
Manne, Kate (2014) 'Internalism about Reasons: Sad but True', *Philosophical Studies* 167, pp. 89–117.
Markovits, Julia (2011a) 'Why Be an Internalist about Reasons?', in *Oxford Studies in Metaethics* 6, Russ Shafer-Landau (ed.) (Oxford: Oxford University Press), pp. 255–79.
Markovits, Julia (2011b) 'Internal Reasons and the Motivating Intuition', in *New Waves in Metaethics*, Michael Brady (ed.) (Basingstoke: Palgrave Macmillan), pp. 141–65.
Markovits, Julia (2014) *Moral Reason* (Oxford: Oxford University Press).
Mill, John Stuart (1979/1861) *Utilitarianism*, George Sher (ed.) (Indianapolis: Hackett Publishing Company).
Nagel, Thomas (1970) *The Possibility of Altruism* (Oxford: Clarendon Press).
Olsson, Erik (2013) 'Coherentist Theories of Epistemic Justification', in *The Stanford Encyclopedia of Philosophy* Spring 2013, Edward N. Zalta (ed.): http://plato.stanford.edu/archives/spr2013/entries/justep-coherence/.
Parfit, Derek (1984) *Reasons and Persons* (Oxford: Oxford University Press).
Parfit, Derek (2011) *On What Matters* (Oxford: Oxford University Press), vols 1 and 2.
Railton, Peter (1986) 'Facts and Values', *Philosophical Topics* 14, pp. 5–31.
Rawls, John (1971) *A Theory of Justice* (Cambridge: Harvard University Press).

Scanlon, T.M. (1998) *What We Owe to Each Other* (Cambridge: Harvard University Press).
Scanlon, T.M. (2002) 'Replies', *Social Theory and Practice* 28, pp. 337–40.
Setiya, Kieran (2012) 'Introduction: Internal Reasons', in *Internal Reasons: Contemporary Readings*, Kieran Setiya and Hille Paakkunainen (eds) (Cambridge: MIT Press), pp. 1–34.
Shakespeare, William (2005/1595) *A Midsummer Night's Dream*, in *William Shakespeare: The Complete Works* (second edition), John Jowett, William Montgomery, Gary Taylor and Stanley Wells (eds) (Oxford: Oxford University Press), pp. 401–23.
Sidgwick, Henry (1981/1874) *The Methods of Ethics* (Indianapolis: Hackett Publishing Company).
Smith, Michael (1994) *The Moral Problem* (Oxford: Blackwell).
Smith, Michael (1995) 'Internal Reasons', *Philosophy and Phenomenological Research* 60, pp. 109–31.
Sobel, David (2005) 'Pain for Objectivists: The Case of Mere Matters of Taste', *Ethical Theory and Moral Practice* 8, pp. 437–57.
Street, Sharon (2009) 'In Defense of Future Tuesday Indifference: Ideally Coherent Eccentrics and the Contingency of What Matters', in *Philosophical Issues* 19 (a supplement to *Noûs* on 'Metaethics'), Ernest Sosa (ed.), pp. 273–98.
Street, Sharon (forthcoming) 'Nothing "Really" Matters, but That's Not What Matters', in *Does Anything Really Matter: Parfit on Objectivity*, Peter Singer (ed.) (Oxford: Oxford University Press).
Williams, Bernard (1981) 'Persons, Character, and Morality', in his *Moral Luck* (Cambridge: Cambridge University Press), pp. 1–19.
Williams, Bernard (1993) *Morality: An Introduction to Ethics* (Cambridge: Cambridge University Press).
Williams, Bernard (1995) 'Internal Reasons and the Obscurity of Blame', in his *Making Sense of Humanity* (Cambridge: Cambridge University Press), pp. 35–45.

4

THE BUCK-PASSING ACCOUNT OF VALUE

Assessing the negative thesis

Philip Stratton-Lake

Introduction

The buck-passing account of goodness (BPA) is a specific analysis of goodness in terms of reasons and pro-attitudes. According to BPA to be good is roughly to have properties that give everyone reason to have a pro-attitude towards the thing that has those properties. This is a metaethical thesis so should not have any substantive implications for first-order normative theory. So its truth does not affect Parfit's views in normative theory – his Triple Theory.[1] But it is an important part of his metaethical view, and the central role he gives to reasons – his reasons-fundamentalism. Furthermore, Parfit deviates from Scanlon's version of BPA in an interesting way. This revision is interesting not only because Parfit claims it makes BPA more plausible, but also because it contributes towards a broader issue in the theory of reasons – namely the way in which reasons 'add up' and how literally we are to understand the metaphor of the weight of a reason.

Parfit on buck-passing

In *On What Matters* Parfit endorses Scanlon's buck-passing account of value. BPA consists of a positive and a negative thesis.

> *The positive thesis* – for X to be good is for X to have properties that give us reason to have a certain pro-attitude towards X and to act in certain positive ways towards X.[2]

> *Negative thesis* – goodness itself is never reason-providing – that is, the fact that X is good is never a reason to have a pro-attitude, or act in certain ways, towards X.[3]

In what follows I will identify BPA with the positive thesis and regard the negative thesis as a view that buck-passers may (arguably) either accept or reject depending on other views they hold.

I think BPA needs refining in various ways.[4] First, I do not think reasons to act should be included in the analysis – only reasons to have pro-attitudes should (which is not to say that we typically, if not always, have reasons to act in various ways in relation to good things). Second, the reasons to have a pro-attitude must be provided by properties of, or facts about, the object to which the pro-attitude is directed. Finally, the reasons that involve goodness (the right kind of reasons) are universal – they are reasons that everyone has. But since Parfit (and others) often ignore these refinements in their discussion of BPA, I too will put them to one side in assessing his view on the matter.

Scanlon seems to assume that the negative thesis follows from the positive thesis, and on the face of it this seems right. It is hard to see how goodness could be reason-providing if BPA is true, for according to BPA the fact that X is good is, crudely, the existential fact that there is reason to care about X. *Prima facie* it is very odd to suppose that this existential fact is a reason to care about X. It would be like supposing that the fact that there is an argument for *p* is itself an argument for *p*.

Parfit, however, disagrees. He denies that BPA implies the negative thesis. He writes:

> When something is in this [the reason-involving] sense good, Scanlon claims, this thing's goodness could not give us reasons. Such goodness is the property of having *other* properties that might give us certain reasons, and the second-order fact that we had these reasons would not itself give us any reason not [sic] to act in this way.
>
> This view needs, I think, one small revision. If some medicine or book is the best, these facts could be truly claimed to give us reasons to take this medicine, or to read this book. But these would not be *further, independent* reasons. These reasons would be *derivative*, since their normative force would derive entirely from the facts that made this medicine or book the best. That is why it would be odd to claim that we had *three* reasons to take some medicine: reasons that are given by the facts that this medicine is the safest, the most effective, *and* the best. Since such derivative reasons have no independent normative force, it would be misleading to mention them in such a claim.[5]

If Parfit is right to think that the negative thesis is implausible, then this seems to cause a problem for buck-passers. If the fact that something is good is, roughly, the existential fact that there is reason to admire it, then it should be as counter-intuitive to suppose that goodness is reason-providing as it is to suppose that this existential fact is reason-providing. Parfit tries to get round this problem by trying to make it more plausible to accept that the fact that there is reason to admire something is a reason to admire it. He does this by claiming that the reason provided by this existential fact (which on the buck-passing account of value is goodness itself) is derivative, and thus does not add to the other reasons present. Understood in this way, he claims, buck-passers may plausibly deny the negative thesis.

I will later consider further why buck-passers might want to deny the negative thesis. Before I do that I want to get clearer on Parfit's view.

Non-additive reasons

Parfit tries to avoid the apparent oddity of denying that goodness, analysed in buck-passing terms, is reason-providing by claiming that the reason it provides is derivative and consequently does not add weight to the reasons from which it is derived. In a certain way this view is quite attractive, as it means that buck-passers are not forced to claim that people are mistaken when they say, for example, that we should read a certain book because it is so good, or that we should exercise regularly because it would be good for us.

Parfit claims three things about the reason provided by goodness, which should be distinguished.

1   Goodness is a dependent reason.
2   Goodness is a derivative reason.
3   Goodness is a non-additive reason.

A dependent reason is one that is not independent and so is one that we have only when and because we have some other reason. It need not be dependent on the particular reasons on which it actually depends. A medicine might be good because it will reduce our fever, but it could be good in some other way. It might be good at relieving the pain of aching joints. So the reason provided by the fact that the medicine is good will not depend on the reason provided by the actual good-maker – the fact that it will reduce our fever. It will, however, depend on the reason provided by whatever makes the medicine good.

I'm not sure that (1) and (2) are different claims, for Parfit claims that a derivative reason is one that has no independent normative force – independent, that is, from the force of the reasons provided by the facts that make the medicine or the book good, and presumably this is true of a dependent reason.[6] Perhaps a derivative reason is different from a dependent reason in the sense that one reason might depend on another without being derived from it. For instance, the reason we have to feel guilty if we do not Φ is one that we have only if there is some other reason – the reason that generates the duty to Φ. So the reason to feel guilty is a dependent reason. But it is not obvious that the reason to feel guilty if we do not Φ is derived from the reason to Φ.[7]

Parfit seems to understand a non-additive reason in two distinct ways. First, he understands it as a reason that does not add to the *number* of other reasons we have to take the medicine or read the book. This is suggested when he denies that the reason provided by goodness is not a further reason, and when he claims that it is odd to say that goodness is a third reason (assuming there are two good-making features that each provides its own reasons). So if there were two other reasons to take the medicine – for example, because it would lower our fever and ease our aching joints – Parfit would say that the medicine's goodness is not a third reason to take it.[8]

The second way in which he understands a non-additive reason is as one that does not add *normative force* to the other reasons present. I take this to mean that a reason is non-additive in the sense that it does not imply that we have more, or stronger, reason to Φ when it is added to the other reasons to Φ. This way of understanding a non-additive reason does not commit one to the first. Although it may at first sound odd, one might think of the reason provided by goodness as a distinct, extra reason, but one that does not add normative weight to the reasons provided by the good-making features. This is the view that Mark Schroeder holds. So whereas Parfit claims that goodness is a non-additive reason in the first and second sense, Schroeder, as I understand him, maintains that it is non-additive only in the second sense.

I do not think Parfit's view can be sustained. If Parfit takes seriously the idea that goodness itself *provides* a reason – rather than say that *there is* a reason to do what is good (which everyone can accept), or that we may carry on talking *as if* goodness is reason-providing – then he cannot, I think, understand a non-additive reason in the first way. The fact that some medicine will relieve a fever and the fact that it is good are clearly distinct facts, so the reasons provided by each of these facts would be distinct reasons – that is, there would be two reasons rather than one.[9] This reason is not independent of the other reasons, but that is quite compatible with its being distinct from them.

If this is right, then Parfit should not say that the reason provided by goodness is non-additive in the sense that it does not add to the number of reasons provided by whatever makes the thing good. Rather he should say only that this further reason does not add weight to the reasons provided by the facts that make the thing good. If what makes the medicine good is that it will reduce my fever, then the fact that it will reduce my fever gives me a reason to take it. That the medicine is good (or best) gives me a distinct and, therefore, a second reason to take the medicine. But because this second reason is derivative, Parfit should say that the fact there is this second reason does not mean that we have more, or stronger, reason to take it. The reason to take the medicine provided by the fact that it will reduce our fever has the same weight or strength as this reason together with the reason provided by the fact that the medicine is good.

This revision to Parfit's view eliminates the difference between him and Schroeder on this matter. But to sustain his view Parfit would also have to deny additivity.

> *Additivity*: if A and B are each reasons for S to Φ, then A&B must be a better reason for S to Φ than either individually.[10]

Given additivity, the fact that X is good can be a reason for me to desire X only if it adds weight to the reasons provided by the properties that make it good. But, as everyone agrees, it is implausible to suppose that the grounding properties together with the goodness they ground would be a better reason than the reason provided by the grounding properties alone. It is this that tends to lead buck-passers to endorse the negative thesis. But if we abandon additivity, we do not need to accept the negative thesis, and this seems to be what Parfit does.

The plausibility of additivity

But abandoning additivity seems to generate another problem. On the face of it additivity seems very plausible: if I am aware of one reason to Φ and you point out another reason for me to Φ, then I would now think that I have even more reason to Φ. This extra reason might be important, as it might decide the matter of whether to Φ. So if the best version of BPA forces us to abandon additivity, that would seem *pro tanto* to count against BPA, even if it makes BPA better in some other way. Schroeder, however, argues for abandoning additivity on the ground that abandoning it allows us to capture better the two most important roles of reasons. These two roles are:

1 Reasons determine what we ought to do.
2 When we act well, they are the reasons for which we act.[11]

The first of these roles seems to count in favour of additivity. Take what Schroeder calls 'buck-passing facts'. A buck-passing fact is the fact that someone has reason to act in some way. Buck-passing facts do not seem to contribute to the explanation of what we ought to do, as all of the explanatory work is done by the reasons that make the buck-passing fact true. Suppose the reason I have to act is that it will further my career. That doing this act will further my career will figure in an explanation of why I ought to do it. It also makes the buck-passing fact true – that is, it makes it true that I have reason to do this act. But the buck-passing fact plays no role in explaining why I ought to do this act, since all the work is done by its truth-maker. This gives us a good reason to suppose that buck-passing facts are not reasons.

But if buck-passing facts are reasons they would clearly be dependent reasons, depending on the facts that make them true. And Schroeder notes that we can revise the first role of reasons so that it applies only to independent reasons:

> even though all reasons are *taken into account* in the balance of reasons, which determines what we ought to do, when reasons fail to be *independent*, they may not contribute more to that balance together than either does separately.[12]

At this point in his argument that is just an option. Why should we go this way rather than simply deny that buck-passing facts are reason-providing? Schroeder's argument here moves on to the second role of reasons – that when things are going well reasons are things for which we act. Since sometimes we might act on the basis of buck-passing facts, that supports denying additivity. Schroeder illustrates his point with the example of Nate, who loves surprise parties but hates unsuccessful surprise parties. Now the fact that there is a surprise party in the living room is a reason for Nate to go there. But his friend Calvin cannot tell Nate this reason as it would spoil things. So he tells him that he has a good reason to go into the living room, and, trusting his friend Calvin, Nate goes into the living room. It would seem that Nate went into the living room because he had good reason, and this seems fine. But given the linking principle that, when things go well, the reason for which we act is the reasons we have to act, this would seem to imply that the buck-passing fact is a reason for Nate to go into the living room.[13] If we hold onto additivity we could not say that and would have to say that Nate acted for no reason.

So abandoning additivity enables Nate's reason to be a good one and avoids the implausible implication that he acted for no reason at all. Allowing buck-passing facts to be reasons also enables buck-passers to allow that when people choose something because it is good, they are acting for a reason. This makes a decent case for abandoning the negative thesis, as Parfit proposes. But even if this argument is good, it is not clear to me that Parfit can accept the conclusion, as he wants to.

The coherence of abandoning additivity

Because Schroeder has a different conception of a reason from Parfit, it is easier for him to abandon additivity. But given Parfit's understanding of a reason, it is not clear that he can abandon additivity. I think that Parfit's understanding of a reason as a consideration that counts in favour of some attitude or action means that he cannot coherently abandon additivity.

Parfit agrees with Scanlon that for some fact, F, to be a reason for me to Φ is for F to count in favour of me Φing. Such facts can count in favour of acts in different degrees. They can favour them strongly or weakly. The fact that by Φing I would avoid bruising my elbow and the fact that by Φing I would avoid being blinded each give me a reason to Φ, but the latter fact is a much stronger, or weightier, reason to Φ than the former. This latter fact counts in favour of Φing much more strongly than the former fact. So, on this view, reasons not only count in favour of certain attitudes or actions but do so with a certain strength or weight.[14] It is because reasons have a certain weight that they can be defeated by being outweighed by opposing reasons – that is, a reason to Φ can be defeated by a stronger, or weightier, reason not to Φ, although this is not the only way in which reasons can be defeated. The same is true of reasons to believe.

So for Parfit every reason must (a) count in favour of a certain act or attitude and (b) do so with a certain weight. That I have said that I will go to dinner with you this evening and that going to dinner with you this evening will be very pleasant are each a distinct reason to go to dinner this evening. Each fact counts in favour of going to dinner, and each does so to a certain degree. Cases like this are quite compatible with additivity.

The cases that Parfit (and Schroeder) thinks cast doubt on additivity involve derivative reasons – the sort of reason that is provided by goodness if the buck-passing account of value is true. Derivative reasons, they claim, are non-additive reasons. But now that we have got clear on the notion of a non-additive reason, making sense of the rejection of additivity will prove quite tricky. For now the issue of making sense of the rejection of additivity becomes the issue of making sense of derivative reasons being distinct from (though not independent of) the reasons they are derived from, whilst not adding to the strength of those reasons.

Parfit's view seems to be something like the following: suppose N is what makes X good and gives us a non-derivative reason to Φ, and G is the derivative reason provided by the goodness of X. Parfit might say that both N and G stand in a favouring relation to Φing, and that G stands in this relation because N does. So we get something like the following:

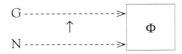

The arrows from left to right represent the counting-in-favour-of relation, and the vertical arrow represents the explanatory relation. But if G is a distinct reason, we have to ask what weight the reason provided by G has – to what degree does G count in favour of Φing. At first sight we seem to have two options:

a   The derivative reason provided by G has no weight.
b   The derivative reason provided by G has a weight, but this weight does not add to the weight of the basic reason provided by N.

According to (a) N and G each count in favour of Φing, but, although N favours Φing to a certain degree (with a certain strength or weight), G favours it to no degree – that is, the reason provided by G has no strength or weight. That explains why the reason provided by G does not add to the reason provided by N. The trouble is that it is very hard to see how G could count in favour of Φing but not do so to any degree. That looks indistinguishable from its not counting in favour of Φing at all, and the claim that G does not count in favour of Φing at all is what is being denied.

I appreciate that the notions of strength and weight are metaphors, but they are metaphors for the idea of normative force of reasons – and illuminating metaphors at that. To say that G is a reason to Φ that is distinct from the reason to Φ provided by N, but has no weight, is to say that G is a normative reason with no normative force. To me that makes as much sense as saying that some event is a cause yet has no causal power. Labelling it a *derivative* cause would not help.[15]

If, then, we are to make sense of the idea of distinct, non-additive, derivative reasons, we must think of them as having a weight or strength of their own, but one that does not add to the weight of the basic reason. How are we to make sense of this? Presumably the thought is that, qua derivative reason, any normative weight it has is inherited from the basic reason from which it is derived. But the metaphor of inheritance militates against the view that the basic reason retains the same weight that it passes on to its progeny. This metaphor makes sense of non-additivity, for all of the normative force of the basic reason is here handed over to the derivative reason. But this has the absurd result that the basic reason has no normative force. It has given it all away!

One need not understand the metaphor of inheritance in this way. We might say that I have inherited my genes from my parents, without supposing they have lost their genes by bequeathing them to me.[16] But even here the metaphor is not illuminating, for the genes I inherit from my parents have the full range of powers that they have in my parents. But to make sense of a non-additive reason Parfit needs the derivative reason not to inherit all of the powers of the reason from which it is derived, for the grounding reason has weight of its own and the derivative reason is not supposed to inherit this.

So if Parfit is to hold onto his account of a reason as something that counts in favour of an act or attitude, then he owes us an account of how a derivative can count in favour of something without adding weight.

Weighing reasons

Perhaps the problem I have with Parfit's view stems from the fact that I think of normative weights as an amount of something, an amount that attaches to individual reasons. But weights may not be best understood as amounts and may attach to sets of reasons rather than to individual reasons. Once again, Schroeder's views on this subject are helpful. I will not lay out the details of his account, as my main interest here is whether Parfit can make use of some key elements of Schroeder's account of weight to give sense to his view that goodness is reason-providing, whilst maintaining that this reason does not add weight to the reasons provided by the good-making facts.

Schroeder argues that we should abandon the view of weights just mentioned, in part because it does not allow us to abandon additivity. In its place he offers an alternative account of the weight of reasons. Schroeder has a Humean account of reasons, which Parfit would reject. But his account of the weight of reasons is not distinctively Humean.[17] So as far as that goes it could be used by Parfit to give sense to his claim that goodness provides a non-additive reason.

The two relevant parts of Schroeder's view are:

1 The weight of a reason is the weight that it is correct to place on it.
2 "Strictly speaking ... it is not reasons that have weights, but only *sets* of reasons".[18]

Correctness is determined by the balance of reasons of the right kind, and the right kind is "those which are generated by an activity, very broadly construed".[19] Parfit need not analyse correctness in terms of the right kind of reasons to give weight to reasons or accept Schroeder's account of the right kind of reasons. He may claim that correctness is indefinable, and thus basic, or offer some alternative account of correctness.

Schroeder often departs from (2) and talks as if weights attach to individual reasons. But I take it to be an essential part of his account that weights apply to sets, for it is this that allows him to suppose that some reasons added to the set add weight, whereas others do not. The ones that do not are the ones which, when added to the set of other reasons, do not imply that it is correct to give that set more weight in our deliberation. One need not assume that the individual reasons carry their weight with them for them to add weight to the set. On the view under consideration, all we need assume is that it is correct to give more weight to the enlarged set in our deliberation if the additional reason is additive, and that it is not correct to do this if it is a non-additive reason that is added to the set.

So can Parfit accept (1) and (2)? Let's start with (2). Perhaps Parfit should abandon his view that individual facts count in favour of certain attitudes and acts. Perhaps he should claim, instead, that it is sets of such facts that do this and so could be said to have a weight. But that would undermine the very claim he wants to make – namely that the fact that something is good is a reason. If only sets count in favour of certain acts and attitudes – that is, they are reasons for those acts or attitudes – then the fact that something is good would not be a reason but would be part of a reason. The reason is provided by the set of such facts.

As I argued above, such a view would not have the radical implication that most of our reasons claims would turn out false. For we could regard most people's reasons claims as incomplete descriptions of reasons, and it does not seem to me that that would imply their claims are false. But if Parfit accepted that it is only sets of facts that provide reasons for attitudes and actions, rather than individual facts, he would be denying the very thesis he wanted to defend – namely that the fact that something is good is a reason. So he cannot accept (2).

Perhaps Parfit could maintain that weight attaches to individual reasons, but each weight is determined by the weight it is correct to give to those individual facts in our deliberation. Parfit might then say that the reason provided by goodness is non-additive in the sense that it is not correct to give weight to this in our deliberation if the good-making facts have been taken into account, but it is correct to give weight to the reason provided by goodness if those other facts have not been taken into account. In the latter case, the weight it is correct to give to goodness in our deliberation is the same as the weight it would be correct to give to the good-making facts alone.

Once again, I doubt this could work with Parfit's understanding of a reason as a fact that counts in favour of some act or attitude. But even if it could work with his understanding of a reason, I think there is a fundamental problem with any such attempt to analyse the weight of reasons (or sets of reasons) in terms of the weight it is correct to give it in our deliberation. For this reason I think we should not understand the weight of reasons in this way.

The problem is that one of the reasons (or set of reasons) for some action may be excluded by an exclusionary reason. An exclusionary reason is a reason not to give any weight in one's deliberation to some reason for or against a certain act.[20] An exclusionary reason does not cancel the reason it excludes. It does not imply that it is really no reason after all. Rather the thought is that the relevant fact continues to be a reason to Φ, and may even be a very good reason to Φ, but nonetheless should not figure in our deliberation.

So, for example, the fact that a judge has ruled that some piece of evidence, E, against the accused is inadmissible, perhaps because it has been obtained in some illegitimate way, means that the jury should not give any weight to E in deciding whether the accused is guilty. But although the jury ought not to give E any weight in their deliberation, E may nonetheless be a strong reason to believe that the accused is guilty and so will have a weight.

To make this clear, suppose that the only reason to believe that the accused is guilty is given by E, and that this evidence is stronger than the evidence in favour of innocence. If we understand weight of a reason as the weight it is correct to give it in our deliberation, then it would turn out that in reaching a verdict it is correct to give more weight to E in our deliberation than to the reasons in favour of the accused's innocence. But this is not correct. Because E is excluded from consideration, the jury ought not to give any weight to this piece of evidence in their deliberation. So it would not be correct for them to give more weight to it in their deliberation than to the considerations in favour of the accused's innocence. But then it would turn out that it has less weight than the reasons in favour of an innocent verdict. This has the unfortunate implication that the thought that it has more weight than the opposing evidence has been lost completely.

So this account of weight cannot account for the idea that some reason might be a very good reason to Φ – which I take to mean a weighty, or strong, reason – even though it ought not to figure in our deliberation about whether to Φ at all. Since this account of the weight of a reason (or set of reasons) cannot leave room for the idea that certain reasons to Φ ought not to figure in our deliberation about whether to Φ, this account should, I think, be rejected.

There are other accounts of the weight of a reason. For example, Kearns and Star argue that for F to be a reason to Φ is for F to constitute evidence for the belief that we ought to Φ. Evidence for p is understood in terms of the probability that p is true, and the strength of that reason is determined by the strength of that evidence, i.e. the degree to which it makes it more probable that p is true.[21] But clearly this account of weight involves buying into an account of a reason that Parfit would not, I think, accept – namely an account that defines all reasons as epistemic reasons.

Parfit's examples: being attributively best and being good for you

In the passage cited earlier Parfit gave the example of attributive value as a plausible reason-giving fact when he claims that "if some medicine or book is the best, these facts could be truly claimed to give us reasons to take this medicine, or to read this book. But these would not be *further, independent* reasons". He also claims that the fact that something would be good for you is plausibly reason-providing.

I think what we should ask is not whether the negative thesis contradicts what we would naturally say here, but whether we would persist in thinking that goodness after some Socratic questioning. This questioning would involve asking why we think this thing is good, whether the good-makers are reason-providing and whether, once we recognise these features as reason-providing, we would still be inclined to think of goodness as reason-providing. So, for example, you might initially and quite naturally cite the fact that the medicine will be good for me as a reason to take it. I ask you what makes it good for me, and you reply that it will reduce my fever. You accept that this good-maker gives me reason to take the medicine. I would suggest that, at this point, if I then asked you whether you still regarded the fact that it was good as a further reason to take it, you would lose your inclination to say that the fact that the medicine will be good for me is also a reason to take it, for you would have acquired the (negative) buck-passing intuition. Because I think that people would lose their inclination to say that goodness is reason-giving after asking the above-mentioned questions, I do not think we should be too bothered by the fact that the negative thesis is contrary to what many people will quite naturally say prior to asking those questions.

Their intuition that goodness is reason-providing would be further weakened if we could persuade them that BPA is true. For then they would see that claiming that the fact that X is good is (roughly) the fact that there are reasons to care about X, and, as I noted above, it is very implausible to suppose that this fact is reason-providing.

But what if I do not know the good-making fact and only know that something is good? Surely in that situation it is plausible to say that the fact that it is good is a reason to have a pro-attitude towards it? This may well be true and does not require us to abandon additivity. For the idea here is that there is an epistemic filter on certain practical reasons, such that certain reasons are not reasons *for me* if I do not, or cannot, know them. This may be true of basic, non-derivative reasons and the reasons derived from them. If I am not in a position to know the non-derivative reasons (the good-maker), then the derivative reason provided by goodness may well be a reason to have a pro-attitude. But in this scenario the non-derivative is not a reason for me. Only the derivative reason is, so we need not abandon additivity. If, however, I know the good-maker – that is, the non-derivative reason – then the derivative reason provided by goodness is not a reason for me. This captures everything a buck-passer might want, for although both facts are reasons in the abstract, the derivative reason is only a reason for some individual if she is not in a position to know the non-derivative reason.

It may help to make this idea clear to illustrate it with an example of a derivative epistemic reason.[22] Suppose the fact that the car is in the garage is a reason to think people are at home. And suppose that the muddy tyre tracks leading to the garage are a reason to think the car is in the garage. The tracks are a reason to believe that a car is in the garage, but, because of that, also seem to be a reason to think that someone is home. If we do not already know the car is in the garage, knowledge of the tracks would raise our subjective probability that there is someone in the house. But if we already know that the car is in the garage (because we looked in the window and saw it), we should not raise our credence that people are home. Knowledge of the car's being in the garage (itself a reason to think people are home) screens off the probability-raising force of our knowledge of the tracks on the driveway.

If that is right it makes perfectly good sense to say that these two reasons are not additive. If you do not know through other means that there is a car in the garage, learning that there are muddy tracks leading to it raises the probability that there are people home and so is a reason to believe this. Learning that there is a car in the garage also raises the probability that there are people home and so is itself a reason to believe that people are home. But if we learn that there is a car in the garage, then learning that there are muddy tracks on the driveway does not raise further the probability that people are home. It is a reason to believe that people are home, but it does not add to the reason provided by the fact that a car is in the garage.

This seems to me to be a perfectly cogent model and allows us to make sense of the idea of a distinct but non-additive reason to act. So one thing a buck-passer might say is that the fact that some medicine is good is a reason for me to take it, but only on the condition that I do not know why it is good. If I know why it is good, the fact that it is good is still a reason in the abstract, but it is not a reason *for me* to take the medicine. For I know the non-derivative reason to take it, and the derivative reason is only a reason for me to take the medicine if I do not know the non-derivative reason. I think this is a perfectly respectable model and one all buck-passers might accept. But what it allows is not quite what the negative thesis aimed to rule out – namely that if I know why something is good, its being good does not give me a reason. What I have been struggling to give substance to is the idea that the good-maker and the goodness made is each a distinct reason to act at the same time, but that the second does not add any weight to the first. The idea suggested here does not allow that these facts are reasons at the same time, but rather allows that ignorance can enable the transmission of the normative force of the non-derivative reason to the derivative reason. That fits perfectly well with the idea of a reason being a fact that counts in favour of some act or attitude.

Conclusion

I have argued that once the notion of a non-additive reason is disambiguated between denying distinctness and denying extra weight, it becomes very hard to give a clear sense to the claim that goodness is a non-additive reason. I considered whether Schroeder's account could support Parfit's view, but concluded that it does not, and that, in any case, it has serious problems of its own. There may be some other account of weight that can make sense of this claim, but I do not know of any that Parfit could use. Without such an account, I think Parfit must give up the claim that goodness is a derivative, non-additive reason and so should not reject the negative thesis. But he can allow the weaker thesis that ignorance of the good-making qualities can enable the fact that something is good to be a reason, but only on the condition that one is ignorant of the more basic reason.

Notes

1. OWM 1, pp. 411–17.
2. Scanlon (1998), pp. 11, 95.
3. Scanlon (1998), p. 11.
4. Stratton-Lake (2013), pp. 78–80.
5. OWM 1, p. 39.
6. OWM 1, p. 39.
7. Thanks to Alex Gregory for this example.
8. OWM 1, p. 39.
9. I assume here that it is a sufficient condition for there being two different reasons to Φ that these reasons are provided by different facts.
10. Schroeder used this term in an earlier draft to Schroeder (2009). Although it did not make its way into the published paper, I think it is for my purposes a useful principle.
11. Schroeder (2009), p. 342.
12. Schroeder (2009), p. 344.
13. Schroeder (2009), p. 345.
14. Of course one might try to abandon the idea that reasons must have a weight, but this is not something Schroeder seems inclined to do; see Schroeder (2007b), p. 122. He abandons the view that the weight or strength of a reason is in some way proportional to the strength of the desire it explains, or how effectively it satisfies the desire it explains. For him, the weight of a reason is determined by the weight it ought to have in our deliberation.

    > If reasons are the kinds of thing to which we are supposed to pay attention in our deliberations about what to do, then stronger reasons are the ones to which we are supposed to pay *more* attention, and which we are supposed to find more *decisive*.
    >
    > (Schroeder 2007b, p. 122)

15. Although normative reasons are very different from causes in a variety of ways, they are analogous in the respect that causes have a certain causal force, and normative reasons have a certain normative force.
16. Thanks to Richard Rowland for this point.
17. Schroeder (2007a), p. 139.
18. Schroeder (2007a), p. 126.

19 Schroeder (2012), p. 471. Schroeder (2007a) develops this view with reference to first-order, second-order, third-order, etc. reasons to give more weight to sets of reasons. He argues that this does not lead to an infinite regress, as such reasons are simply undercutting defeaters, and we may assume undercutting defeaters run out at some point.
20 Raz (1975), pp. 35–48.
21 Kearns and Star (2009), pp. 231–2.
22 Many thanks to an anonymous referee for this suggestion.

References

Kearns, Stephen and Star, Daniel (2009) 'Reasons as Evidence', in *Oxford Studies in Metaethics 4*, Russ Shafer-Landau (ed.) (Oxford: Oxford University Press), pp. 215–42.
Parfit, Derek (2011) *On What Matters* (Oxford: Oxford University Press), vols 1 and 2.
Raz, Joseph (1975) *Practical Reason and Norms* (Oxford: Oxford University Press).
Scanlon, Thomas (1998) *What We Owe to Each Other* (Cambridge, MA: Harvard University Press).
Schroeder, Mark (2007a) *Slaves of the Passions* (Oxford: Oxford University Press).
Schroeder, Mark (2007b) 'Weighting for a Plausible Humean Theory of Reasons', *Nous* 41, pp. 110–32.
Schroeder, Mark (2009) 'Buck-passers' Negative Thesis', *Philosophical Explorations* 12, pp. 341–7.
Schroeder, Mark (2012) 'Reply to Shafer-Landau, McPherson, and Dancy', *Philosophical Studies* 157, pp. 463–74.
Stratton-Lake, Philip (2013) 'Dancy on Buck-passing', in *Thinking about Reasons: Themes from the Philosophy of Jonathan Dancy*, David Bakhurst, Brad Hooker and Margaret Little (eds) (Oxford: Oxford University Press), pp. 76–96.

5

NORMATIVITY, REASONS AND WRONGNESS

How to be a two-tier theorist

David McNaughton and Piers Rawling

In *On What Matters*, Derek Parfit powerfully advances what we have elsewhere called the *two-tier view* of practical reasons – a view that we ourselves have advocated. We open by revisiting this view and go on to discuss, among other things, our view of the nature of practical reasons and their strengths, drawing some contrasts with Parfit's views along the way. In addition to discussing Parfit, then, we shall also lay out parts of our own view on how to be a two-tier theorist. Having laid out the basics of the two-tier view in the first section, the next two sections explore some of the primitive notions that are required on such a view (we differ from Parfit here). There are, of course, many objections to realist views such as Parfit's and ours, and the fourth section looks at a constructivist alternative. In the fifth section, we venture beyond our discussion of Parfit to address a pair of issues that confront our own two-tier account. We look, first, at the relation between what an agent has most reason to do and what she ought to do. And, second, we respond to the worry that, if the future is indeterminate, there are insufficient facts to serve as practical reasons. We conclude with a return to Parfit, contrasting our view of wrongness with his and suggesting that his model of morality may not be ours.

The two-tier view

Donald Davidson[1] famously argues that practical reasons are mental states with causal powers. But we, like Parfit,[2] adopt a different usage, according to which practical reasons are facts – the fact, say, that it is cold outside is a reason for you to wear your coat.

It is important to note that there are two facts lurking here. Your reason is the first: it is cold. But there is also a second: the fact that the first fact is a reason.

We have, then, a two-tier view of practical reasons. At tier one are the reasons; at tier two are the facts that the tier one facts are reasons. Experience tells us that it is easy to muddle this distinction, so perhaps it helps to appreciate that the two tiers give rise to different possibilities for error: you might be mistaken about the weather (tier-one error); or you might fail to realize that cold weather is a reason to wear a coat (tier-two error).

For Davidson, 'reason' refers, in psychological contexts, to a cause that rationalizes – if, say, he wanted to persuade her to go, and he believed he could do so by texting her, then, according to Davidson, if this desire – belief pair caused his texting, it constituted his reason for doing so. And this notion of a reason is normative: if his belief was well-grounded, and he lacked countervailing desires, he did as he should. Our notion of a reason is also normative: if it is cold, and this fact is a reason for you to wear your coat, then (roughly speaking), in the absence of countervailing reasons, you should wear your coat. But note that it is the tier-two fact here that is normative[3] – not the fact that it is cold but, rather, the further fact that the cold is a reason for you to wear your coat.

According to Parfit, "[w]hat is normative are certain truths about what we have *reasons* to want, or will, or do".[4] And he sees these truths, as we do, as "fundamental".[5] But he might be interpreted as denying that there are any other irreducible normative concepts. (We will address this in more depth in 'Parfit's reductionism', below.) We disagree – we see, for example, the concepts of value, harm and benefit as central, normative and irreducible. And there are numerous further, perhaps less central, though no less irreducible, normative concepts, such as desert, justice, fidelity, gratitude, and reparation. While, however, these normative concepts are irreducible, they are interrelated. W.D. Ross,[6] for instance, takes justice to be concerned with the distribution of benefits and harms in accord with desert. (The normative is also tied to the non-normative, of course, by supervenience.)

What about the possibility of reasons themselves having normative content? That is, in our jargon, can there be normative tier-one facts? According to what we will call the *simple* two-tier view, the answer is negative. A practical reason on this view is never itself a normative fact (it is the fact that you have it that is normative). But is the simple view correct? Suppose you are contemplating an act that would cause undeserved harm. Is this a reason against doing it? To say 'yes' is to deny the simple view, since 'undeserved harm' is a normative notion. But any harmful act has non-normative features that make it harmful. So perhaps the simple view might be retained by citing these features as reasons, rather than citing the harm. For example, suppose you are deciding whether to cast the deciding vote on a piece of legislation that will increase sales taxes. This increase will cost the poor more, relative to their incomes, than it will cost the wealthy, and thereby cause undeserved harm to the former group, let us suppose. What is your reason for voting against the increase? It seems that you might cite the first fact about relative cost; or you might cite the second, concerning undeserved harm. We see no problem with citing either, provided you do not cite both. It is fine for you to cite the harm as a reason for your vote, but this is not a *further* reason to vote against the increase, independent of the relative cost to the poor. Thus we reject the simple view, with the caveat that care must be taken not to 'double-count' when citing reasons with normative content.

Harm, then, is not a further, independent reason against your voting – a reason in addition to the facts that would make your voting harmful. And, in our view, the same applies in all cases of putative reasons with normative content – including the case of wrongness. Herein lies another difference with Parfit, to which we shall return in the final section. But we first address some other disagreements and points of accord.

Parfit's reductionism

Parfit sees 'impersonal goodness' and 'good for' as derivative normative concepts, reducible to the concept of a reason. He begins with the following definition:

> When we call one event *better* in the *impartial-reason-implying* sense, we mean that everyone would have, from an impartial point of view, stronger reasons to want this event to occur, or to hope that it will.[7]

And he associates 'impersonal goodness' with this notion of 'better'. There is also the idea that an event can be 'good for someone':

> When we call some event *good for someone*, in the *reason-implying* sense, we mean that there are certain facts that give this person self-interested reasons to want this event to occur, and that give other people altruistic reasons to want or hope, for this person's sake, that this event will occur.[8]

Parfit acknowledges that the fact that an event would be impersonally good or good for someone can be a reason "to want this event to occur". But he sees such reasons as "derivative, since [their] force would derive from facts that would make this event good for this person, or impersonally good". As we will discuss below, we might agree with Parfit thus far. But we part company when he goes on to assert that unlike "the concept of *a reason* . . . these versions of the concept *good* are not fundamental".[9] We see a distinction between the claim that facts about goodness are not fundamental reasons ('reasons reductionism') and the claim that goodness is not a fundamental concept ('conceptual reductionism'). And we claim that the second (which we deny) does not follow from the first (which we might accept).

We see matters as follows. In acting you modify the state of the world. Some states are better than others; some states are better than others for you; and some states are better than others for the neighbourhood dogs. The 'better than' relation ranks states in accord with their goodness or value; the 'better for x than' relation ranks states in accord with how beneficial they are to x. Terminology can be confusing here: some authors distinguish between impersonal and personal value, but, as we use the term, value is always impersonal; it is benefits that are personal. Each is measured on an objective scale – it is not the case, for example, that x's benefit scale varies in accord with the perspective of the evaluator. And care must be taken not to conflate benefit scales with the value scale. Consider, for instance, the following case from Ross:

> Suppose . . . that the fulfillment of a promise to A would produce 1,000 units of good for him, but that by doing some other act I could produce 1,001 units of good for B, to whom I have made no promise, the other consequences of the two acts being of equal value.[10]

Ross thinks he should keep the promise to A, and sees the view that right acts are those "productive of the best possible consequences" as denying this.[11] But if units of benefit are independent of units of good, then it might be that Ross's keeping his promise to A, and thereby providing 1,000 units of benefit to him, has value x; his providing 1,001 units of benefit to B has value y; and he should keep his promise because x>y.[12]

So far so good – we and Parfit could be in agreement. In addition, we are in rough agreement with him when he says:

> We ought . . . to accept some *wide value-based objective* theory. On such views, when one of two possible choices would make things go in a way that would be impartially better, but some other choice would make things go better either for ourselves or for those to whom we have close ties, we often have sufficient reasons to make either choice.[13]

But now let us look to some details. Suppose Anne is confronted with the choice of saving five strangers (by A-ing) or her own child (by B-ing). Let us first leave the comparison of A-ing and B-ing aside and address the question of why the fact that Anne's A-ing would save five strangers is a reason for her to A. On our view, this is because Anne's A-ing would be *better* than doing nothing. And the *strength* of her reason to A is a matter of the value of saving five lives in comparison to saving none. On Parfit's view, by contrast, to say that it is better, and to say that the impartial reasons are stronger, is to say the same thing. Thus, whereas we think there is an irreducible concept of 'betterness' that does explanatory work, Parfit apparently denies this.

Parfit could respond by pointing out that he is simply replacing talk of value and the 'better than' relation with talk of impartial reasons and their strengths, where the latter are conceptual primitives. So the dispute is merely verbal. We are sceptical, however, on various grounds. For example, this move does not account for the following asymmetry: whereas each of us has reason to save lives because doing so is valuable, if someone asks why saving innocent lives is valuable, pointing to the fact that we have reason to do it seems not to be a satisfactory response. Or, to take another example, Parfit believes that we all have impartial reasons to want earthquakes not to kill people.[14] We agree, but we think this holds because such killings are bad. In part, of course, it is a question of where the explanatory buck stops – what are the metaphysical primitives? We have extra such, which we will say more about below. But now let us turn to the comparison between Anne's A-ing and her B-ing.

When benefits to ourselves or those to whom we have special ties are involved, we think that yet more primitives must be invoked. That Anne's B-ing would save her child, Bert, is a reason for her to B not only because it is better than doing nothing (a child's life would be saved; and, perhaps, parenting is valuable), but also because it would benefit *her* child more than her doing nothing. And the combined strength of her reasons to B is perhaps greater than that of her reason to A. But Parfit apparently eschews such an account in terms of benefits and the good, given not only his conceptual reduction of 'better' but also that of 'good for'.

And Parfit's account of "good for" raises some other concerns. Given his accounts of self-interested and altruistic reasons (see note 8), Parfit's definition is equivalent to:

> An event would be *good for someone* (S) in the *reason-implying* sense, just in case everyone has reasons to want this event to occur due to the fact that it would enhance S's well-being.

One issue is the degree to which this is circular, given the tight connection between 'good for' and well-being. We maintain that an event enhances someone's well-being just in case it is good for her, thus we have:

> An event would be *good for someone* (S) in the *reason-implying* sense, just in case everyone has reasons to want this event to occur due to the fact that it would be good for S.

Further, setting the definitional problem aside, we doubt the truth of the following:

> If an event would be good for someone, then we all have reason to want it to occur because of this.

Suppose we are playing a competitive game. Winning will enhance my well-being. But you, my competitor, need have no reason to want me to win because of this. Or suppose I am a justly imprisoned felon. Arguably, escape will enhance my well-being. But you need have no reason to want me to escape because of this. One might try to add *ceteris paribus* clauses to evade this difficulty, but we are dubious – no matter the number of clauses, there will always remain the possibility that another is needed, so that, in the end, the effort will end with the uninformative:

> If an event would be good for someone, then, absent countervailing circumstances, we all have reason to want it to occur because of this.

We are sceptical, then, of Parfit's conceptual reductionism about good and benefit. But care needs to be taken in distinguishing his claims about conceptual reduction from reasons reductionism. We see degree of benefit or value as contributing to reason *strength*, but despite this we need not disagree with Parfit when it comes to citing goodness or benefit ('goodness for') as reasons for some act. Someone might say, for example, that she did something because it would do some good. On the one hand, this is a remark about the strength of her reasons – the act was, presumably, better than doing nothing. But, on the other, it might at the same time be giving her reason. Of course, there will be underlying features of the act that made it good, and perhaps these are the more "fundamental" reasons for her action – so that, as Parfit suggests,[15] goodness and benefit are "derivative" reasons rather than further independent such (cf. harm in 'The two-tier view', above).[16]

We need not, then, oppose this reduction of good and benefit, qua reasons, to the relevant underlying features. That good and benefit are not fundamental reasons does not entail, however, that they are not fundamental *concepts*.

First, the fact that every good act or state has non-normative features that make it good does not entail that there is a finite list of non-normative features to which the concept of goodness can be reduced (and the same applies, obviously, to the concept of benefit). Indeed, in our view, there may be no finite lists of non-normative good-making or beneficial features, let alone such lists that would serve a reductive function. Just as the fact that everyone has a mother does not entail that some poor woman is the mother of all, so the fact that each good act has non-normative features that make it good does not yield, by logic alone, the conclusion that there is some finite list of non-normative features that all good acts have in common – an additional argument is needed.[17]

Second, even if we could list all the potential good-making and beneficial features, we could make no sense of such lists without the concepts of good and benefit to bind them together. And when presented with novel features to consider, we would not know how to categorize them as good, or beneficial, or neither, without a grasp of the concepts of good and benefit. As an analogy, take the functional concept of a tin opener. From the perspective of pure physics, the placing of all actual and potential tin openers into one category makes no sense; and without a grasp of the notion at the functional level we could not categorize novel objects as tin openers (or not).

So much for our differences with Parfit on the reduction of good and benefit. When it comes to another area of reductionist debate, however, we and Parfit are in agreement: tier-two facts are irreducibly normative (that is, no tier-two fact is identical to any non-normative fact – see note 3) and metaphysically basic. This latter metaphysical point of agreement will reappear in 'Constructivism and the two-tier view', below. In the next section, however, we consider another point of possible contrast between our view and Parfit's: the issue of constraints.

Benefits, value and constraints

We are not consequentialists, but we think that consequentialism can cover more of the practical territory than some of its opponents suppose. And it is useful to define our position by contrasting it with a simple consequentialist view according to which the strength of your reason to perform an act is proportional to its value (which includes that of its consequences).[18] Value, then, determines reason strength on this view, but it need not enter reason content. Your reason to put on your coat is that it is cold; its strength is a matter of its value relative to your alternatives.

But what determines the value of an act? Hedonistic utilitarianism is, perhaps, the simplest view. It can be seen as the conjunction of:

1 (a) pleasure is always beneficial, pain always harmful and (b) nothing else is beneficial or harmful; and
2 (a) welfare (i.e. benefit) is always good, harm always bad and (b) nothing else is good or bad.

The simple consequentialist need not, of course, be a hedonistic utilitarian. The latter, for instance, has no room for the thought that one distribution of welfare is better than another, whereas the simple consequentialist can incorporate the view that justice – in the sense of distributing welfare in accord with desert – is itself good.[19] This adds to the list of goods in denial of (2b); and (2a) fails also, since benefits going to someone who deserves harm is bad.

Setting aside the issue of (1), let us turn to consider reason strength. According to simple consequentialism, you might say, have most reason to pursue your own welfare in some circumstance, but only if the state you produce in that pursuit is the best (in the sense of maximizing value) you can achieve.[20] Welfare is relevant to reasons here but only indirectly: while welfare is relevant to the value of a state, the strength of your reason(s) to produce that state is proportional only to its value.

We now have three notions in play: value, welfare and reason strength. The simple consequentialist sees reason strength as a matter only of value. But, of course, there are other possibilities. According to the normative egoist, for instance, value is irrelevant to reason strength – rather, the strength of your reason to do something is a matter only of how much it would benefit you. We try to occupy an intermediate position between these two extremes. Like the advocate of egoism, we see welfare as playing a direct role in our practical reasons. And, like simple consequentialism, we also see the good as playing such a role.

On our position, you have reason to perform some act only if, in comparison to doing nothing, either so acting will give rise to benefits (for someone or something), good, or both.[21] And, *pace* simple consequentialism, the act that you have most reason to perform will often not be one that would maximize the good. The strength of your personal and special reasons (respectively reasons to benefit yourself and reasons to benefit those with whom you have 'special relationships') may exceed whatever contribution the conferral of such benefits would make to the general good. You may have reason to benefit someone to whom you bear no special relationship, but the strength of such a reason, we claim, is a function only of how much good would be accomplished – when benefiting such people you should, other things being equal, distribute the benefits so as to do the most good. When it comes to personal and special reasons, however, we contend that their strength can outstrip value. And this is not so far from Parfit's 'wide value-based objective theory', cited above. Parfit sees matters in terms of having "sufficient reasons" to choose either, say, to do a favour for your friend or to do something for the general good. He does endorse a degree of weighing but believes our "partial and impartial reasons [to be] only *very imprecisely* comparable".[22] We agree that such comparison lacks precision – there is certainly a degree of vagueness – but we suspect that we see less vagueness here than Parfit does.[23]

What are the special relationships we have in mind? On the one hand, there are the ties you have with your friends and family and so forth. On the other hand, there are the ties you can also have with strangers in virtue of such things as making promises,[24] accepting benefits, or inflicting harm.[25] Consider, for instance, Ross's "duties of reparation".[26] In our framework, these become special reasons to benefit those whom you have unjustifiably harmed – that is, you may have a reason to benefit someone that you have unjustifiably harmed, the strength of which is greater than the value of the act of reparation would warrant. The simple consequentialist could incorporate reparational thoughts along the following lines: the world goes better if wrongdoers themselves make reparation to their victims. But we are not sure that this goes far enough – for example, it would require that if you could ensure more such reparation by failing to make reparation yourself, that is what you should do.

We see the simple consequentialist as confronting at least a *prima facie* dilemma (among other difficulties). Either she acknowledges the existence of benefits and harms or she doesn't. If she doesn't, she is in the position of having to deny even the possibility of a debate over distributional concerns: in order even to *raise* the issue of whether one distribution is better than another, there must be something to be distributed – namely, benefits and harms. If she does acknowledge their existence, she has to counteract the plausible thought that, on occasion at least, we have personal and special reasons the strength of which is disproportionate to the value of the acts in question. Suppose you could benefit me or yourself, and both acts would be of equal value. Does this rule out the possibility that you have more reason to benefit yourself here? Or consider a case in which your receiving some benefit would make the world worse: might you not have some reason to pursue it? (Consider again the escape of a justly imprisoned felon.)

Vis-à-vis personal and special reasons, then, we disagree with the simple consequentialist. But what about those moral restrictions that are now standardly known as constraints – rejected by consequentialists but accepted by many traditional deontologists?[27] A constraint is a prohibition against harming people, even in pursuit of good ends – even, indeed, to prevent a greater amount of the very kind of harm that is prohibited by the constraint in question. Proponents of constraints differ in how stringent they take them to be. Some think them absolute: Roman Catholic moral theology, for example, has traditionally held that one may never intentionally kill an innocent person – even to prevent others killing many more innocents. Other deontologists have held that, though constraints are always a significant consideration, they may be overridden, especially if that is the only way to avoid catastrophe. Constraints that are seen, in this latter fashion, as having some threshold beyond which the bad consequences of adhering to them dictate that we should violate them, are known as threshold constraints.

There is much debate, then, over constraints qua putative moral principles of a certain sort. On our account, however, morality is not a system of principles to which constraints might belong in this form. Rather, we see morality as continuous with the rest of practical reason; and, on our view, reasons are central to both. Hence, in order to assess the possibility of our advocating constraints we need an account of them in terms of moral reasons. But what are moral reasons? While, in our view, there is no sharp division of practical reasons into the moral and the nonmoral, examples can be provided that are clearly on one side or the other. Your reason to choose a peach over an apple – that the former is sweeter – is nonmoral. Your reason to give to Oxfam, on the other hand – that doing so will reduce innocent suffering – is moral. Or suppose that you promised to repay a debt on Thursday; this fact is a moral reason to do so. What about your reasons to favour your friends? Some object to the idea that any of these are moral on the grounds that there is something less than ideal about doing things for friends out of a sense of obligation. But that is to confuse the issue of reason with that of motivation: it is quite possible to act on a moral reason – to refuse to betray a friend, say – out of affection.

The moral reasons just mentioned fall within two categories: some are associated with promoting the good, and some with special ties. And some personal reasons may also be moral. But the advocate of constraints can be seen as claiming that there is a further category of moral reasons. Suppose, for instance, there were a constraint against killing the innocent. Then there would a possible occasion on which the strength of A's moral reason not to kill an innocent stranger would be greater than that which would correspond to the disvalue of the killing. On such occasions, A's killing the innocent stranger would be bad but not doing so would be worse (in the sense of being more disvaluable – more innocents would be killed by others, say); yet the constraint would dictate that A has more moral reason not to kill. So the strength of A's moral reason not to kill an innocent stranger does not vary only with the badness of doing so – call such a reason a *constraining reason*.

Our view is that the strength of your reason to perform a given act is a matter only of how much benefit or harm to yourself or those to whom you stand in special relations, and/or how much good or bad, would result. Thus we leave no room for constraining reasons. The badness of harm cannot do the job: the constraint *violator* in the previous paragraph would ensure that less bad comes about. And special relations do not help either. Constraints are independent of relations such as friendship, and the only relation to strangers that might appear relevant is the tie that grounds reasons for reparation. But that tie results from the infliction of *unjustified* harm. Even if harming a stranger is necessary to do greater good, the advocate of constraints will still see this as unjustified. But that is to beg the question against the simple consequentialist (and us, in this case), who sees the doing of greater good as justifying the harm.[28]

Constraints (in the form of constraining reasons), then, would require, from our perspective, a further primitive concerning reason strength – they cannot be accommodated by appeal to welfare or value. We see little prospect of a plausible rationale for including such an added extra.[29] But arguing this case in detail here would take us too far afield (although we do say something more in the next section).[30] Rather, we will pursue the issue of whether Parfit endorses constraints – particularly in light of his attempt to incorporate both Kantianism and rule consequentialism into his Triple Theory.[31]

First, some brief background. Traditionally, Kantians endorse constraints – perhaps the most extreme example is Kant's own absolute proscription against lying, whatever the circumstance. Rule consequentialists, on the other hand, standardly endorse only what we might call *quasi-constraints*, in a sense we will now explain.

As Parfit himself points out, if the rule consequentialist appeals to the claim that

(Q) all that ultimately matters is how well things go[32]

she has trouble when it comes to cases in which the best act does not conform to the optimific rules – how could the best act be wrong if (Q) holds? And, of course, if the rule consequentialist denies that there could be such acts, her position collapses into something akin to our simple consequentialism. This is, of course, a standard complaint against rule consequentialism. The rule consequentialist must, then, deny (Q) if her position is to be distinctive, and argue for rule consequentialism on a different basis. One way of doing this is first to contend that morality is a system of rules that meets certain criteria (such as, say, simplicity and publicity, among others) and then argue that morality comprises the set of rules (for simplicity, we are assuming there is exactly one) that both meets these criteria and whose general acceptance would maximize expected value, where the "calculation of a code's expected value includes all costs of getting the code internalized".[33] Call the rules in this set, following Parfit, the "optimific principles".[34]

These principles will be contingent in the sense that they will depend on, for example, the society in which they are to be introduced. Suppose, say, that animal cruelty is widespread in society A and would be very costly to stamp out, so that principles banning animal cruelty would not make it into the optimific set in A due to the fact that the internalization costs would be too high. And now suppose that such cruelty is regarded, on the whole, with abhorrence in society B, so that such principles would make it into the optimific set in B. Thus certain acts that would be considered wrong in B would be morally permitted in A. We might put this by saying that there is a constraint against animal cruelty in B, but not in A.

For a Kantian, however, constraints are not society-dependent in this way: if there's a constraint against animal cruelty, then that constraint holds in society A; the cost of inculcating a change in conscience is simply irrelevant. The principle banning animal cruelty in society B is contingent in a way that genuine constraints are claimed not to be. But it is constraint-like in that it does not permit you to be cruel to an animal even if that is the only way to minimize animal cruelty overall – it is a 'quasi-constraint'.

Parfit, however, seeks to reconcile the two theories – so does he opt for constraints (forcing the rule consequentialist into the Kantian mould), quasi-constraints (forcing the Kantian into the rule consequentialist mould), or neither? We are not sure.

Parfit, of course, does not base his rule consequentialism on (Q). Rather, he offers[35] an argument from his Kantian Contractualism to rule consequentialism. He begins with the premise that everyone ought to follow the set of principles whose universal acceptance everyone could rationally choose. This is his Kantian Contractualist Formula, and it claims, as we suggested above, that morality must be a system of principles that meet certain criteria – it is just that in Parfit's case it is a single criterion, namely rational choiceworthiness. Parfit then notes that everyone could rationally choose whatever they would have sufficient reasons to choose. Next he considers principles that we have the strongest impartial reasons to choose – these are the principles whose universal acceptance would make things go best, the optimific principles. He then argues that these impartial reasons are not decisively outweighed by any conflicting reasons. Thus we have sufficient reasons to choose the optimific principles. Therefore, provided there are no other sets of principles that everyone has sufficient reasons to choose, the optimific principles are identical to the Kantian principles – the only principles that everyone has sufficient reasons to choose as the principles that everyone ought to follow.

One key claim, then, is that:

(E) No one's impartial reasons to choose [the optimific] principles would be decisively outweighed by any relevant conflicting reasons.[36]

As Parfit notes, "we might have strong personal and [special (to use our terms)] reasons *not* to choose the optimific principles".[37] So why mightn't these decisively outweigh the impartial reasons to choose the optimific principles? Parfit has his arguments,[38] but we won't go into those. Rather, our interest here is in constraints, which, as we have seen, correspond neither to personal nor special reasons. Can constraints serve to decisively outweigh one's impartial reasons to choose the optimific principles? Parfit does make specific reference to constraints[39] but insists that they be backed by further reasons – that an act would violate a constraint is not by itself a reason that can play a role at this stage in the argument, or so Parfit apparently claims. Let us explain.

Parfit sees the wrongness of an act as a further independent reason not to perform it – further, that is, to the features of the act that make it wrong.[40] However, in challenging (E), Parfit claims[41] that it is illicit to appeal to the fact that if everyone accepted the optimific principles, this would lead people to act wrongly. But why? If wrongness is an independent reason, why can't we dig in our heels and say that someone's impartial reasons are decisively outweighed by the wrongness of an act those reasons endorse? Parfit seems to be saying that we can't appeal to wrongness – a "deontic reason", as he puts it – until he has finished his argument from Kantian Contractualism to rule consequentialism. But why not? The answer lies in Parfit's claim that he is *applying* the Kantian Contractualist Formula,[42] the idea being that wrongness is determined by the application. But in our view this is not what he is doing. Rather, he is giving an argument from this formula as premise to rule consequentialism as conclusion.

Be that as it may; but how does this relate to constraints? In Parfit's example *Bridge*,[43] by killing Parfit you could save five others from a runaway train. But in doing so you would be using him as a means to save the five. This, he agrees, would be to violate a constraint.[44] But, in order to challenge (E), Parfit seems to think that it is not sufficient merely to point out that (E) would sanction constraint violation (if it does). Rather, it must be established that the fact that you would be killing Parfit as means "would give you a decisive non-deontic reason not to choose that everyone accepts [the optimific principle that requires you to kill Parfit, and we] should ask what this reason might be".[45] That is, Parfit apparently sees the fact that some act would violate a constraint as a *deontic* reason against it – akin to the fact that it is wrong. And, as we saw in the previous paragraph, deontic reasons, in Parfit's view, are out of bounds at this point in the argument.

All this is by way of illustrating that Parfit does not seem to rule out constraints. He also suggests that:

> (X) if the optimific principles require certain acts that we believe to be wrong, the features or facts that, in our opinion, make these acts wrong would not give us decisive *non*-deontic reasons not to act in these ways. What might be true is only that, by making these acts wrong, these facts would give us decisive deontic reasons not to act in these ways.[46]

And perhaps the deontic reasons Parfit refers to here correspond, in some cases at least, to constraint violations. If so, it "might be true" that there are constraints on his view. If Parfit endorses constraints, however, it is hard to see how he can also endorse rule consequentialism. And if he does not, his view would not seem to be Kantian.

The issue of constraints is also implicated in a metaethical issue, to which we now turn: that of Kantian constructivism.

Constructivism and the two-tier view

The two-tier view raises a host of well-known questions and challenges, and Parfit addresses many of them. We will content ourselves here with an issue that he does not develop to the extent that he might, namely constructivist variations on the two-tier view.

Broadly speaking, the issue is that of the connection between reasons and the will.[47] While the two positions we are about to discuss – due to Bernard Williams and certain Kantians respectively – are not inconsistent with the two-tier view *per se*, they differ from ours, and from Parfit's, concerning the status of tier-two facts. Parfit and we see these facts as metaphysically basic; Williams and these Kantians deny this.

On Williams' 'internal reasons' view, you have a reason to do something only if, and because, you would (or, on another formulation, could) be motivated to do it under the assumption that you are fully informed (about non-normative matters) and procedurally rational (where, crucially, being procedurally rational does not require having any particular prudential or moral concerns).[48] Thus, if, say, an anorexic's current motivations are such that, no matter how well informed he becomes and how well he reasons, he cannot be brought to desire food, then he has no reason to eat, according to Williams. We reject this account: it may be that the anorexic has no reason to eat, but, if so, this is not dependent on rational procedure and his current motivations in the way that Williams supposes.

Certain Kantians also claim that there is a connection between reasons and the will. Consider the following passage from Stephen Darwall:

> In [the Kantians'] view, as in that of Humean internalists, something's standing as a normative reason ultimately depends on its being motivating (treated as a reason) in fully rational deliberation, where the latter is determined by internal, formal features of the deliberative process, not by its responsiveness to independently establishable normative reasons.[49]

Where, then, do these Kantians differ from the Humeans? For present purposes we will count Williams as a Humean, and this Kantian view might be seen as simply extending Williams' notion of procedural rationality to include the requirement that practical reasoning accord with the categorical imperative (CI) or some suitably Kantian substitute. Like Williams, these Kantians deny that practical reasons are metaphysically basic. Rather, on both accounts, whether you have a reason to φ depends on what you would be motivated to do if fully informed and procedurally rational. The difference comes in what is to be included under the procedural umbrella. Kant himself, for example, saw self-destruction as ruled out by the CI, and thus, on his account, the anorexic does have reason to eat.

This Kantian position (like Williams' in this respect) is constructivist about reasons in the sense that if you have a reason to do something that is because you would be motivated to do it if you followed the appropriate rational procedure – the fact that you have a reason is 'constructed' via the procedure. This view, as we saw Darwall noting, stands in contrast to one in which the dependence runs in the opposite direction – one for which deliberation being fully informed and fully rational depends on "its responsiveness to independently establishable normative reasons". That is, whereas this Kantian (roughly speaking) sees tier-two facts – facts to the effect that we have practical reasons – as "constructed" in accord with a procedure that respects the CI (or some similar metaprinciple), her opposition here, which includes us, sees such facts as freestanding. We fit the intuitionist mould in this respect.[50]

Parfit too is opposed to constructivism about reasons. AsScanlon puts it, according to the Kantian constructivist about reasons, justification "never runs . . . from claims about reasons to claims about what rationality requires". But Parfit, by contrast, appeals "to an idea of 'what one can rationally will' that presupposes an independently understandable notion of the reasons that a person has and their relative strength".[51]

The Kantian idea here is that the construction of practical reasons emanates from the reasoning of a rational will – where the rational will is autonomous in the sense that it is beholden to no standard external to it. There have been, of course, numerous arguments proposed in favour of this account. Darwall points out flaws in Christine Korsgaard's approach and, indeed, in Kant's original line of thought in the *Groundwork*.[52] So, since we do not have the space to cover multiple varieties of constructivism, we will focus on Darwall's own account.[53]

The key notion for Darwall is that of a 'second personal reason':

> a distinctive kind of reason for acting . . . that, to exist at all, must be able to be *addressed* second-personally ("I" or "we" or "you") by free and rational agents to other agents.[54]

By way of illustration, he contrasts "two different ways in which you might try to give someone [a stranger, we'll assume] a reason to stop causing you pain, say, to remove his foot from on top of yours".[55] One way would be to try to persuade him that pain is bad and that removing his foot will improve the state of the world – call this the *consequentialist*, or C, strategy. The other strategy (call it the D, for *deontological*, or *Darwallian*) strategy would be to

> insist that the other move his foot as a way of advancing a valid demand, from one equal member of the moral community to another, that he stop *causing* you pain. This would address a second-personal reason that presumes on your equal authority as members of the moral community to demand that people not step on one another's feet. Here the reason would be agent-relative, addressed distinctively to the person causing another pain rather than implicitly to anyone who might be in a position to relieve it. . . . [This] reason would purport . . . to be independent of the agent-neutral value of outcomes.[56]

These two strategies differ not only in their rationales but also in their practical upshots. On the C approach, the idea is that treading on others' feet is bad and should be minimized. According to D, by contrast, each of us should simply avoid stepping on others' feet ourselves. If (in admittedly unlikely circumstances) by treading on a stranger's foot I could prevent several people from treading on further strangers' feet, then the advocate of C would have me do it, whereas the advocate of D would not.

Darwall argues for autonomy by arguing that there are second-personal reasons, and that their existence presupposes that rational agents possess autonomy of the will and respect the CI. As he puts it, "[b]ut what authority is a free and rational agent bound to accept and recognize? Only, it would seem, whatever authority one is committed to in making and considering second-personal claims and demands in the first place". And "second-personal reasoning presupposes both autonomy of the will *and* the CI".[57]

But what is Darwall's case for the existence of second-personal reasons – that is, for the claim that second-personal demands and claims are normatively authoritative for rational agents (and, indeed, are the only claims and demands that possess this property)? It apparently hinges on the idea that even strangers are in a certain kind of relationship – one that is a necessary condition of the very possibility of second-personal demands having normative authority: "[m]aking and entertaining demands and claims second-personally at all is *already* to be in a relation in which each reciprocally recognizes the other and gives him an authority as a free and rational person".[58]

As it stands, however, this is no argument for the normative status of second-personal demands – rather, it seems to presuppose it: given that we do make normatively authoritative demands, we must already be in the appropriate relationship. And there is a further difficulty. In the unlikely case above, in which I am treading on one stranger's foot to prevent others from treading on further strangers' feet, why does my 'relationship' with the first stranger take precedence over my 'relationships' with those strangers whose feet I am protecting? Given Darwall's emphasis above on the demand that the treader "stop *causing* you pain", perhaps the idea is that it is the direct causal nature of my relationship to the pain of the stranger on whose foot I am treading that accounts for this. But, of course, we need to be told what counts as direct causation and why it makes such a difference.

For example, consider a 'trolley case' in which five strangers will be killed unless you divert the driverless runaway train by switching the points so that it kills only one (this is Parfit's example *Tunnel*[59]). If you do not intervene, do you directly cause the death of the five? If Darwall says 'yes', then why would I not be directly causing pain to the strangers whose feet I can protect by treading on the one? So let us assume he says 'no'. But by switching the points you surely would directly cause the death of the one, so on Darwall's view perhaps you should not do it. But, if so, why not? Why does the one have the authority to demand of you that you not switch the points, whereas the five lack the authority to demand that you do, even though your relationship with all six strangers would appear to be the same?

Further, if a direct causal relationship makes a difference in cases of harm, what about in cases of benefit? Suppose you could cause someone to benefit directly, versus allowing several others to be similarly benefitted indirectly – you could, say, save one swimmer yourself or make way for the lifeguard to save several. It strikes us that, *ceteris paribus*, you have more reason to do the latter. But, if Darwall agrees, he then has an asymmetry to explain.

In short, we are no more convinced by Darwall's constructivism than by any other form. And with that we return to further development of the non-constructivist alternative – recall the subtitle of the chapter: 'How to be a two-tier theorist'. In the next section, we address some issues that arise on our own two-tier account.

Oughts, degrees of belief and future contingents

Parfit considers several different senses of 'ought';[60] we'll restrict ourselves to one, but one that we regard as central. We begin with the question: what is the relation between what I ought to do and what I have most reason to do?

One simple proposal is:

(O) 'A ought to ϕ' is equivalent to:

'A has most reason to ϕ (and ϕ-ing is an option)'.

We label it '(O)' because it is, in H.A. Prichard's sense, an objective view of ought. Here is one of his examples against such views:

> 'Ought we to stop, or at least slow down, in a car, before entering a main road?' If the objective view be right, (1) there will be a duty to slow down only if in fact there is traffic; (2) we shall be entitled only to think it likely – in varying degrees on different occasions – that we are bound [i.e. morally obligated] to slow down; and (3) if afterwards we find no traffic, we ought to conclude that our opinion that we were bound to slow down was mistaken.[61]

Given that there is no traffic, what you have most reason to do, according to us, is proceed apace – regardless of your state of knowledge. But, surely, if you are uncertain about the traffic, what you ought to do, counter to (O)'s rash prescription, is slow down.

In defence of an objective view of ought, one might suppose that there is an objective probability that a car is coming, and that the agent should slow down because this probability is greater than zero. Prichard rejects this sort of account because there are no such things as probabilities in nature. There cannot, e.g., be such a thing as the probability that someone has fainted, since either he has fainted or he has not. No doubt it is extremely difficult to formulate the precise nature of the fact which we express, for instance, by the statement: 'X has probably fainted'. But at least we must allow that, whatever its precise nature may be, the fact must consist in our mind's being in a certain state or condition. And, once this is realized, it becomes obvious that most of our ordinary thought involves the subjective view.[62]

This passage is suggestive of a subjectivist Bayesian view, according to which all probabilities are subjective. One key feature of such a view is that subjective probability, or degree of belief, is a property of the believer rather than of the object of belief: if your degree of belief that a tossed coin will come up heads is one half, this is a property of you rather than the coin. On pure Bayesianism, probability assignments held by an agent are criticizable if and only if they collectively violate Kolmogorov's axioms.[63] This comports with the idea of rationality as internal consistency: internal consistency of subjective probabilities – or 'coherence' – is conformity to Kolmogorov's axioms. And you can have quite, shall we say, unconventional degrees of belief that are yet coherent.

On our view, like Prichard's, (O) is false. However, we maintain that there is a reading of 'ought' that is less subjective than Prichard's. We disagree, for instance, with Prichard's view that if a "would-be torturer [were] in a very high degree confident that torturing, and torturing only, would save the heretic, he would be bound to inflict the torture".[64] Such a "high degree" of confidence strikes us as unreasonable, and hence the would-be torturer ought not to torture. Admittedly, the notion of a reasonable subjective probability is vague; but we do not have the space here to do more than appeal to intuitions and take the notion as given.[65]

Our claim is that what a person ought to do depends upon what it is reasonable for her to surmise about her practical reasons and their strengths. Surmise and supposition here involve degrees of belief. The idea is that agents have (rough) degrees of belief about tier-one propositions, tier-two propositions and reason strength. And some degrees of belief are more reasonable than others. (Spelling out the formal aspects of our position in detail would require delving into decision-theoretic equations, which we will not do here.) What is reasonable, of course, may be hotly disputed, particularly when it comes to tier-two propositions – expressivists and error theorists, who deny that it is ever true that we have a reason to do anything in our sense, may well assign degree of belief zero to all claims that some fact is a reason for a certain action, for example.

When you ought to slow at a traffic junction, then, this is not because you happen to have a non-zero degree of belief that traffic is present but because such a degree of belief is reasonable, as is a high degree of belief in the proposition that the presence of traffic is a very strong reason to slow. Admittedly, if there is no traffic, you have no reason to slow – but this just shows that you may have no reason, on our view, to do as you ought. When we engage in practical reflection, we try to determine what we have most reason to do. But ignorance intrudes, and verdicts concerning what we ought to do take account of this, forcing a conceptual separation from what we have most reason to do.

So far, so good, perhaps. But we have been supposing that there are tier-one facts to have degrees of belief about. Sometimes, however, we look to the future in deciding what to do. Should you take an umbrella? This depends upon whether it will rain later in the day – a causally contingent matter (let us suppose), if one holds an indeterministic view of the world. On the indeterministic view we (or, at least, one of us) favour(s), no such future contingent is true (or false) now (call this view *NTV*). But how, then, are we to incorporate degrees of belief concerning future contingents? Given the forecast, it seems reasonable to have a high degree of belief that it will rain. But on NTV the only reasonable degree of belief to have concerning the *truth* of the proposition that it will rain is zero.

Richard Thomason,[66] building on the work of A.N. Prior[67] and Bas Van Fraassen,[68] develops a temporal logic for NTV according to which there are various world 'histories' that coincide up to any given time, α, and then diverge into disjoint branches (to reflect indeterminism). Each history respects bivalence, but nothing of the form:

p will be true τ time units in the future $(F(\tau)p)$[69]

is true *simpliciter* at time α (as opposed to being true in a particular history at α) unless it is true at α in every history that contains α. If $F(\tau)p$ is true at α in some histories that contain it, but not in others, then $F(\tau)p$ lacks an overall truth-value at α although $F(\tau)p \lor F(\tau)\sim p$ is true at every time in every history, as is $F(\tau)\ p \lor \sim F(\tau)p)$.[70] But we will typically want to assign a non-zero subjective probability to $F(\tau)p$, even when it lacks a truth-value. So we need some way of thinking of it as an 'event' to which we can apply Kolmogorov's axioms. We suggest using the set of histories in which it is true, so that, for purposes of assigning subjective probabilities, events are considered to be sets of histories.[71]

The idea, then, is that, even in the absence of facts about the contingent future, we can still appeal to reasonable degrees of belief concerning it. And this enables us to give a univocal account of what you ought to do that is consistent with the two-tier view. Your reason for taking your umbrella cannot be (on NTV) that it will rain. And claiming that the forecast is your reason would not comport well with the thought above, that, in the absence of traffic (as opposed to the absence of evidence of traffic), you have no reason to slow. Maybe, as in this latter case, then, you have no reason to take your umbrella even though you ought to. But now reasons seem to have become irrelevant – all that matters is the reasonableness of your degrees of belief. Consistency with the two-tier view appears to have been bought at the expense of rendering it redundant. However, returning to Thomason's temporal logic, the two-tier view is not redundant within histories. Given, say, a history in which it rains, you have a reason to take your umbrella in that history – the two-tier view is now relativized to histories.

Moral wrongness

We turn, finally, to the issue of moral wrongness, and whether the fact that an act would be morally wrong is a further independent reason against doing it, in addition to the facts that make it wrong. Briefly put, Parfit thinks it is; we do not.

On our view, an act's wrongness involves reasonable degrees of belief (in line with our view of 'ought' in the previous section) – if it would have been reasonable, say, for you to have had a high degree of belief that your act would inflict suffering on an innocent, with nothing to be said in its favour, then this constitutes the wrongness of your act. This approach accounts for cases in which (setting aside worries about future contingents) what you have most moral reason to do is the wrong thing. Suppose you are a doctor and have at your disposal two pills: one will either cure the patient of her non-lethal rash or kill her, and you have no way of knowing which; the other will merely effect a partial cure.[72] In this case (unbeknownst to you, of course) the first pill would cure, so it is what you have most moral reason to prescribe. But prescribing it is surely the wrong thing to do – given your state of ignorance, having a zero degree of belief that it is lethal would be unreasonable.

So, according to us, to say that some act would be wrong is to say, among other things, that certain facts about reasonable degrees of belief obtain. But these latter facts are not further reasons against performing the act in question. Given that there is nothing to be said in its favour, the fact that your act would harm an innocent is a decisive moral reason against doing it; that it would be reasonable for you to have a high degree of belief that this is so is not a further independent reason against the act. According to Parfit, by contrast, "when certain acts would be wrong . . . we *can* claim that the wrongness of these acts gives us further, independent reasons not to act in these ways".[73]

Parfit, then, 'double-counts': the moral reasons against an immoral act contribute twice, once in their role as reasons against the act and once in their role as contributors to the act's moral wrongness, which then itself gets counted as a further independent reason against the act. But does this double-counting pose a difficulty for Parfit's view? Perhaps not. There would appear to be two different models of morality in play, and it may be that, if we accept Parfit's model, double-counting is not a problem. Ours is a thoroughgoing non-constructivist two-tier view, whereas Parfit, while a non-constructivist about reasons, is a constructivist about wrongness – in one sense, at least. He does consider constructivism about wrongness and rejects it. But the version he rejects is a form of scepticism, according to which (in a phrase, but not a view, that he attributes to Rawls), "it's for us to decide what the moral facts are to be".[74] However, this is not the constructivism that we see him as holding.

His Triple Theory merely asserts a biconditional:

> An act is wrong just when such acts are disallowed by some principle that is optimific, uniquely universally willable, and not reasonably rejectable.[75]

But this triple test is not merely epistemic – rather, being disallowed by a principle that passes the test is a wrong-*making* feature: "The Triple Theory should claim to describe a single. . . wrong-making property".[76] Parfit, then, claims that acts are wrong (in part) because they fall foul of "triply supported" principles,[77] rather than falling foul of such principles because they are wrong. This 'Euthyphro switch' is a hallmark of constructivism.

Such constructivism is itself symptomatic of what we might call a *legal model* of morality. Just as an illegal act is made so by its violation of the law, so an immoral act, on this way of looking at matters, is made so by its violation of some moral principle. And moral principles gain their normative authority, in turn, via their selection by some higher-level process, just as laws gain their authority via their enactment by a governing body. The selection and enactment can be regarded as 'constructive' processes in the sense that they are what make the principles and laws authoritative. Parfit, of course, does not deny the existence of moral reasons,[78] but his Triple Theory adds additional materials, otherwise it would be metaphysically redundant. On our alternative picture, by contrast, even if there were a non-trivial set of principles that circumscribed morality (which we doubt), morality would not depend upon it metaphysically. Setting aside epistemic worries, and concerns about future contingents, our basic idea is that when moral reasons weigh sufficiently heavily against an act, it is wrong, and there is nothing further to which to appeal, and nor is any such needed.

The view that the wrongness of an act is a further independent reason against it is another mark of a legal model – the analogy being that an act's illegality may be an independent reason against it, further to any other reasons.[79] Each of us, for example, has good reasons (R) not to pollute. But now suppose that the relevant authority enacts a law against it, in response to R. Arguably, each of us now has a further independent reason not to pollute: it is illegal. Of course, the prospect of punishment is one further reason not to pollute once the law is in effect. But perhaps the mere fact of illegality is itself a reason against – it may, for instance, be part of what we owe to each other (to borrow Scanlon's phrase) that we obey the laws of our society.[80] If so, R are counted twice in determining whether I have more reason than not to stop polluting: once directly and once indirectly, when its illegality (to which R contributed) is weighed.

What considerations can be advanced concerning these competing models? In part, it is a matter of which model is more compelling when taken as a whole. But Parfit does offer arguments, of course, for his Triple Theory; and he provides others in favour of seeing wrongness as a further independent reason against immoral acts.

For example, if the latter were not the case, then,

> it would always be enough to ask whether we have [decisive moral reasons] not to act in some way. We would never need to ask, as a separate question, whether some act would be wrong.[81]

But, Parfit claims, when certain people considered, for example, *Bridge*:

> they did not first decide that you would have a decisive reason not to save the five by killing me, and only then conclude that this act would be wrong. These people were struck first by the belief that this act would be wrong, and only then concluded that the wrongness of this act gave you a further, and perhaps decisive reason not to act in such a way.[82]

The argument seems to be that, since people may come to believe that acts are wrong without first considering the moral reasons against them, there is more to wrongness than moral reasons. But this is akin to arguing that, because on occasion people can read a passage and see that it harbours a non sequitur without first working out which canons of logic are violated, there is more to invalidity than violation of logical canons.

In a related argument Parfit complains that, on views such as ours,

> it would have no practical importance whether some act would be wrong. When we were trying to decide what to do, it would always be enough to ask whether we had decisive reasons for or against acting in any of the possible ways. If we decided that we had such reasons, we could then ask whether these were *moral* reasons... But this would not be a question about what we ought to do, or had reasons to do. This question would be merely conceptual, like the questions of which are the kinds of reason that can best be called legal, or aesthetic.[83]

Suppose we are, say, confronting an awkward student who asks why she shouldn't plagiarize. We might respond by pointing out the various moral reasons against plagiarism. But according to Parfit it would add something of practical weight if we also brought her to see that plagiarism is *wrong*. And we might agree – but what it would add is not the recognition of an extra reason. Rather, it would give her an appreciation of the strength and significance of the reasons against plagiarism and the ways in which she might be justifiably criticized if she were to engage in it. The exercise is, perhaps, conceptual. But reconceptualization is not without practical upshot.

Alternatively, of course, the student might have phrased her question as 'what's wrong with plagiarism?', in which case, as we see it, she is asking about the moral reasons against it – and wrongness is not among them. Parfit might, however, respond by claiming that the student already sees that the wrongness of plagiarism is a decisive reason against it and now wants to know what makes it wrong. The answers to both questions, however, ultimately rest on moral considerations – appealing to such notions as harm, justice and so forth. And these alone decide the matter – wrongness, if it were an extra reason, would be superfluous. So, at best, we see the legal model as adding idle cogs to the moral machinery.

Parfit's triple superstructure, then, even if adequate in the sense of rendering correct verdicts, lacks metaphysical significance. In short, he should eschew constructivism about morality, just as he does about reasons, and join us in advocating a thoroughgoing non-constructivist two-tier theory.

Notes

1. Davidson (1980).
2. For example, OWM 2, pp. 279–80.
3. By a normative fact we mean one that has normative content – normative facts can be referred to using non-normative vocabulary, at least on occasion: for instance, 'the first fact David thought of when waking today' might refer, in non-normative vocabulary, to the normative fact that he has reason to go into the office. In our view, as in Parfit's, normative facts are irreducibly so – no normative fact is identical to any non-normative fact. We, like Parfit, are non-reductive normative realists; but we shall not here explicitly defend this view.
4. OWM 2, pp. 424–5.
5. OWM 1, p. 148.
6. Ross (1930), p. 21.
7. OWM 1, p. 41. By an impartial point of view, Parfit means one in which "we are considering possible events that would affect or involve people who are all strangers to us"; and "[w]hen our actual point of view is not impartial [we can adopt an imaginary one] by imagining possible events that are relevantly similar, except that the people involved are all strangers to us" (OWM 1, pp. 40–1).
8. OWM 1, p. 41. Self-interested reasons are "reasons to care about our own well-being", and altruistic reasons are "reasons to care about the well-being of other people" (OWM 1, p. 40).
9. All from OWM 1, p. 42.
10. Ross (1930), pp. 34–5.
11. Ross (1930), p. 34.
12. Ross's failure to distinguish good from benefit is made explicit in his discussion (in Ross (1930), p. 35) of a variant of the above example, where he starts by speaking of a disparity in the provision of "units of good for A" and ends by speaking of "a disparity of good" *simpliciter*.
13. OWM 1, p. 186; see also p. 137.
14. OWM 1, p. 41.
15. OWM 1, p. 42.
16. See also Scanlon's discussion of buck-passing in Scanlon (1998), pp. 97ff.
17. We are more optimistic when it comes to a *normative* list of goods and benefits, albeit a non-reductive one – although the various attempts are certainly not without controversy. Ross, for example, sees justice as a good, whereas Rawls famously denies this.
18. This definition of simple consequentialism differs from earlier definitions we have proposed – for example, in McNaughton and Rawling (2006). Also, it should be noted that we are setting aside recent moves to 'consequentialize' all moral theories. Consider, for example, Portmore (2009). His leading idea is that any theory that determines the deontic status of an act "by how its outcome ranks relative to those of the available alternatives on *some* evaluative ranking" (Portmore (2009), p. 330, italics ours) is a form of consequentialism. The evaluative ranking here can be, for example, egoist, so that egoism is a form of consequentialism on this account (pp. 334–5). For Portmore, the appeal of consequentialism, as he defines it, rests on the thought (roughly) that outcomes can be ranked in accord with what we have reason to prefer,

and we should perform the act at the top of the ranking. Disputes then arise over what we in fact have reason to prefer – is it, for instance, what would be good for me or what would be good *simpliciter*? For us, by contrast, the appeal of consequentialism, as we define it, is the thought that the good *simpliciter* plays a central role in practical reason.

19 See, for instance, Ross (1930), pp. 26–7 and 138.
20 Note that on our account, consequentialism is not a doctrine solely concerned with what one is morally required to do – your reason to pursue your own welfare here, for example, need not be a moral one. Parfit (OWM 1, p. 168) attributes something like our view of consequentialism to Sidgwick – at least to the extent that he sees Sidgwick's version of consequentialism as concerned only with impartially assessed reasons. But Parfit then goes on to say that this "kind of Consequentialism may be better regarded, not as a moral view, but as. . . an external rival to morality". We disagree, but this is a result of many further differences between our view and his that we do not have the space here to address.
21 Two aspects of this claim might initially appear puzzling. First, why the comparison to doing nothing? This is to accommodate cases in which, if you act, either harm or badness will result, but if you do nothing, even more harm will arise, or things will go even worse. We do not want to rule out your having reason to act in such unfortunate circumstances. (Implicit in our view, then, is the thought that reducing harm counts as producing benefit; and reducing badness counts as producing good.) Of course, the notion of 'doing nothing' is tricky, and we certainly do not want to enter the debates about acts and omissions. What it would be to do nothing will, however (we hope), be clear in any given case. Second, why not strengthen the claim from 'only if' to 'if and only if'? Well, suppose you could benefit a justly imprisoned felon by helping him escape. His benefit notwithstanding, you may have no reason to. However, if an act would do some good (in comparison to doing nothing), then you do have some reason to perform it.
22 OWM 1, p. 137.
23 The problem of vagueness, of course, is notorious, and we have nothing much to add to the debate. But, given the ubiquity of the problem, that our view is subject to it is not, we think, a major strike against it. But there is a challenge to the possibility of any weighing of reasons on views such as ours, according to which the strength of reasons varies with context. Both Berker (2007) and Gert (2007) contend that in order to make sense of a reason having weight, its weight must be invariant. (Gert also proposes a positive view, to which Parfit's may have some affinities, on which reasons can have two different kinds of strength that vary independently of one another.)

We, naturally, deny this contention. Consider, for example, the diminishing marginal utility of money. The more money you have, the less you care about losing or gaining the odd dollar. And claiming that your decreasing preference strength here reflects varying reason strength is certainly not incoherent – that φ-ing would earn you a dollar is a reason for you to φ, but the strength of that reason to φ depends on your current wealth.
24 Some might claim that you have reason to keep a promise even though it will benefit no one and not do any good (and the same might apply to refraining from stealing). If this is correct, it is a counterexample to our view. Consider, for instance, a confidential death-bed promise to do something posthumously for the promisee that, as things turn out, will dishonour the promisee's memory. Is there room on our view for the thought that, even if you have most reason not to keep the promise, nevertheless you do have some reason to do so? It is open to us to maintain that the very keeping of a promise, regardless of its consequences, can be either beneficial to the promisee, valuable, or both. We are not sure about this. But in our view, of course, whether you do have some reason to keep the promise is precisely a matter of whether it will benefit anyone (or thing) or do some good.

25 Ross (1930), p. 21.
26 Ross (1930), p. 21.
27 For example, Alexander and Moore (2008).
28 What about personal reasons? Admittedly, violating a constraint might harm the violator (consider the psychological trauma, for example). But such harms to the violator do not provide her with *moral* reasons not to violate, and thus are not, presumably, what the advocate of constraints has in mind as grounding them.
29 In many ways our view is similar to that of Ross (1930) and (1939). But there are also many points of difference. For example, we see practical matters in terms of reasons, moral and otherwise; Ross, by contrast, sees practical reason as comprising only moral obligations. This leads to many further differences – for example, Ross (1930), pp. 24–6, claims that we have a "duty to produce pleasure for ourselves"; we think only that you often have a reason to pursue your own pleasure. Constraints may constitute another point of difference. Ross speaks of the "duty of non-maleficence" (pp. 21–2) in a way that may imply he thinks of it as (what we would now call) a constraint against injuring others. However, one of Ross's main concerns in contrasting non-maleficence with beneficence is to emphasize that the former is 'a duty of a more stringent character'; but this point can be accommodated without any appeal to constraints once we distinguish (as Ross does not do as sharply as he might: see 'Parfit's reductionism') between benefits and harms on the one hand and value on the other: the bad of injury outweighs the good of benefit.
30 For instance, one of the issues that we lack the space to address here is arguments to the effect that admitting personal reasons without constraints yields counter-intuitive results – see, for example, Kagan (1984) and McNaughton and Rawling (2006).
31 OWM 1, p. 413.
32 OWM 1, p. 417.
33 Hooker (2000), p. 32.
34 For example, OWM 1, p. 378.
35 OWM 1, pp. 378ff.
36 OWM 1, p. 378.
37 OWM 1, p. 379.
38 OWM 1, pp. 379ff.
39 OWM 1, p. 396.
40 For example, OWM 1, pp. 173 and 448ff.
41 For example, OWM 1, p. 386.
42 OWM 1, p. 386.
43 OWM 1, p. 218.
44 OWM 1, p. 396.
45 OWM 1, p. 396.
46 OWM 1, pp. 395 and 448.
47 For further discussion see, for example, McNaughton and Rawling (2004), the references listed there and OWM 2, pp. 269–94.
48 Williams (1981).
49 Darwall (2006), p. 299.
50 Darwall (2006), p. 298.
51 In his response to Parfit in OWM 2, p. 121.
52 Darwall (2006), pp. 299–302.
53 Why not a general argument against constructivism about practical reasons, i.e. a general argument to the effect that tier-two facts are metaphysically basic, rather than arguments against individual constructivist positions? The danger is that such general attempts to persuade the constructivist will degenerate into mutual incomprehension. Perhaps the best general strategy is to paint a compelling picture of practical reason with metaphysically basic tier-two facts playing a crucial role – something that Parfit is attempting to do.

54 Darwall (2006), p. 305.
55 Darwall (2006), p. 307.
56 Darwall (2006), p. 307.
57 Darwall (2006), p. 310.
58 Darwall (2006), p. 310.
59 OWM 1, p. 218.
60 For example, OWM 1, pp. 33–8 and 158–74.
61 Prichard (1949), p. 29.
62 Prichard (1949), p. 30.
63 Kolmogorov (1950).
64 Prichard (1949), p. 30.
65 The notion of a reasonable subjective probability, requiring more than mere coherence, is to be found in, for example, Ramsey (1931), §5. Ramsey links it to the idea of a "useful [mental] habit"; we shall not commit ourselves that far here, however.
66 Thomason (1970).
67 Prior (1967).
68 Van Fraassen (1966) and (1968).
69 Thomason does not employ time indices, but they are helpful for our purposes, despite Thomason (1970, p. 267, n. 5).
70 $F(\tau)\sim p$ is equivalent to $\sim F(\tau)p$ on this view.
71 To apply Kolmogorov's axioms (setting aside the requirement of countable additivity), we need the objects to which probabilities are assigned to form a Boolean algebra, and using sets of histories fits the bill since they constitute a field of sets, which is a standard example of such an algebra. (The fact that excluded middle holds means that the 'one' of the algebra does correspond to the necessarily true proposition.) And there is precedent for probabilities that are not probabilities of truth – consider, for instance, E.W. Adams' view that the probability of a conditional is a conditional probability. See Arlo-Costa (2016), Bennett (2003), pp. 58 and 104, and Edgington (2014).
72 This is a variant of one of Jackson's cases in Jackson (1991).
73 OWM 1, p. 173.
74 OWM 1, p. 367.
75 OWM 1, p. 413.
76 OWM 1, p. 414.
77 OWM 1, p. 413. Incidentally, Parfit gives us remarkably few examples of triply supported principles, which is grist to our particularist mill, but we won't pursue that further here – although we do wonder whether Parfit agrees with Scanlon (1998), p. 201, that there are an "indefinite number" of "valid moral principles". If virtually every case requires its own principle, this would explain the lack of examples of general principles that are triply supported.
78 For example, OWM 1, p. 414.
79 Parfit in fact endorses *triple* counting. An act's wrongness, he claims, is distinct from its falling foul of a triply supported principle – the latter is (part of) what *makes* it wrong; and its falling foul of such a principle is in turn distinct from the properties that make it fall foul. So we might have the fact that, say, an act inflicts pointless suffering, the fact that it falls foul of a triply supported principle, and the fact that it is wrong, with each fact making it the case that the next one holds. And, as we read him (OWM 1, pp. 173–4, 413–4 and 448–51), Parfit claims that all three of these facts are independent reasons not to perform the act in question. There is a disanalogy here with the law, because Parfit has certain definitional concerns (for example, OWM 1, pp. 369–70) that lead him to deny that wrongness just *is* (in part) violating a triply supported principle, whereas illegality just is violation of the law – thus law abiders need only double count. But this disanalogy is unimportant for our purposes.
80 Scanlon (1998).

81 *OWM* 1, p. 450.
82 *OWM* 1, p. 451.
83 *OWM* 1, pp. 172–3.

References

Alexander, Larry and Moore, Michael (2008) 'Deontological Ethics', in *The Stanford Encyclopedia of Philosophy* (Fall 2008 Edition), Edward. N. Zalta (ed.): http://plato.stanford.edu/archives/fall2008/entries/ethics-deontological/

Arlo-Costa, Horacio (2016) 'The Logic of Conditionals', in *The Stanford Encyclopedia of Philosophy* (Fall 2016 Edition), Edward N. Zalta (ed.): http://plato.stanford.edu/archives/fall2016/entries/logic-conditionals/

Bennett, Jonathan (2003) *A Philosophical Guide to Conditionals* (Oxford: Oxford University Press).

Berker, Selim (2007) 'Particular Reasons', *Ethics* 118, pp. 109–39.

Darwall, Stephen (2006) 'Morality and Practical Reason: A Kantian Approach', in *The Oxford Handbook of Ethical Theory*, David Copp (ed.) (Oxford: Oxford University Press), pp. 282–320.

Davidson, Donald (1980) *Essays on Actions and Events* (Oxford: Oxford University Press).

Edgington, Dorothy (2014) 'Indicative Conditionals', in *The Stanford Encyclopedia of Philosophy* (Winter 2014 Edition), Edward N. Zalta (ed.): http://plato.stanford.edu/archives/win2014/entries/conditionals/

Gert, Joshua (2007) 'Normative Strength and the Balance of Reasons', *The Philosophical Review* 116, pp. 533–62.

Hooker, Brad (2000) *Ideal Code, Real World* (Oxford: Oxford University Press).

Jackson, Frank (1991) 'Decision-Theoretic Consequentialism and the Nearest and Dearest Objection', *Ethics* 101, pp. 461–82.

Kagan. Shelly (1984) 'Does Consequentialism Demand Too Much? Recent Work on the Limits of Obligation', *Philosophy and Public Affairs* 13, pp. 239–54.

Kolmogorov, Andrei (1950/1933) *Grundbegriffe der Wahrscheinlichkeitsrechnung*, Nathan Morrison (trans. and ed.) (Springer: Berlin).

McNaughton, David and Rawling, Piers (2004) 'Duty, Rationality and Practical Reasons', in *The Oxford Handbook of Rationality*, Al Mele and Piers Rawling (eds) (Oxford: Oxford University Press), pp. 110–31.

McNaughton, David and Rawling, Piers (2006) 'Deontology', in *The Oxford Handbook of Ethical Theory*, David Copp (ed.) (Oxford: Oxford University Press), pp. 424–58.

Parfit, Derek (2011) *On What Matters* (Oxford: Oxford University Press), vols 1 and 2.

Portmore, Douglas W. (2009) 'Consequentializing', *Philosophy Compass* 4, pp. 329–47.

Prichard, H.A. (1949/1932) 'Duty and Ignorance of Fact', in *Moral Obligation*, W.D. Ross (ed.) (Oxford: Clarendon Press), pp. 18–39. First given as Annual Philosophical Lecture, Henriette Hertz Trust, British Academy.

Prior, A.N. (1967) *Past, Present and Future* (Oxford: Oxford University Press).

Ramsey, F.P. (1931/1926) 'Truth and Probability', in *The Foundations of Mathematics and other Logical Essays*, R.B. Braithwaite (ed.) (London: Routledge and Kegan Paul), pp. 156–98.

Ross, W.D. (1930) *The Right and the Good* (Oxford: Clarendon Press).

Ross, W.D. (1939) *The Foundations of Ethics* (Oxford: Clarendon Press).

Scanlon, T.M. (1998) *What We Owe to Each Other* (Cambridge, MA: Harvard University Press).

Thomason, Richard. H. (1970) 'Indeterminist Time and Truth-Value Gaps', *Theoria* 3, pp. 264–81.
Van Fraassen, Bas (1966) 'Singular Terms, Truth-value Gaps, and Free Logic', *Journal of Philosophy* 63, pp. 481–95.
Van Fraassen, Bas (1968) 'Presupposition, Implication, and Self-reference', *Journal of Philosophy* 65, pp. 136–52.
Williams, Bernard (1981) 'Internal and External Reasons', in his *Moral Luck* (Cambridge: Cambridge University Press), pp. 101–13.

6

WRONG-MAKING REASONS

Kieran Setiya

At the heart of Derek Parfit's magisterial book is a defense of Kantian Contractualism and an argument for convergence in moral theory. According to "*the Kantian Contractualist Formula*: Everyone ought to follow the principles whose universal acceptance everyone could rationally will."[1] Although it uses the concept *ought*, this is meant to be a principle of moral right and wrong. It does not assume that there is decisive reason not to act wrongly, so that we ought never to do so, all things considered—though Parfit is sympathetic to that claim. Instead, it gives the condition under which an act is morally wrong.[2] The condition is that the act is forbidden by principles whose universal acceptance everyone could rationally will.

This formula needs explanation. To accept a principle, in the relevant sense, is to believe that the acts this principle forbids are wrong, and the acts it allows permissible.[3] To will that something be the case is to make it the case by an act of will.[4] So to will the acceptance of a principle is to make it the case that everyone believes that the acts this principle forbids are wrong and the acts it allows permissible.

When is it rational to will the acceptance of a principle? In general, what it is rational to do depends on one's beliefs, not on the relevant facts.[5] If one has false beliefs, it can be rational to act in ways for which one has no reason. In contrast, the condition for an act to be wrong, according to Kantian Contractualism, turns on the principles whose universal acceptance there is *reason* to will. More precisely, it turns on a subset of these reasons. In applying the Kantian formula, "we should not appeal to our beliefs about which acts are wrong."[6] Parfit calls these "our *deontic beliefs*" and adds: "[n]or should we appeal to the *deontic reasons* that an act's wrongness might provide."[7] On a natural reading, deontic reasons are reasons that consist in deontic facts, to the effect that some act is wrong; all other reasons are nondeontic.[8] In its most explicit formulation, Kantian Contractualism takes this form:

KANTIAN CONTRACTUALISM: an act is wrong if and only if it is disallowed by principles whose universal acceptance everyone has sufficient nondeontic reason to will.

To apply this test, we perform a series of thought experiments, one for every person, in which we imagine that he or she is choosing principles for everyone to accept, and compare the non-deontic reasons for and against. A principle passes the test if no one has stronger non-deontic reason to will the acceptance of any alternative principle.

Kantian Contractualism is a recognizable adaptation of Kant's Formula of Universal Law, though Kant does not appeal to reasons, as Parfit does. I won't pursue Kant interpretation here or the more elusive question, whether Parfit's adaptation of Kantian materials is in the spirit of Kant. Instead, I will look directly at Kantian Contractualism, its application, its role as a guide to action, and its relation to principles of other kinds. Using Parfit's argument as a platform, I will raise questions about our capacity to apply the Kantian formula when we do not already know what we have reason to do. There is a threat of redundancy for Kantian Contractualism.[9]

Before we turn to these arguments, it is useful to sketch how the application of Kantian Contractualism is meant to go. It is essential to the success of the Kantian project that in situations that call for moral judgment, there are principles whose universal acceptance everyone has sufficient non-deontic reason to will. If this were not the case, Kantian Contractualism would be too permissive: it would fail to condemn actions that are morally wrong. This existence condition may seem hard to meet. In many situations, the effects of a principle's acceptance on different agents will be different. Some principles benefit one more than others, some the reverse. Consider, for instance, the question of how to divide a quantity of unowned goods, where an equal division would produce the greatest sum of benefits.[10] Won't we each have decisive reason to will the principles that give us more? As Parfit argues, there are conceptions of practical reason on which that is true. If each of us has non-deontic reason to do only what will benefit us, or what will satisfy our final desires, there will be no principle we all have sufficient non-deontic reason to will. Parfit argues instead for a "wide value-based objective view," on which we have non-deontic reason to benefit others, and when

> one of our two possible acts would make things go in some way that would be impartially better, but the other act would make things go better either for ourselves or for those to whom we have close ties, we often have sufficient reasons to act in either of these ways.[11]

(An outcome is impartially better when it is favored by the balance of impartial reasons, reasons that do not depend on other people's relationships with us.) Applied to the case of division, Parfit's claim is that we all have sufficient non-deontic reason to will the acceptance of a principle of equal shares, and there is no alternative principle—of giving more to some than others—that we all have sufficient non-deontic reason to will. If this is right, the existence condition is met. Kantian Contractualism tells us that it would be wrong not to divide the unowned goods equally, producing the greatest sum of benefits for those concerned.

In this example, not only is there a principle that seems to pass the Kantian test, it is the only principle that does so. Things are more complicated if there are distinct principles, each of which we have sufficient non-deontic reason to will. In Parfit's formulations, Kantian Contractualism appeals to "the principles" that satisfy this condition. He suggests that, when uniqueness fails because "everyone could rationally choose two or more seriously conflicting principles," the Kantian formula goes wrong in much the way it does when there are no principles everyone could rationally will.[12] He adds:

> It would not matter, though, if everyone could rationally choose any of several similar principles. Such principles would be different versions of some more general higher-order principle, and the choice between these lower-level principles could then be made in some other way.[13]

This remark is puzzling. How can principles that differ in what they permit fail to be distinct from one another in the sense that is relevant to Kantian Contractualism? How to individuate principles if not by their prescriptions? If Kantian Contractualism condemns actions only when the uniqueness condition is met, even modest failures of uniqueness yield permissive conclusions. Suppose two principles pass the Kantian test. In a choice among A, B, and C, both forbid A, but the first forbids B, allowing C, and the second forbids C, allowing B. If Kantian Contractualism requires uniqueness, it fails to condemn any action in this circumstance. On a more plausible interpretation, the Kantian formula claims that an act is wrong if and only if it is disallowed by *all* relevant principles whose universal acceptance everyone has sufficient non-deontic reason to will. There need not be a single principle that passes the test. In the case described, it is wrong to do A but permissible to do either B or C.

With this clarification, we set the issue of uniqueness aside. In the following section, I explain Parfit's argument for the consistency of his Kantian principle with Rule Consequentialism. Although the argument itself is not our main concern, it serves to introduce our principal question, about the reason-giving force of wrong-making features. According to

> WRONG-MAKING REASONS: when an act would be wrong, the non-deontic facts that make it wrong are decisive reasons against it.

I argue that Wrong-Making Reasons is significant for more than the success of Parfit's derivation: it threatens our ability to learn important truths from Kantian Contractualism. In the next section, I make a tentative defense of Wrong-Making Reasons. And, in the third, I ask whether Kantian Contractualism can be revised to avoid the problem and consider what is at stake in this dispute.

1

One of Parfit's more surprising claims is that, far from being incompatible, the most plausible versions of Contractualism and Consequentialism in fact agree. He defends this claim by deriving a form of Rule Consequentialism from Kantian Contractualism. According to the universal acceptance version of Rule Consequentialism, the standard of right and wrong is fixed by the principles whose universal acceptance would be "optimific" in that, among the outcomes being compared, it is the one we have the strongest impartial reasons to will. For simplicity, I will talk about willing a principle instead of willing its universal acceptance. In these terms, Parfit argues as follows:[14]

(1) There are optimific principles, ones we have the strongest impartial reasons to will.

(2) No one's impartial reasons to will these principles are decisively outweighed by other non-deontic reasons.

(3) There are no other principles that everyone has sufficient non-deontic reason to will.

It follows that the optimific principles are ones that everyone has sufficient non-deontic reason to will, and that no other principles pass this test. Given

KANTIAN CONTRACTUALISM: an act is wrong if and only if it is disallowed by principles whose universal acceptance everyone has sufficient non-deontic reason to will,

we can infer the truth of

RULE CONSEQUENTIALISM: an act is wrong if and only if it is disallowed by principles whose universal acceptance would be optimific.

This argument is valid, and, like Parfit, I will not question premise 1 or premise 3. The basis for the latter is that, if we have the strongest impartial reasons to will a certain principle, A, then while some of us might have sufficient reason to will another principle, B, because it benefits us or those with whom we have close ties, others will not.[15] Since B is nonoptimific, there must be some who would benefit from principle A; given the strength of the impartial case for A, and the benefits to them, these individuals would have decisive non-deontic reason not to will B.

For our purposes, the most interesting premise of the argument is the second: that no one's impartial reasons to will the optimific principles would be outweighed by other non-deontic reasons. This premise could be challenged in several ways. For instance, in *Lifeboat*, I am stranded on one rock and five people are stranded on another.[16] The optimific principles would require you to save them, not me. But it might be argued that, since my life is at stake, I have stronger reason to will an alternative principle. Suppose I am on the nearest rock and the Nearness Principle requires one to save the nearest group. Do I have decisive non-deontic reason to will the Nearness Principle even though it is not optimific? Parfit argues that I do not: on his wide value-based objective view, I have sufficient non-deontic reason to will the optimific principles. That is, I have sufficient if not decisive reason to will the acceptance of principles that would save five lives at the cost of mine. What is more, even if this were not the case—even if I had decisive non-deontic reason to will that my life be saved at the cost of five—I would not have decisive non-deontic reason to will the *universal* acceptance of the Nearness Principle. If everyone accepted this principle, it would be applied to countless scenarios, and millions of lives would be lost. On any plausible view, I have sufficient reason to will the acceptance of principles that would save millions of lives, even at the cost of mine. Parfit makes a similar move when the reasons against the optimific principle are ones of partiality to friends or family.[17] Given the scale of what is at stake in the universal acceptance of a principle, we have sufficient non-deontic reason to will the optimific principles even at great cost to those we love.[18]

The most serious threat to premise 2 appeals not to reasons of self-interest or partiality but to the features of an act that make it morally wrong. According to Wrong-Making Reasons, the non-deontic facts about an act that make it wrong give decisive reasons against it. Parfit worries that, if we accept this principle, we may find exceptions to premise 2. Thus, in *Bridge*, a runaway train will kill five people unless you cause me to fall in front of it, resulting in my death.[19] According to the Wrong-Making Features Objection, the principle of saving five in *Bridge* is optimific, but there is decisive non-deontic reason not to save the five and therefore not to will the optimific principle. This reason might consist in the fact that, if you cause me to fall in front of the train, you would be harming one as a means to helping others.

Parfit responds to this objection in three ways. He argues, first, that if the fact of harming one as a means to helping others gives decisive reason not to save the five in *Bridge*, there is impartial reason to will that others act accordingly and so to will the universal acceptance of a principle that forbids us to harm one as a means to helping others, at least in cases of this kind.[20] On this assumption, the principle of saving five in *Bridge* is not optimific: we have impartial reason to will a principle that conflicts with it. Parfit argues, second, that wrong-making features do not give decisive reason to act in ways that violate the optimific principles.[21] And he argues, third, that even if they did, we would not have decisive reason not to will these principles. You might have reason not to harm one as a means to helping others and so to oppose the universal acceptance of a principle that requires you to save five in *Bridge*; but this is not enough to outweigh the impartial reasons that make this principle optimific.[22]

Rather than dispute these claims, I want to address the wider significance of Wrong-Making Reasons. It is striking that Parfit treats such reasons only as an objection to the convergence argument. He does not ask what they imply for the application of his formula. But there is a serious puzzle here. The truth of Wrong-Making Reasons would raise doubts about the value of Kantian Contractualism as a way of knowing what to do. We can see this if we think through the application of the Kantian test to *Bridge*. Our task is to consider the various principles that might be applied to the case and to ask which principles we have sufficient non-deontic reason to will. In ordinary conditions, we must rely on knowledge of the non-deontic reasons for and against these principles. But, according to Parfit's first response, the non-deontic reasons for and against the principles are not independent of the non-deontic reasons for and against the relevant acts. There may be non-deontic reasons for or against a principle that do not correspond to reasons for or against the acts that fall under it, reasons that derive from the effects of its general acceptance. But there is a definite constraint: "If everyone had . . . decisive non-deontic reasons *not* to act in some way, we could not . . . have [sufficient] impartial reasons to *want* everyone to act in that way. That would be a schizophrenic view."[23] We can state the relevant connection as follows:

> ACTS AND PRINCIPLES: if there is decisive non-deontic reason not to act in some way, there is decisive impartial reason not to will the universal acceptance of a principle that permits such actions.

Given Acts and Principles, most realistic cases will be ones in which we cannot know the balance of non-deontic reasons for and against a principle unless we know the non-deontic reasons for and against the relevant acts. And now the problem appears. For each possible act, we can ask: is there decisive non-deontic reason against it? For instance, in *Bridge*, is there decisive non-deontic reason not to save the five by killing one? If we do not know, we cannot apply the Kantian formula. Suppose, then, that we do. If the answer to the question is 'Yes, there is decisive non-deontic reason against the act,' we can infer that there is decisive reason against it, all told. It cannot be morally required, since if it were, there would be decisive non-deontic reason not to do otherwise, in light of Wrong-Making Reasons. So the act is either permissible or wrong. If it is permissible, we can ignore deontic reasons and the non-deontic reasons carry the day. If it is wrong, that only adds another reason against it. Either way, the act is one we should not perform. If the answer to the question is no, it follows by Wrong-Making Reasons that it would not be wrong to perform the act. In fact, there is sufficient reason to do so, since there is sufficient non-deontic reason to perform the act and no deontic reason not to.

The upshot is that, by appeal to Wrong-Making Reasons, we can determine the set of acts for which we have sufficient reason, none of which is morally wrong. In realistic cases, if we have the knowledge required to apply the Kantian formula—knowledge of the non-deontic reasons for and against the relevant actions—the truth of Wrong-Making Reasons would remove the need to do so. It already answers the questions—how to avoid acting wrongly and what to do—that motivate our inquiry.

The problem here is one of practical worth. It is about the useful application of Kantian Contractualism, not about its truth. This point comes out in at least two ways. First, the test inspired by Wrong-Making Reasons identifies the acts for which we have sufficient reason, none of which are morally wrong. It does not tell us which acts are permissible, among those for which we lack sufficient reason. But that is a merely theoretical question. It has no bearing on how to act.[24] Second, one could in principle know the balance of non-deontic reasons for and against a series of principles without already knowing the non-deontic reasons for and against the corresponding acts. One might be told how the reasons for the principles compare, instead of working this out by weighing the reasons oneself. In this unusual circumstance, one could discover what to do by Kantian reasoning but not by Wrong-Making Reasons. Ordinarily, however, the attempt to balance non-deontic reasons for and against principles will assume knowledge of the non-deontic reasons for and against the actions they prohibit and permit. Given Wrong-Making Reasons, this knowledge allows us to shortcut the elaborate thought experiments called for by Kantian Contractualism. We can know what to do without it.

Although it does not refute the Kantian formula, this line of thought casts doubt on its power to guide and illuminate practice. The problem here is not about the bad effects of embracing this formula, as we might fear that it would impede the maximization of utility if we were all committed utility-maximizers, so that act-utilitarianism is "self-effacing."[25] The problem is rather that, if we accept Wrong-Making Reasons, what we have to learn from Kantian Contractualism is not of practical value. What then is the point of the Kantian project?

2

Parfit might concede that the Kantian formula, while true, is practically redundant. Its interest is merely theoretical. But he might also resist the argument of the first section. This argument assumes the truth of Acts and Principles and of Wrong-Making Reasons. We will focus on the latter.

In the sections of his book that respond to the Wrong-Making Features Objection, Parfit considers the reason-giving force of facts we take to make an action wrong. He suggests that

> (X) if the optimific principles require certain acts that we believe to be wrong, the features or facts that, in our opinion, make these acts wrong would not give us decisive *non*-deontic reasons not to act in these ways. What might be true is only that, by making these acts wrong, these facts would give us decisive deontic reasons not to act in these ways.[26]

It is worth noting that this principle does not conflict with Wrong-Making Reasons. (X) is concerned with the strength of non-deontic reasons to act against the optimific principles and thus with premise 2 of the convergence argument.

I have been supposing that this premise holds, in light of Acts and Principles. If there is decisive non-deontic reason to act against certain principles, there is decisive impartial reason not to will those principles, which therefore do not count as optimific. Conversely, if principles are optimific, the acts they require cannot be wrong. There is no need for the advocate of Wrong-Making Reasons to question principle (X).

In defending (X), Parfit considers an argument against this principle that would support Wrong-Making Reasons. According to this argument, "when some act is wrong, this fact is the second-order fact that certain other facts give us decisive moral reasons not to act in this way."[27] Parfit rejects this conception of wrongness on the ground that such higher-order facts "would not give *further, independent* reason[s]" against the relevant actions, while "an act's wrongness does give us strong or even decisive further reasons not to do it."[28] It is not obvious to me why a higher-order fact could not provide a further reason. But we need not take that up. Those who defend Wrong-Making Reasons can agree with Parfit about the conception of wrongness as a higher-order property and about the reason-giving force of deontic facts. They can endorse

DEONTIC REASONS: that an action would be wrong is a decisive reason against it.

Deontic reasons are not redundant, even if the non-deontic facts that make an action wrong are decisive reasons too. When an act is wrong, the case against it is over-determined; but reasons of both kinds are significant. They do not pre-empt or undermine each other. Sometimes, deontic reasons matter more. If you know that it would be wrong to act in a certain way but do not know the facts that make that action wrong, you cannot respond directly to those facts. Still, it is irrational to perform the act, assuming deontic reasons.

If this is right, Parfit's claims do not refute, or count against, Wrong-Making Reasons. For all he says, this principle might be true. But it might also be false. Is there any reason to accept it? A case can be made for Wrong-Making Reasons from reflection on the rational authority of right and wrong. Parfit is sympathetic to Moral Rationalism, according to which there is decisive reason not to act in ways that would be wrong.[29] The truth of Moral Rationalism follows from Wrong-Making Reasons. But, on the face of it, the converse implication fails. Moral Rationalism might be true even if the non-deontic facts that make an action wrong are not decisive reasons. Most plausibly, its truth would be explained instead by deontic reasons. Against this, I will argue that we cannot have Moral Rationalism without Wrong-Making Reasons.

Begin by supposing the contrary: Moral Rationalism holds without Wrong-Making Reasons. On the natural alternative, it is the fact that an action would be wrong that is the reason against it, not the facts that make it wrong. We thus accept deontic reasons. Now, it is not a condition of practical rationality, as such, that the beliefs on which one acts be epistemically rational.[30] It is not a failure of *practical* reason that one's beliefs about means and ends, or about the effects of acting in a certain way, go against one's evidence. But, as Parfit insists, there are exceptions to this rule. It *is* a failure of practical reason if one has irrational beliefs about what there is reason to do.[31] In general, practical rationality involves epistemic rationality in the domain of practical reason. Even if they are not facts about reasons, as such, facts about wrongness are, given the truth of deontic reasons, of central importance to this domain. Those who cannot conceive such facts, or who fail to consider them in practical reasoning, or whose beliefs about right and wrong are epistemically unjustified, fall short of practical rationality. More strongly, assuming deontic reasons, a practically rational agent who knows the non-deontic facts that make an action wrong will conclude that the action is wrong and thus refrain from doing it. Finally, if knowledge of certain facts would prevent a practically rational agent from performing an action, those facts provide decisive reason not to act in that way. It follows that we must accept

> WRONG-MAKING REASONS: when an act would be wrong, the non-deontic facts that make it wrong are decisive reasons against it.

To summarize this argument: Moral Rationalism would be explained by Wrong-Making Reasons; if that explanation is false, the most plausible alternative appeals to deontic reasons; but the truth of Wrong-Making Reasons follows from deontic reasons, on modest assumptions about the nature of practical reason. Parfit might dispute these premises, but if they are true, we cannot ignore the problems raised in the first section.

3

In closing, I will look at a response to these arguments that revises the Kantian formula, or the definition of 'deontic reason,' and discuss the larger question it provokes.

The revision is inspired by the fact that, in the argument of the second section, what follows from deontic reasons is that the non-deontic facts that make an action wrong are reasons against it *because* they are grounds on which a rational agent would conclude that the act is wrong. Their status as reasons turns on the fact that they are wrong-making features. Why not exclude, in the application of Kantian Contractualism, not only deontic reasons but reasons of this kind? Alternatively, why not adjust the definition of "deontic reason" to apply to reasons whose status as such turns on the fact that they make acts wrong?[32] Either way, what matters is the balance of reasons whose status as such does not depend on being, or being grounds for, deontic facts. This revision makes it possible to apply the Kantian formula without knowledge of Wrong-Making Reasons: the information required to apply the formula is no longer sufficient for the shortcut framed in the first section.

There are three things to say about this line. First, it is not clear how much the revision helps with the practical redundancy of Kantian Contractualism. In balancing the reasons for and against conflicting principles, it may be hard to say whether the status of a non-deontic fact as a reason turns on making an act wrong unless one already knows the deontic facts. Second, although the argument of the second section does not prove that the status of wrong-making facts as reasons is independent of the fact that they make acts wrong, it is perfectly consistent with that view.

Finally, and most importantly, the success of the revision turns on a double standard. Consider Parfit's wide value-based objective view, on which we have non-deontic reason to act in ways that benefit others, despite the cost to us or those we love. The facts that provide these impartial reasons are often among the facts that make an action wrong—for instance, because it harms another person. Now, there are two views we can take about the rational significance of such facts where they do not make an action wrong. One view denies that they are reasons in that case. When they fail to make an action wrong, reasons of harm and benefit to others do not count as reasons at all. On this view, the rational significance of such facts is deontically mediated. This view is fatal to Kantian Contractualism, on the revision just proposed. The revision forbids appeal to reasons of this kind; but if we cannot appeal to reasons of benefit and harm in applying the Kantian formula, its existence condition will fail. There will be no principles we all have sufficient reason to will. On the alternative view, the rational significance of benefits and harms to other people is immediate. Even when they fail to make an action wrong, such reasons have weight. Their status as reasons is independent of wrong-making. But then we should take the same view of all impartial reasons. It would be arbitrary not to. Just as facts about harm to others can make an action wrong, but count as reasons even when they don't, so facts about harming as a means, if they can make an action wrong, may count as reasons even when they don't. In general, the rational force of wrong-making features is partly independent of deontic facts. Such reasons must be weighed in applying the Kantian formula even when it has been revised. On neither view does the revision save Kantian Contractualism from the arguments above.

The larger question here is why Parfit is willing to make the assumptions he needs about impartial reason in order to apply the Kantian formula. Parfit defends the wide value-based objective view by attacking subjective and desire-based theories of practical reason.[33] He does not give a direct argument for this view. And there are many conceptions of non-deontic reason he does not discuss. We have considered one of them: the principle of Wrong-Making Reasons. Even if my claims about this principle are mistaken, we can ask why Parfit begins just where he does.

Of course, we can always question premises, and it would be unfair to expect an argument every time. But there is more going on. If someone has a practical interest in knowing right from wrong, their real concern is knowing what to do. How difficult their challenge is, and what form it takes, will depend on what they already know about reasons. Nothing at all? Just formal constraints? Or more than that? These questions apply to Parfit's book. What state of knowledge does the Kantian project address? It does not speak to those who are largely ignorant of reasons or who doubt that they have reason to benefit others, even at some cost to themselves. It assumes that we have knowledge of impartial reasons. But it does not assume more. It does not assume that we have decisive reason to sacrifice ourselves for the sake of others or that we know what is right and wrong. Why focus our attention here? Why is this state of limited knowledge—knowledge of impartial but not deontic reasons—an urgent target of ethical thought? Why not assume less knowledge and set a more ambitious challenge? Why not confront the normative skeptic? Or if that seems hopeless, why not aim for much less? A modest project would begin with those who know what to do, and why to do it, and defend their claim to know.

The fundamental question posed by Wrong-Making Reasons concerns the shape of Parfit's approach. On any account, the use of Kantian Contractualism assumes a delicate balance of known and unknown normative facts. I have argued that we almost never satisfy these constraints and that the Kantian formula is practically inert. Even if I am wrong, why fixate on this epistemic state? Why address someone who knows all there is to know about non-deontic reasons, including ones that bear on the treatment of others, but is oddly blind to deontic facts? There is nothing to prevent us from doing this, but why expect to learn valuable truths?[34]

Notes

1 OWM 1, p. 342.
2 Parfit sometimes equates the question of what I ought morally to do with the question of which acts would be wrong (OWM 1, p. 144); his considered view is that the sense of wrong is primitive and that what I ought morally to do is explained by asking what it would be wrong to do in various states of information (OWM 1, pp. 162, 165, 172–4). For the most part, Parfit states his Kantian principles as claims about wrongness; he shifts to formulations with "ought" in discussing the Golden Rule and in his subsequent treatment of Contractualism and Consequentialism.
3 OWM 1, p. 341.
4 OWM 1, p. 285: "When we apply Kant's formula, we suppose or imagine that we have the power to will, or choose, that certain things be true."
5 OWM 1, p. 34.
6 OWM 1, p. 287.
7 OWM 1, p. 287; see also OWM 1, p. 201.
8 I consider an alternative below, in the third section.
9 The threat in question bears comparison with a problem for Scanlon's contractualism in Scanlon (1998). In describing what it is for an act to be wrong, Scanlon cites what we can "reasonably reject" in a partly moral sense of "reasonable." Critics have asked whether we can short-circuit the contractualist machinery and determine what is wrong by direct appeal to what is reasonable. My objection is similar, though I think it can be made more definite here because Parfit is so explicit about the reasons to which his principle refers.
10 OWM 1, pp. 359–60.
11 OWM 1, p. 137.
12 OWM 1, p. 358.
13 OWM 1, p. 358.

14 *OWM* 1, p. 378. Premise 1 corresponds to Parfit's (C), premise 2 to Parfit's (E), and premise 3 to Parfit's (G).
15 *OWM* 1, pp. 399–400.
16 *OWM* 1, pp. 380–2.
17 *OWM* 1, pp. 387–8.
18 A peculiar feature of this argument is that it is sensitive to the number of people for whom I imagine choosing. If the future population is very small, non-deontic reason to will principles that favor those I love may outweigh my impartial reasons to choose the optimific principles, so that different actions would be right or wrong.
19 *OWM* 1, pp. 390–1.
20 *OWM* 1, pp. 391–4.
21 *OWM* 1, pp. 394–5, 448–51.
22 *OWM* 1, pp. 395–8.
23 *OWM* 1, p. 393.
24 I set aside the role of moral judgment in guilt and blame and in the justification of punishment. While these are practical matters, one would expect moral thought to have a more immediate bearing on the question what to do.
25 A claim defended by Parfit himself, in *RP*, Part One.
26 *OWM* 1, pp. 395, 448.
27 *OWM* 1, pp. 448–9.
28 *OWM* 1, pp. 172–3.
29 *OWM* 1, p. 141. Parfit formulates Moral Rationalism in a way that implies deontic reasons; I will keep these principles distinct.
30 *OWM* 1, pp. 112–17.
31 *OWM* 1, pp. 119–20.
32 There are hints of this in Parfit's book, as when he suggests that features of an act that make it wrong "might give you a decisive reason not to act in this way" but "only by making this act wrong." He goes on to say, "[this] decisive reason would have to be deontic" and that "[you] would not have decisive non-deontic reason not to act in this way" (*OWM* 1, p. 395). These remarks can be interpreted in two ways. On one reading, Parfit adopts the broad definition according to which non-deontic facts that count as reasons because they make acts wrong are themselves deontic reasons. On the second reading, he claims that they "give us" deontic reasons, which consist in deontic facts, since they make such facts obtain.
33 *OWM* 1, pp. 58–110.
34 For comments on earlier versions of this material, I am grateful to Mike Otsuka, Derek Parfit, Karl Schafer, and three anonymous readers.

References

Parfit, Derek (1984) *Reasons and Persons* (Oxford: Oxford University Press).
Parfit, Derek (2011) *On What Matters* (Oxford: Oxford University Press), vols 1 and 2.
Scanlon, T.M. (1998) *What We Owe to Each Other* (Cambridge, MA: Harvard University Press).

7

PARFIT ON REASONS AND RULE CONSEQUENTIALISM

Douglas W. Portmore

According to rule consequentialism, an act is morally permissible if and only if, and because, it is permitted by the ideal code of rules. And a given set of rules counts as the ideal code if and only if the expected value of the world in which it is adopted is greater than that of any alternative world in which some other set of rules is adopted. Now, I will argue that we don't always have sufficient reason to act as rule consequentialism requires us to act. And this means that either rule consequentialism is false or we don't always have sufficient reason to act as morality requires.[1] Either spells trouble for Parfit. On the one hand, if rule consequentialism is false, then Parfit's Triple Theory is false, for Triple Theory entails rule consequentialism. And although Parfit doesn't explicitly endorse Triple Theory, he claims that we have strong reasons to accept it.[2] On the other hand, if we don't always have sufficient reason to act as morality requires, then, by Parfit's own lights, morality is undermined, and his assumption that we always have strong reasons to avoid acting wrongly is called into question.[3]

The chapter has the following structure. In the first section, I argue that for us to have a consequence-based reason to perform an act, the reason for us to perform the act must be provided either by the fact that the act itself has good consequences or by the fact that the act is part of a set of acts that, if realized, would have good consequences. But, in the second section, I argue that we have a reason to perform an act in virtue of the fact that it is part of a set of acts that, if realized, would have good consequences only if we are able to see to it that this set and its good consequences are realized. Yet, as I show in the third section, rule consequentialism implies that we can be morally required to perform an act in virtue of this sort of fact even if we are unable to see to it that the relevant set and its good consequences are realized. Thus, from these arguments, it follows that, in many situations, we have no consequence-based reason for acting as rule consequentialism requires us to act. And, in the fourth section, I argue that whatever non-consequence-based reasons we may have for acting as rule consequentialism requires us to act in these situations are not strong enough to give us sufficient reason to so act. It follows, then, that either rule consequentialism is false or we do not always have sufficient reason to act as morality requires us to act. And, in the fifth section, I argue that this presents a dilemma for Parfit. Parfit must concede either that rule consequentialism (and, hence, Triple Theory) is false despite the putatively strong reasons that he believes we have for accepting it or that morality doesn't have the importance he seems to attribute to it given that its importance has been undermined by his own substantive account of morality.

Reasons and consequences

It is relatively uncontroversial to suppose that if your φ-ing would have good consequences, then you have a reason to φ. For instance, if your pushing a button would have the effect of draining a mine shaft of otherwise rising floodwaters, thereby saving the five miners trapped inside, then you have at least some reason to push the button. But beyond supposing that the consequences of individual acts matter, we might further suppose that the consequences of sets of acts matter. For instance, we might suppose that you can have a reason to φ, not because your φ-ing would itself have good consequences, but because your φ-ing is part of a set of acts that, if realized, would have good consequences. Suppose, for instance, that the miners will be saved if and only if you push both button A at t_2 and button B at t_3. Here, your pushing A at t_2 is not itself sufficient to do any good. But we might say that you have a reason to push A at t_2, because it is part of a set of acts (i.e. the set consisting in your pushing both A at t_2 and B at t_3) that, if realized, would have good consequences.[4]

Of course, one might object that, in determining whether you have a consequence-based reason to push A at t_2, all that matters is whether the way the world would be if you were to push A at t_2 would be better than the way the world would be if you were to perform some alternative act instead.[5] And it may be that if you were to push A at t_2, you would not, as a matter of fact, follow up by pushing B at t_3. In which case, the world would be no better for your pushing A at t_2. According to this objection, then, you would have no consequence-based reason to push A at t_2. For, on this view, what matters in determining whether you have a consequence-based reason to φ is not whether your φ-ing is part of a set of acts that, if realized, would have good consequences, but whether your φ-ing would itself have good consequence. Call this the *standard view*.

The standard view is, I believe, mistaken.[6] For there are cases in which it is plausible to suppose that you have a consequence-based reason to perform an act, not because your performing it would have good consequence, but because it is part of a set of acts that, if realized, would have good consequences. Here is one such case:

> *The Five:* Five miners will be saved from drowning in rising floodwaters if and only if Faisal pushes both A at t_2 and B at t_3. Now, as a matter of fact, Faisal *wouldn't* push B at t_3 even if he were to push A at t_2. This is

true, not because he *couldn't* push both buttons. Indeed, if he were to form at t_1 the intention to push both buttons, he would do precisely that. The reason, then, that he wouldn't push both buttons is that, as a matter of fact, he is not going to form at t_1 the intention to push both buttons—and this despite the fact that he has, as of the present (that is, as of t_0), the capacity to form this intention in response to the decisive reasons he has for doing so. Instead, he is, as a result of his malice towards the five miners, going to form at t_1 the intention to refrain from pushing B at t_3 irrespective of whether or not he has pushed A at t_2. And, if this is the intention that he will form (and I am stipulating that it is), then he *would* not push B at t_3 even if he were to push A at t_2. Again, this is not to say that he *could* not see to it that he pushes both buttons. He could, for all he would need to do is to form at t_1 the intention to push both buttons, an intention that he would then carry out.

Given both that Faisal would not push B at t_3 even if he were to push A at t_2 and that his pushing A at t_2 will do no good unless he follows up by pushing B at t_3, it follows that, on the standard view, he has no reason (or, at least, no consequence-based reason) to push A at t_2. For his pushing A at t_2 would have no good consequences. But, in this case, it seems plausible to suppose that he has a reason to push A at t_2 in virtue of the fact that it is part of a set of acts whose realization he can see to and whose realization would have good consequences: the saving of five lives.

Consider that it would be a mistake for Faisal to deliberate at t_0 as follows:

(1) I would not push B at t_3 even if I were to push A at t_2. (2) There is no reason for me to push A at t_2 unless I'm going to follow up by pushing B at t_3. (3) Given premise 1, I can conclude that I would not so follow up. (4) Therefore, I have no reason to push A at t_2.

The problem with his deliberating in this way is that it inappropriately treats premise 1 as fixed for the purposes of his deliberations. But when deliberating about whether or not to do x, one should not hold fixed the fact that one is (or is not) going to do x, nor should one hold fixed the fact that one is (or is not) going to do y if whether one does y is just as much under one's present control as whether one does x is.[7] So when deliberating about whether or not to push A at t_2, Faisal should not hold fixed the fact that he isn't going push A at t_2, nor should he hold fixed the fact that he isn't going to push B at t_3.

Perhaps, though, the reader will balk at my suggestion that Faisal could presently see to it that he pushes both buttons, even though he would not push B at t_3 even if he were to push A at t_2. In that case, let me just stipulate that I will use the phrase 'see to it' such that:

S can at t see to it that a set of actions, α, will be realized if and only if there is some set of intentions such that S has at t the capacity to form these intentions at t' and α would (via some non-deviant causal process) be realized if S were to form these intentions at t', where t' is immediately subsequent to t.

Still, some readers may question whether my being able to see to it (in this stipulative sense) that some set of acts and its good consequences are realized is itself *sufficient* for my having a reason to perform each of the acts in that set.[8] But this does not matter for my purposes. For I will be arguing that my being able to see to it that some set of acts and its good consequences are realized is *necessary* for my having a consequence-based reason to perform the acts within that set that do not themselves have good consequences.

Two types of case

To begin to see why we should think that this is a necessary condition, consider the following two types of case:

> *Securability cases*: (1) S_1 is deliberating at t about whether or not to φ at t'; (2) although S_1's φ-ing at t' would not itself have good consequences, good consequences would ensue if both S_1 φs at t' and S_2 ψs at t''; (3) as a matter of fact, though, S_2 will not ψ at t''; but (4) S_1 *can* (but won't) at t see to it that S_2 ψs at t'' (S_1 may or may not be identical to S_2 and $t < t' \leq t''$).
>
> *Insecurability cases*: (1) S_1 is deliberating at t about whether or not to φ at t'; (2) although S_1's φ-ing at t' would not itself have good consequences, good consequences would ensue if both S_1 φs at t' and S_2 ψs at t''; (3) as a matter of fact, though, S_2 will not ψ at t''; and (4) S_1 *cannot* at t see to it that S_2 ψs at t'' (S_1 may or may not be identical to S_2 and $t < t' \leq t''$).

I will argue that although S_1 has a reason to φ at t' in securability cases, this is not so in insecurability cases. And this, as I will show, suggests that my being able to see to it that some set of acts and its good consequences are realized is a necessary condition for my having a consequence-based reason to perform the acts within that set that do not themselves have good consequences.

For my purposes, it will be helpful to demonstrate how we can divide each of the above two types of case into three main sub-types, depending both on whether S_1 is identical to S_2 and on whether t' is identical to t''. Consider, for instance, the three main sub-types with respect to securability cases. First, there is the sub-type in which S_1 is identical to S_2 and t' is identical to t''. One such case is *The Car*: while driving, Carl is deliberating about whether or not to accelerate as there is a slow-moving truck up ahead in his lane and a Ferrari coming up fast from behind in the only adjacent lane.[9] Given the circumstances, his accelerating will have good consequences if and only if he does so while changing lanes. If he changes lanes without accelerating, he will be rear-ended by the Ferrari. And if he accelerates without changing lanes, he will crash into the back of the truck. As a matter of fact, though, Carl would not change lanes even if he were to accelerate, because he is so frustrated with the slow-moving truck that he intends to rear-end it. Yet it is extremely important that he instead accelerates while changing lanes, for that is the only way he will make it to his meeting on time, and his job depends on it. Moreover, if he were to intend to accelerate while changing lanes, then that is precisely what he would do.

Second, there is the sub-type in which S_1 is identical to S_2 but t' is earlier than t''. *The Five* is such a case. Faisal's pushing A at t_2 will have good consequences if and only if he is going to follow up by pushing B at t_3. But, unfortunately, Faisal would not push B at t_3 even if he were to push A at t_2—although he certainly could see to it that he pushes both buttons merely by intending now to do so.

Third, there is the sub-type in which S_1 and S_2 are not identical and t' is earlier than t''.[10] To illustrate, consider a variation on *The Five*, which I'll call *The Second Five*: five miners will be saved if and only if Abe pushes A at t_2 and Beatrice pushes B at t_3. Assume that although Beatrice would not push B at t_3 even if Abe were to push A at t_2, this is only because Beatrice doesn't know that she needs to push B at t_3, and, unfortunately, Abe has no intention of telling her this. Thus, even though Abe could see to it that the five are saved merely by pushing A at t_2 while simultaneously telling Beatrice at t_2 to push B at t_3, Abe has no intention of doing either. In this case, Abe's pushing A at t_2 will have good consequences if and only if Beatrice is going to push B at t_3, which is something that Beatrice isn't going to do given that Abe isn't going to tell her to do so.

It is fairly uncontroversial to suppose that, in *The Car*, Carl has a reason to accelerate in virtue of the fact that it is part of a set of acts (namely, the set consisting in his accelerating while changing lanes) that, if realized, would have good consequences: his keeping his job. The fact that Carl doesn't intend to change lanes doesn't mean that he has no reason to accelerate any more than the fact that, say, Hitler, facing an ultimatum from Britain, had no intention of ordering his troops to withdraw from Poland meant that he had no reason to do so. One can't avoid having a reason to φ merely by lacking the intention to φ, and this is so whether φ is a singular act (such as issuing an order) or a compound act (such as accelerating while changing lanes). Moreover, one can't avoid having a reason to perform each of the conjuncts of some compound act merely by lacking the intention to perform that compound act.

And why should it matter whether the individual acts that make up some compound act are contemporaneous or not if the agent has just as much present control over whether the compound act will be realized in either case? So if we claim that Carl has a reason to accelerate in *The Car* despite the fact that he doesn't intend to change lanes, then we should also claim that Faisal has a reason to push A at t_2 in *The Five* despite the fact that he doesn't intend to push B at t_3. And likewise we should further claim that Abe has a reason to push A at t_2 in *The Second Five* despite the fact that he doesn't intend to tell Beatrice at t_2 to push

B at t_3. It seems that what is relevant is whether the agent can see to it that the relevant set of acts is realized, not whether the acts in the set have identical agents or occur at identical times.[11] So we should, I think, say that S_1 has a reason to φ at t' in securability cases regardless of whether S_1 is identical to S_2 and regardless of whether t' is identical to t''.

Should we go further and say that S_1 has a reason to φ at t' in insecurability cases—that is, regardless of whether S_1 can at t see to it that S_2 ψs at t''? Should we say, for instance, that Carl would have a reason to accelerate even if he could not see to it that he changes lanes, as where, say, the steering wheel was stuck? And should we say that Abe has a reason to push A at t_2 even if he could not see to it that Beatrice pushes B at t_3, as where, say, he has no way of communicating with Beatrice. It seems not, for such acts would be entirely pointless, if not harmful. It seems, then, that the mere fact that S_1's φ-ing at t' is part of a set of acts (i.e. the set consisting in S_1's φ-ing at t' and S_2's ψ-ing at t'') that, if realized, would have good consequences is insufficient to provide S_1 with a reason at t to φ at t'. For such a fact to constitute a reason at t for S_1 to φ at t', it must be that S_1 could at t see to it not only that she φs at t', but also that S_2 ψs at t''. We should conclude, therefore, that an agent has a reason to φ in virtue of the fact that her φ-ing is part of a set of acts that, if realized, would have good consequences only if she is able to see to it that this set and its good consequences are realized.

Rule consequentialism

I have argued that an agent has a reason to φ in virtue of the fact that her φ-ing is part of a set of acts that, if realized, would have good consequences only if she is able to see to it that this set and its good consequences are realized. Yet rule consequentialism implies that an agent can be morally required to φ in virtue of this sort of fact even if she is unable to see to it that the relevant set and its good consequences are realized. To see this, consider that, on rule consequentialism, whether I'm obliged to φ (for example, to keep a promise) doesn't depend on whether my φ-ing would have better consequences than my not φ-ing, but on whether everyone's following a code of rules that requires me to φ would have better consequences than everyone's following any code of rules that doesn't require me to φ. Thus, on rule consequentialism, I am obliged to φ because φ is a member of a set of acts that would have the best consequences—namely, the set consisting in everyone's following the ideal code. And rule consequentialism holds that I am required to φ in virtue of its being a member of this set even if I cannot see to it that this set and its good consequences are realized. That is, I am required to follow the ideal code even if I cannot see to it that everyone else follows the ideal code.

Now, strictly speaking, it is only one version of rule consequentialism that implies that I am obliged to φ in virtue of the good consequences resulting from the set of acts consisting in everyone's following the ideal code—namely, the *universal following* version of *rule consequentialism*, or

UFRC: an act is wrong if and only if, and because, it is disallowed by the UF-optimific set of principles, where a set of rules, R1, is UF-optimific if and only if there is no alternative set of rules, R2, such that the expected value of the world in which R2 is universally followed is greater than the expected value of the world in which R1 is universally followed.[12]

Shortly, I will be considering other versions of rule consequentialism, but for now let me demonstrate that UFRC does indeed have the above-noted implication. To illustrate, consider

The Unsolved Climate Case: if everyone (or even just nearly everyone) makes the significant sacrifices required to drastically reduce their carbon footprints, then the climate disaster that will otherwise ensue in the next century will be averted. Unfortunately, no one is making, nor is anyone going to make, these sacrifices. Moreover, each individual has control over only his or her own actions. Thus, regardless of what any individual does, climate disaster is going to ensue. Indeed, let's assume that no individual can make the slightest difference to the likelihood that the disaster will occur, to when it will occur, or to how morally bad it will be if it occurs.[13] But individuals can make a significant difference as to how well their own families will fare over the next century by not pointlessly making the sacrifices required to drastically reduce their own carbon footprints.[14]

In *The Unsolved Climate Case*, UFRC implies (1) that I am required to make significant sacrifices so as to drastically reduce my own carbon footprint, (2) that I am required to do so in virtue of the fact that my doing so is part of a set of actions (namely, the set of actions consisting in everyone's following the UF-optimific set of rules) that, if realized, would have good consequences, and (3) that this is so despite the fact that I cannot see to it that this set or its good consequences are realized. The only way UFRC wouldn't have these implications is if the UF-optimific set of rules were such as to permit people in my situation to refrain from making such sacrifices. But since, in this case, everyone is in exactly the same situation that I am in vis-à-vis potential climate disaster, any such rule would permit not just me, but everyone else, to refrain from making such sacrifices.[15] And the UF-optimific set of principles would not permit everyone (or even nearly everyone) to refrain from making such sacrifices, for any such set of principles would be one that, if universally followed, would inevitably result in climate disaster, which is, I will stipulate, much worse than a world in which everyone follows a set of rules requiring them to make the sacrifices needed to drastically reduce their carbon footprints.

It might be thought that the ideal (or optimific) code would include a rule saying that one is required to bear the burdens of doing one's part in some possible cooperative venture only if one's doing so would not be pointless due to the unwillingness of others to do their parts.[16] But even if the ideal code would include such a rule in certain possible worlds, it would not include such a rule in the possible world that I am imagining, which is one in which climate disaster would ensue if everyone (or nearly everyone) were to follow (or even accept) such a principle. After all, given how bad climate disaster is, it is clear that no code whose universal (or near universal) following (or acceptance) would result in climate disaster could possibly be the ideal code—that is, UF-optimific. So we know that the UFRC-optimific code of rules would not permit everyone (or even nearly everyone) to refrain from making significant sacrifices in *The Unsolved Climate Case*.

So UFRC implies that I am morally required to make significant sacrifices because my doing so is part of a set of actions that, if realized, would have good consequences, and UFRC implies this despite the fact that I cannot see to it that this set or its good consequences are realized, and despite the fact that my making these sacrifices would have no good consequences for anyone and some bad consequences for me and my family. Yet I have argued that the fact that some act is part of a set of acts that would, if realized, have good consequences constitutes a reason to perform that act only if the agent can see to it that the relevant set and its good consequences are realized. This means that unless there is some other fact that constitutes sufficient reason for me to make these sacrifices, UFRC must either be false or be such that agents don't always have sufficient reason to act as it requires. Either would, I believe, be disappointing for Parfit.

Of course, Parfit needn't endorse UFRC; he remains neutral as to which version of rule consequentialism is best. But, as I will show, every version of rule consequentialism faces the same dilemma: either that version is false or morality isn't as significant as Parfit thinks. For, as I will show, every version of rule consequentialism implies that agents are sometimes required to perform acts that they lack sufficient reason to perform, and if agents sometimes have decisive reason to do wrong, that would undermine morality's importance. So either the strong reasons that Parfit claims that we have for accepting rule consequentialism are decisively opposed by the reasons that we have for rejecting it or morality isn't as important as Parfit seems to think.

Let me turn now to showing how all other versions of rule consequentialism face the same dilemma: the dilemma of being either false or relatively unimportant. All versions of rule consequentialism hold that an act is wrong if and only if, and because, it is disallowed by the ideal code—that is, the optimific set of rules. Different versions of rule consequentialism differ only with respect to how we are to determine which alternative code is ideal. The two main points of contention are (1) whether we are to look at the expected value of each alternative code's being *universally* or *partially* "adopted" and (2) whether we are to understand the "adoption" of a code in terms of *accepting* or *following* the code. On what I will call *universal* versions of rule consequentialism (such as UFRC), we look only at the expected value of the various alternative codes being universally adopted. On *partial* versions of rule consequentialism, we look also, or instead, at the expected value of the various alternative codes being partially adopted. And whereas, on *following* versions of rule consequentialism, we look at the expected value of the various alternative codes being (partially and/or universally) followed, on *acceptance* versions of rule consequentialism, we look at the expected value of the various alternative codes being (partially and/or universally) accepted, where the acceptance of a code involves more than just a disposition to follow it. It involves, among other things, believing what the code says.

So there are three types of rule consequentialism besides UFRC: (1) universal acceptance rule consequentialism, or UARC, (2) partial following rule consequentialism, or PFRC, and (3) partial acceptance rule consequentialism, or PARC. And, with these distinctions in place, I am now in position to explain how each of these other three face the same dilemma that UFRC faces, starting with PFRC.

PFRC is to be defined exactly as UFRC was defined above except that we are to replace 'partially' for 'universally' and 'PF' for 'UF' throughout. Now, there are many different versions of PFRC, for there are many different ways of understanding how we should think of the partial following of a code. On *fixed-rate* PFRC, for instance, we assess each alternative code by the expected value of its being followed by some fixed rate—say, by 90 percent of the population. On *variable-rate* PFRC, we look at each alternative code and the expected value of its being followed at every rate from 0 percent to 100 percent (inclusive) and then take the average expected value of the consequences for all of these rates. The ideal code, then, is the one with the highest average. On Parfit's *best-at-every-rate* version of PFRC, "everyone ought to follow the rules whose being followed by any number of people rather than by no one would make things go [expectably] best."[17]

Unfortunately, each of these has significant problems. The problem with Parfit's best-at-every-rate version of PFRC is, as Michael Ridge points out, that it "entails that if there is no single code which is [expectably] best *for each and every single* [rate of following] . . . then nothing is morally required."[18] In a couple of endnotes, Parfit makes clear that he is aware of this problem, and he seems to be inclined to adopt something like Ridge's variable-rate version in response to the worry.[19] But, unfortunately, Ridge's variable-rate version of rule consequentialism is subject to its own devastating objections, as are all the other versions of PFRC mentioned above.[20]

The best version of PFRC is, perhaps, *maximizing-expectation-rate* PFRC, which holds that the ideal code is the one whose expected value is at least as high as the corresponding expected value of any alternative code.[21] The *weighted* expected value of a code *at a given rate* of following is the product of the expected value of that code at that rate of following and the probability that that code will be followed at that rate. And the expected value of a code is just the sum of that code's weighted expected values at every rate of following from 0 percent to 100 percent (inclusive). Since I take this to be the best version of PFRC, I will focus on it. But my arguments would work, *mutatis mutandis*, against any other version of PFRC.

If the expected value of a code is to be calculated in terms of subjective probabilities, then there is no way for maximizing-expectation-rate PFRC to avoid implying that agents will be required to make pointless sacrifices in certain more fully specified versions of *The Unsolved Climate Case*.[22] After all, if the comparative value of a world in which climate disaster ensues is low enough and/or the subjective probability that nearly everyone will follow a code requiring significant sacrifices is high enough, then the ideal code—that is, the code with the highest expected value—will require agents to make significant sacrifices in *The Unsolved Climate Case* even though, as a matter of fact, there is, in this case, no objective chance that anyone will be making these sacrifices.[23]

Of course, the defender of maximizing-expectation-rate PFRC could claim that the expected value of a code is to be calculated in terms of objective probabilities. And, in that case, the ideal code would not require agents to make significant and pointless sacrifices in *The Unsolved Climate Case*. For one of the stipulations of the case is that "no one is making, nor is anyone going to make," the necessary sacrifices. Thus, we can assume that there is zero objective chance that a code requiring significant sacrifices will be followed. In which case, the code with the highest expected value could not be a code requiring significant sacrifices. But even if maximizing-expectation-rate PFRC avoids problematic implications in *The Unsolved Climate Case*, it has problematic implications in the following case.

> *The Solved Climate Case*: if everyone makes the fairly minor sacrifices required to drastically reduce their carbon footprints (assume that, in this possible world, the needed sacrifices are fairly minor), then the climate disaster that would otherwise ensue sometime in the next century will be averted. As it turns out, everyone is doing far more than their fair share, as this is what they believe that they ought to do. That is, everyone believes that they should do more than their fair share (making significant as opposed to minor sacrifices) so as to ensure that even if many don't do their fair share, climate disaster will nonetheless be averted. Yet, unbeknownst to anyone, everyone is indeed doing far more than his or her fair share. Thus, regardless of what any individual does, climate disaster is going to be averted. Indeed, no individual can make the slightest difference to the likelihood that the disaster will occur—it won't. But individuals can make a significant difference as to how well their own families will fare over the next century by not making any significant (as opposed to minor) sacrifices themselves.

In this case, there is no *objective* chance that anything other than a code requiring each to do more than his or her fair share will be followed (or accepted for that matter). So the ideal code will include such a requirement, for, on the objective version of maximizing-expectation-rate PFRC, any principle with a 100 percent objective chance of being adopted will necessarily be part of the ideal code—assuming, that is, that there is some code that includes that principle that has a non-zero weighted expected value at some rate of following. After all, the expected value of any code lacking that principle would be zero given that it will have a 100 percent chance of being followed at a zero rate and a 0 percent chance of being followed at any non-zero rate.

So, on the objective version of maximizing-expectation-rate PFRC, individuals are, in *The Solved Climate Case*, required to make significant sacrifices even though these sacrifices would be entirely pointless and constitute doing far more than their fair shares. I find this implication of the objective version of maximizing-expectation-rate PFRC to be at least as problematic as the subjective version's implication in *The Unsolved Climate Case*. For the fact that making these sacrifices is part of a set of acts that, if realized, would have good consequences does not seem, in either case, to be any reason at all to make such sacrifices given that the relevant agents cannot see to it that this set of acts or its good consequences are realized. So I conclude that PFRC faces the same dilemma that UFRC faces.

What about UARC? On this view, obligations don't arise from the good consequences of a set of *actions* being *realized* but rather from the good consequences of a set of *rules* being *accepted*. So, unlike UFRC and PFRC, UARC never requires an agent to φ in virtue of the fact that her φ-ing is part of a set of acts that, if realized, would have good consequences. But UARC does require an agent to φ in virtue of the fact that her φ-ing is required by a set of rules that, if universally accepted, would have good consequences. But suppose, as I have argued, that we shouldn't think that the fact that an agent's φ-ing is part of a set of acts that, if realized, would have good consequences constitutes a reason for her to φ if she can't see to it that this set or its good consequences are realized. In that case, we also shouldn't think that the fact that an agent's φ-ing is required by a set of rules that, if universally accepted, would have good consequences constitutes a reason for her to φ if she can't see to it that these rules are universally accepted.

So, although I had earlier drawn the rather limited conclusion that an agent has a consequence-based reason to φ in virtue of the fact that her φ-ing is part of a set of acts that, if realized, would have good consequences only if she is able to see to it that this set and its good consequences are realized, it seems that I can now just as plausibly draw the more general conclusion that an agent has a consequence-based reason to φ in virtue of the fact that her φ-ing is appropriately related to X (where X is something that, if realized, would have good consequences) only if she is able to see to it that X and its good consequences are realized. Insofar as the good consequences of X matter with respect to an agent's φ-ing (whether X be everyone's accepting a set of rules or the set of acts consisting in everyone's following those rules), they matter only insofar as she can see to it that X's good consequences are realized.

It seems, then, that UARC has problematic implications in *The Unsolved Climate Case* just as UFRC did. UARC implies (1) that I am required to make significant sacrifices so as to drastically reduce my own carbon footprint, (2) that

I am required to do so in virtue of the fact that my doing is required by the set of rules that, if universally accepted, would have good consequences, and (3) that this is so despite the fact that I cannot see to it that these rules are universally accepted or that the good consequences stemming from their universal acceptance are realized. So, like UFRC, UARC implies that I am required to make pointless sacrifices in *The Unsolved Climate Case*. And just as PFRC has problematic implications in *The Solved Climate Case*, so does PARC. Both imply that I am required to make significant sacrifices even though these sacrifices would be entirely pointless and constitute doing far more than my fair share. Thus, the move from following versions to acceptance versions of rule consequentialism seems to be of no help in avoiding counter-intuitive implications in the climate cases.

Other reasons

I have argued that the fact that an agent's φ-ing is appropriately related to some X that, if realized, would have good consequences counts as a reason for her to φ only if she can see to it that X and its good consequences are realized.[24] Yet, in certain types of situation, which I will call *unrealizability situations*, rule consequentialism requires agents to φ in virtue of the fact that their φ-ing is appropriately related to some such X even though they cannot see to the realization of X or its good consequences. (Note that depending on which version of rule consequentialism we are considering, at least one of the two climate cases will count as an unrealizability situation.) Of course, this doesn't mean that agents lack sufficient reason to act as rule consequentialism requires them to act in these situations. For even if the fact an agent's φ-ing is appropriately related to some such X doesn't itself count as a reason for her to φ, it may be that some other fact constitutes sufficient reason for her to φ. In this section, I explore this possibility and argue that there is no other fact that constitutes sufficient reason for agents to φ in unrealizability situations.

So, if the fact that an agent's φ-ing is appropriately related to some X that, if realized, would have good consequences is not a reason for her to φ in an unrealizability situation, then what other fact might constitute a reason for her to φ in that situation? One possibility is that some deontological consideration counts in favor of her φ-ing. But in many unrealizability situations there will be no deontological consideration that counts in favor of her φ-ing. In the two climate cases, for instance, there are no deontological considerations that count in favor of my making significant sacrifices.[25] After all, I won't be breaking any promises if I fail to make significant sacrifices. Moreover, I won't be harming anyone if I fail to make significant sacrifices, for it is stipulated in each case that my failing to make significant sacrifices will neither cause harm nor increase the risk of harm to anyone. And fairness doesn't speak in favor of my making significant sacrifices. Indeed, fairness speaks against requiring me to make significant sacrifices in the two climate cases. In *The Unsolved Climate Case*, it would be unfair for me to have to make significant sacrifices when no one else is making such sacrifices. And in *The Solved Climate Case*, it would be unfair for me to have to make *significant* sacrifices when that constitutes doing far more than my fair share.[26] Lastly, it won't do to object: "What if everyone did that?" For in *The Unsolved Climate Case*, it seems sufficient to reply: "Everyone *is* doing that."[27] And in *The Solved Climate Case*, it seems sufficient to reply: "There would be no problem if everyone made only minor sacrifices, for in *The Solved Climate Case*, that is all that is needed to avert climate disaster."

But even if there are no deontological considerations that count in favor of my making significant sacrifices in these cases, perhaps the mere fact that I am morally required to make these sacrifices would itself count as a reason for me to do so. As it turns out, Parfit thinks that the fact that some act is morally required does constitute a reason (what he calls a *deontic reason*) to perform that act. I am skeptical about this, but I must admit that, if Parfit is right and if, as rule consequentialism supposes, I am morally required to make these sacrifices, then there would be at least some reason for me to make these sacrifices. Perhaps, then, this deontic reason will (itself or in conjunction with other facts) constitute sufficient reason for me to make these sacrifices. But, as Parfit admits, the plausibility of supposing that we have sufficient reason to do what morality requires depends on what morality requires. He says, for instance, that if act consequentialism were true, then we could plausibly deny that we always have sufficient reason to do what is morally required, for act consequentialism is very demanding. For instance, act consequentialism requires me to sacrifice my life if I could thereby increase the overall good by even the smallest of increments. And, as Parfit points out, it is implausible to suppose that we have sufficient reason to meet such stringent moral demands.[28] Parfit's thought seems to be that if morality turns out to be very demanding, then it will be implausible to suppose that we always have sufficient reason to act as morality requires. In which case, we should suppose that whatever deontic reason we have to do what is morally required would be decisively opposed by the reasons that we have not to comply with such extreme demands.

Yet it seems to me that rule consequentialism's demands are even more extreme and unreasonable than act consequentialism's demands. At least whenever act consequentialism requires us to make significant sacrifices, there is always some point to our making these sacrifices in that they would produce some greater good. But, as we've seen, rule consequentialism requires us to make significant sacrifices even when doing so is completely pointless, doing absolutely no good whatsoever. So even if the fact that some act is morally required is itself a reason to perform that act, it seems doubtful that it will be strong enough to provide us with sufficient reason to make the sorts of significant and unreasonable sacrifice that rule consequentialism requires us to make in the climate cases.

Although I am quite skeptical about whether the fact that an act is morally required is itself a reason to perform it, I am much less skeptical about whether the fact that an act is one's only blameless and/or justifiable (justifiable to others, that is) option is itself a reason to perform it. But it seems doubtful that such a fact could ever provide sufficient reason for our making the significant sacrifices that rule consequentialism requires us to make in unrealizability cases. For it seems that whatever reasons we have to avoid performing blameworthy and/or unjustifiable actions will not oppose, but coincide with, the (other) reasons that we have to avoid making such sacrifices. And, of course, the reasons that we have to avoid performing blameworthy and/or unjustifiable actions can't possibly provide us with sufficient reason to make such sacrifices unless they oppose the reasons we have to avoid making these sacrifices.

Why think that whatever reasons we have to avoid performing blameworthy and/or unjustifiable actions will not oppose but instead coincide with the (other) reasons that we have to avoid making such sacrifices? Well, I have argued that apart from whatever reasons we have to avoid performing blameworthy or unjustifiable actions, we have decisive reason to avoid making significant sacrifices in the climate cases. After all, we cannot realize any good by making such sacrifices, and we can realize some significant good for ourselves and for our families by refraining from making such sacrifices. Moreover, there are, I have argued, no deontic or deontological reasons that countervail these reasons that we have to avoid making such sacrifices. So the reasons that we have to avoid making such sacrifices are, I believe, decisive. And this, it seems, is sufficient to make our refraining from making such sacrifices both blameless and justifiable. For if we have decisive reason to do something, then others will have to concede that, insofar as they are rational, they would act as we would in the situation. And how can they blame us for acting as they would act insofar as they are rational?[29]

Perhaps, there could be expressive reasons for making significant sacrifices in the climate cases. For it seems that, by making such sacrifices, one could express both one's concern for the environment and one's willingness to cooperate with others. And it may be that we have reason to express such sentiments even when no good consequences will come of it. But even if we do, it seems that these reasons will not be sufficiently strong to countervail the reasons we have to refrain from imposing significant hardships on ourselves and our families, especially when there may be other ways to express such sentiments that are both less costly and more effective. Let's suppose that although there is no way to prevent climate disaster in *The Unsolved Climate Case*, there is a way to reduce the environmental problems resulting from landfills by doing one's part in the "Reduce, Reuse, Recycle" campaign. It would seem, then, that doing one's part in this campaign would be a less costly and more effective way of expressing both one's concern for the environment and one's willingness to cooperate with others in such ventures.

Lastly, one might claim that there is a reason not to be complicit in any wrongdoing and that, in failing to make significant sacrifices in *The Unsolved Climate Case*, I would be complicit in our collectively bringing about climate disaster, which is wrong. But I am doubtful that my failing to make significant sacrifices in *The Unsolved Climate Case* would count as my being complicit in this collective wrongdoing when (1) my own actions made no difference at all, (2) I was willing, and stood ready, to make these significant sacrifices were there any signs from others that they were also so willing, and (3) I clearly expressed my willingness to participate in such a cooperative venture and even actively sought commitments from others to so participate but to no avail. But even if there were such a reason, it seems insufficient to countervail the reason that I have not to pointlessly incur significant hardships for my family and myself.

Above, I have canvassed various sorts of reason that we might have for making significant sacrifices in unrealizability cases: deontic reasons, expressive reasons, deontological reasons, consequence-based reasons, reasons to avoid being complicit in wrongdoing, and reasons to avoid performing blameworthy and/or unjustifiable actions. None of them, taken either individually or collectively, seem to provide sufficient reason for making such sacrifices. But might there not be some other fact that I have failed to consider that constitutes sufficient reason for me to make significant sacrifices in unrealizability cases? I doubt it. If neither the fact that makes such sacrifices morally required on rule consequentialism nor the fact that I am morally required to make such sacrifices provide sufficient reason for me to make such sacrifices (and I have argued that neither does), then whether there would be sufficient reason for me to make such sacrifices would have to be a contingent matter, based on, say, my having promised to make such sacrifices. But presumably, for whatever the contingency we think of, there will always be a way of further specifying the climate cases such that the contingency is not met. For instance, we can just stipulate, as I have, that I have made no such promise. We should, therefore, conclude that we sometimes lack sufficient reason to act as rule consequentialism requires.

Conclusion

We have seen that rule consequentialism sometimes requires us to act in ways that we lack sufficient reason to act. This presents a dilemma for Parfit. Parfit must concede either that rule consequentialism (and, hence, Triple Theory, which entails it) is false, despite the putatively strong reasons that he believes we have for accepting it, or that morality doesn't have the importance he seems to attribute to it, given that it has been undermined by his own substantive account of morality. Parfit could respond, though, that morality would be undermined only if we *often* have decisive reason to act wrongly, and I have shown only that we *sometimes* have decisive reason to act wrongly. How often must these times be to undermine morality? Parfit never says. But it seems to me both that unrealizability cases (on the model of the two climate cases) arise all too frequently and that, in any case, morality would be significantly undermined in terms of its putative rational authority even if we only sometimes have decisive reason to act wrongly. In any case, Parfit admits that "it would be bad if, in such cases [cases where moral duty and self-interest conflict], we and others would have sufficient reasons to act wrongly."[30]

The above-discussed dilemma arises for Parfit because he holds that "moral principles or theories are intended to answer questions about what *all* of us ought to do" (emphasis in original).³¹ By contrast, principles and theories of rationality seem intended to answer a different kind of question: questions about what *each* of us ought to do. And it seems that it is the fact that Parfit thinks of moral principles in this way that leads him to argue for a moral theory that makes what an individual morally ought to do a function of the good consequences that would be realized if all of us acted in a certain way or accepted certain principles. But even if it is plausible to think of moral principles in this way (and I am skeptical), it doesn't seem plausible to think of what an individual has most reason, all things considered, to do in this way.³²

Notes

1 I am not making the well-worn (and, I believe, false) claim that either rule consequentialism collapses into act consequentialism or it is incoherent. Rather, I am claiming that we don't always have sufficient reason to act as rule consequentialism requires us to act. This is not a problem for those rule consequentialists who deny that we always have strong reasons to avoid acting wrongly. But it is a problem for Parfit, for he thinks that if we often have sufficient reason to act wrongly, then morality would be undermined (OWM 1, pp. 147–8).
2 OWM 1, p. 418.
3 OWM 1, pp. 147–8. Strictly speaking, Parfit claims not that morality would be undermined if we *sometimes* had decisive reason to act wrongly, but that it would be undermined if we *often* had decisive reason to act wrongly. Nevertheless, I will spend most of the chapter focused on the issue of whether we sometimes have decisive reason to act wrongly and leave a discussion of the frequency of these times and whether it is sufficient to undermine morality for the chapter's conclusion.
4 A consequence-based reason to φ is a reason to φ in virtue of the fact either that φ-ing would itself promote the impersonal good or that φ-ing is appropriately related to something else that would promote the impersonal good. This allows that there could potentially be both direct and indirect consequence-based reasons. Whereas the fact that S's φ-ing would promote the impersonal good would be a *direct* consequence-based reason for S to φ, the fact that S's φ-ing is appropriately related to an X—where X is something that, if realized, would promote the impersonal good—would be an *indirect* consequence-based reason for S to φ. So if there is a reason for S to push A at t_2 in virtue of the fact it is part of a set of acts (i.e. the set consisting in S's pushing both A at t_2 and B at t_3) that, if realized, would have good consequences, this would be an indirect consequence-based reason for S to push A at t_2.
5 This amounts to the claim that the only consequence-based reasons are the direct ones.
6 What follows is only a brief sketch of an argument against the standard view, but see Portmore (MS) for a more thorough argument.
7 See Portmore (MS) for a further defense of this claim.
8 For more on this issue, see Portmore (2011), chapter 6.
9 I borrow this case, while modifying it for my own purposes, from Goldman (1978), p. 186.
10 A fourth sub-type is where S_1 and S_2 are not identical but t' and t'' are. For reasons of space, I skip discussion of this sub-type.
11 Would it matter if, in *The Five*, Faisal were to undergo some psychology-preserving but identity-destroying process (such as, perhaps, fission or teletransportation) between t_2 and t_3? For more on this, see Portmore (MS).

12 As Parfit admits, this needs to be revised, for there is the possibility that two or more sets of principles with incompatible prescriptions could be UF-optimific—see OWM 1, pp. 407–8.
13 Assume that there is no precise boundary between suffering more and not suffering more, just as there is no precise boundary between being balding and not being balding. And assume that just as the addition or subtraction of a single strand of hair from a man's head cannot make a difference as to whether or not he is balding, the addition or subtraction of a single person's efforts to reduce his or her carbon footprint (because the relevant particulates will be so widely dispersed over the Earth's atmosphere) cannot make a difference as to whether or not any person suffers more. Now, one type of response to this sort of sorites paradox is to deny that there are imprecise and morally relevant boundaries of the sort that I am presupposing. But this is not a response open to Parfit, for he allows for genuine imprecision with respect both to normative truths and to differences in value—see OWM 2, pp. 555–62.
14 I call this The *Unsolved* Climate Case because it is an instance of what Parfit calls an *unsolved each-we dilemma*—see OWM 1, pp. 305–6.
15 Even if the UF-optimific set of principles exempted a few thousand (perhaps, randomly selected) individuals from having to make significant sacrifices, UFRC would still require those who were not exempted to make significant sacrifices despite the fact that their doing so would do absolutely no good and be bad both for them and their families. And note that no set of principles that exempted more than just a few thousand individuals from having to make significant sacrifices would be UF-optimific, for I am stipulating both that, if more than just a few thousand failed to make significant sacrifices, climate disaster would ensue and that no set of rules that permits us to act in ways that allows climate disaster to ensue could be UF-optimific given how bad climate disaster would be.
16 See, for instance, Hooker (2000), pp. 124–5.
17 OWM 1, p. 319.
18 Ridge (2009), p. 68.
19 OWM 1, pp. 469 and 479.
20 Tobia (2013).
21 Tobia (2013), p. 650.
22 Subjective probabilities depend (at least in part) on the evidence available to the subject or subjects in question. By contrast, objective probabilities do not. If determinism is true, then the objective probability of any given event is either zero or one.
23 Parfit may claim that he is giving an account of what agents ought to do in the subjective (evidence-relative) sense as opposed to the objective (fact-relative) sense. But the evidence available to a given agent may suggest that her failing to make significant sacrifices would make absolutely no difference as to whether climate disaster will ensue or to how bad it will be. And it is implausible to suppose that an agent would have a subjective obligation to make significant sacrifices if her evidence suggests that her doing so would make no positive difference.
24 X could, for instance, stand for 'the set of actions consisting in everyone's following the ideal code' or for 'the universal acceptance of a particular set of rules.' And the appropriate relation might be that of being a part of that set or being permitted by that set.
25 It is also unclear how a rule consequentialist could even appeal to deontological moral considerations, for the rule consequentialist holds that the only moral considerations are rule-consequentialist ones.
26 One might suggest that what would be fair is my making the same sacrifices that everyone else is making. But I don't see why the fact that others are irrationally doing more than what each of us needs to be doing makes it unfair for me to do no more than what

each of us needs to be doing. (And I will just stipulate that, in *The Solved Climate Case*, others are irrationally doing more than what each us need to be doing.)
27 Parfit seems to concede as much—see OWM 1, pp. 305–6 and 319. What we might ask instead is whether we could rationally will that everyone as opposed to no one makes significant sacrifices so as to avert climate disaster. But this question isn't equivalent to asking whether any individual should make significant sacrifices, and, as I have argued, the answer to this question depends on whether the individual can see to it that sufficient others do their part.
28 OWM 1, pp. 148–9.
29 For more on this, see Portmore (2011), chapter 2.
30 OWM 1, p. 143.
31 OWM 1, p. 306.
32 For helpful comments and discussions, I thank Justin D'Arms, Dale Dorsey, Pamela Hieronymi, Jeff Moriarty, Shyam Nair, Jussi Suikkanen, Simon Kirchin, two anonymous reviewers, and audiences at both the University of St Andrews and the 2013 New Orleans Invitational Seminar in Ethics.

References

Goldman, Holly S. [now Smith, H.M.] (1978) 'Doing the Best One Can', in *Values and Morals*, Alvin I. Goldman and Jaegwon Kim (eds) (Dordrecht: D. Reidel Publishing Company), pp. 185–214.
Hooker, B. (2000) *Ideal Code, Real World* (Oxford: Oxford University Press).
Parfit, Derek (2011) *On What Matters* (Oxford: Oxford University Press), vols 1 and 2.
Portmore, Douglas W. (2011) *Commonsense Consequentialism: Wherein Morality Meets Rationality* (New York: Oxford University Press).
Portmore, Douglas W. (MS) 'Acts, Attitudes, and Rational Control'. Draft available: http://bit.ly/1Jetb8j
Ridge, Michael (2009) 'Climb Every Mountain?', *Ratio* 22, pp. 59–77.
Tobia, Kevin (2013) 'Rule Consequentialism and the Problem of Partial Acceptance', *Ethical Theory and Moral Practice* 16, pp. 643–52.

8

ADVICE FOR NON-ANALYTICAL NATURALISTS

J.L. Dowell and David Sobel

Volume 2 of Derek Parfit's monumental and magnificent *On What Matters* is primarily devoted to defending Non-Naturalist Cognitivism about normative claims. Such a view maintains that there are normative facts that are not identical with any naturalistic state of the world. Rather, normative facts are over and above any set of natural facts.[1] Much of Parfit's case for such a view rests on showing that all naturalistic alternatives fail. He offers different arguments against different naturalistic views. Here we focus on Parfit's case against what we see as the most promising version of naturalism about the normative—a view that Parfit calls "Non-Analytical Naturalism" (NAN). Parfit has three main named arguments against NAN: The Normativity Objection, The Fact-Stating Argument, and the Triviality Objection. Here we focus on the Triviality Objection. Parfit appears to think of the Triviality Objection as his best argument against NAN. He praises this objection as "livelier" than his other arguments and as showing "more clearly" the depth of his disagreement with naturalists.[2] Further, Parfit names his central chapter against the NAN "The Triviality Objection." He writes of this objection, "This argument, I believe, is sound, and shows that Naturalism cannot be true."[3]

Parfit's Triviality Objection purports to show that NANs are unable to do so much as state informative identities between the normative and the natural, which, if true, would show that the normative is nothing over and above the natural. This is a broad, pre-emptive challenge against a wide range of naturalistic views. It is quite different, and bolder, than merely saying that the thesis they manage to express is in fact false. The argument takes the form of a *reductio* of any NAN position, beginning with the supposition that the NAN's central claims must take the form of identity statements and then showing that no such claim could have all of the features the NAN requires, including informativeness.[4] So, Parfit concludes, no NAN position could be correct.[5]

To spoil any suspense, we think Parfit's challenge to the NAN can be met on its own terms. It will take us a while to lay out Parfit's challenge and our response.

Our suspicion is that Parfit misses the response we offer because he relies on the mistaken assumption that the informativeness of informative identity statements must be explained by their semantics rather than the pragmatics of their use. Dropping that assumption makes available an independently well-motivated Stalnakerian, pragmatic solution to Parfit's challenge. Whatever one thinks about the specifics of Stalnaker's proposal in particular, the need for some such proposal to account for the informativeness of some identities becomes evident once we have accepted a simple, direct reference account of names and kind terms.

Because most of Parfit's case for his non-naturalist alternative hinges on showing that no naturalistic view could be true, if we are able to answer Parfit's challenge to the NAN, this would severely damage Parfit's overall case for Non-Naturalist Cognitivism. While our sympathies tend towards naturalism, we are not here arguing against non-naturalism or for the truth of any particular NAN view. Rather we are claiming that Parfit's argument fails to rule out some NAN views and thus his Non-Naturalist Cognitivism is significantly less well supported by his arguments than he claims.

Parfit's argument against Non-Analytical Naturalism

We should first distinguish the sort of naturalistic view under discussion from other naturalist rivals. According to Analytical Naturalists, "normative words have meanings that can be analyzed or defined by using naturalistic words. On this view, although there is no distinction between normative and naturalistic claims, we can distinguish between normative and naturalistic ways of making the same claim."[6] We might characterize this view using the notion of a conceptual analysis. The meanings of our normative terms are given by our concepts. An analysis of such a concept would give us a list of properties an entity would have to have in order to be in the extension of that concept. According to the Analytical Naturalist, such normative concepts may be given analyses in naturalistic terms. In contrast, according to Non-Analytical Naturalists,

> we use some words to express concepts and make claims that are irreducibly normative, in the sense that these concepts and claims cannot be defined or restated in non-normative terms. When we turn to facts, however, there is no such deep distinction. All facts are natural, but some of these facts are also normative, *since we can also state these facts by making irreducibly normative claims.*[7]

As we will see, this last feature is of some importance to Parfit's argument. As Parfit sees it, once the NAN has given up the Analytical Naturalist's project of analyzing normative concepts in naturalistic terms, she will need some other guarantee that her central claims are about genuinely normative facts. Here he suggests that it would suffice for such claims to be stated using some uncontroversially normative vocabulary.

The NAN claims that we can discover that some normative fact just is some natural fact even when "these discoveries were not implied by the meaning of these words."[8] NANs often attempt to explicate their central claims by exploiting analogies with scientific reductions, such as that of water to H_2O. NANs such as Peter Railton are impressed by the fact that identities such as water being H_2O may be true, though our concepts of water and of H_2O are distinct.[9] Such naturalists might hope to bypass the force of the Moore's Open-Question Argument against naturalism by maintaining that, although there is a conceptually open question about the identity of the favored natural property with a normative property, just as in the case of scientific reductions, such openness does not block non-analytical identities.[10]

The first step in understanding Parfit's argument is to see why he thinks the NAN is required to try to couch her central claims in the form of informative identity statements. Parfit claims that vindicating naturalism requires more than vindicating claims such as 'acts are right iff and because they maximize happiness' or 'one has a reason to O iff and because one has an informed desire to O.' He thinks the non-naturalist can accept such claims. Parfit insists that in claiming that "some natural property is the property that *makes* acts right we are not claiming that this natural property is the property of *being* right."[11] Call *an explanatory tracking claim* any claim of the form 'any x is H iff and because it is L,' where H is some higher-order property and L is some lower-order property. One way to see that explanatory tracking claims are insufficient for showing that the H-properties are not over and above the L-properties is to see that their truth requires no relation stronger than supervenience between the higher- and the lower-order properties. Let us say that the H-properties supervene on the L-properties iff no two objects, *a* and *b*, differ with respect to their H-properties without also differing with respect to their L-properties. Supervenience is compatible with at least two importantly different theses about the relation between H and L. (1) The H-properties are, or their instantiations are constituted by, the L-, or the instantiation of the L-, properties. (2) The instantiation of L-properties, and their instantiation alone, brings about, or otherwise settles, the instantiation of *sui generis* H-properties.

If (1) is true, then the H-properties are not over and above the L-properties. But if (2) is true, then they are. To illustrate the second type of relationship with an example from the philosophy of mind: Emergentists about the phenomenal might hold that the physical properties bring about, or otherwise settle, the instantiation of *sui generis* phenomenal properties.[12] Similarly, Parfit tells us that a non-naturalist utilitarian like Sidgwick might hold that the natural properties bring about or otherwise settle the instantiation of *sui generis* normative ones. This means that a non-naturalist about the H-properties may accept both supervenience and explanatory tracking about the relationship between the H- and the L-properties. So Parfit is right to maintain that views that merely hold that a certain normative status is necessitated and explained by a certain natural property have yet to show that that normative property is not something over and above that natural property. What is required to show this further thing, Parfit claims, is to show that some natural property is identical with some normative property. For this reason, he argues that the NAN must defend claims such as the claim that "when some act would maximize happiness, that is the same as this act's being what we ought to do" or the claim that when some act would satisfy an informed desire, that is the same as the agent having a reason to perform that act.[13] Although one might fuss over the details, we think that something in the neighborhood of Parfit's claim here is quite plausible, so we are inclined to grant it, at least for the sake of argument.[14,15]

So, we will suppose, with Parfit, that NANs must be in the business of defending identity claims between a property denoted using a normative term and that same property denoted by a natural one. Let NORM=NAT stand in for whichever such claim is some NAN's favored claim. If some such claim could be shown to be true for each of our uncontroversially normative properties, then the NAN would have shown that the normative is nothing over and above the natural. And since, by the NAN's lights, any identification between a normative property and a natural property would be *a posteriori* and not secured by an analysis of our normative concepts in naturalistic terms, the statements of those identities would be informative and non-trivial. In other words, once we have granted that the NAN must be in the business of defending identities, we must grant that she must be in the business of defending informative identity statements.

The question of how identity statements can be informative has been a central preoccupation in the philosophy of language at least since Frege. Indeed, explaining the cognitive significance or the informativeness of identity statements of the form 'a=b' provided one of his central motivations for positing the existence of sense. In the next step in his argument, Parfit proposes a solution to Frege's puzzle about the cognitive significance of identity statements that he sees as explaining the informativeness of scientific identities. His final step then aims to show that this solution is of no help in understanding how NORM=NAT identities could meet all of the NAN's requirements.

Frege posited the existence of sense in part to explain how identity statements of the form 'a is b' could be informative. The puzzle is that, if true, such statements would seem to express the same trivial expression as 'a is a.' A solution to that puzzle requires, minimally, identifying some information the former can be used to communicate that the latter cannot. This difference in information, Frege held, is explained by the difference in the sense of the term 'a' and the term 'b.' A term's sense, roughly, provides a route of cognitive access to its referent. Thus Frege's solution was to say that identity statements can be informative because they tell us that the thing that we pick out in one way (as the thing that has one set of features) is the same thing as that which we pick out in another (as the thing that has some different set). For example, Frege suggests that the informativeness of 'Hesperus is Phosphorus' is explained by the different ways of picking out Venus via the different senses of 'Hesperus' and 'Phosphorus.' Such a difference might be that, in using 'Hesperus,' we pick out Venus as that which is in a certain location in the evening sky, while, in using 'Phosphorus,' we pick it out as that which is in a certain location in the morning sky. These two different features that Venus has yield a difference in the way it may be picked out, and this explains the informativeness of 'Hesperus is Phosphorus' in contrast to 'Venus is Venus.' Importantly, we suspect, for understanding Parfit's argument, Frege thought such senses were part of the meaning or semantics of a term.

Parfit's solution to Frege's puzzle possesses several of the distinctive features of Frege's own. According to Parfit, what makes an identity statement of the form "a is b" informative is a difference in the properties associated with the referent by the use of 'a' and those associated with it via the use of 'b.' He illustrates his idea with an explanation of the informativeness of scientific identities such as 'water is H_2O.' His idea is that the pre-scientific concept of water is the concept of "the stuff that has the properties of quenching thirst, falling from the clouds as rain, filling lakes and rivers, etc.," while, in contrast, our concept of H_2O is the concept of "the stuff that is composed of molecules each of which contains two hydrogen atoms and one oxygen atom."[16] Scientists discovered that water is H_2O by discovering that "the stuff that has the properties of quenching thirst, falling from the clouds as rain, etc., is the same stuff that has the *different* property of being composed of such molecules."[17]

Armed with this understanding of how identities can be informative, Parfit then argues that there is no way to extend this model to the NAN's identity statements, compatible with their possession of all of the needed features. Three of these requirements are important for understanding Parfit's argument. The first has been mentioned already: the NAN's identities must be capable of communicating new information. Second, the NAN's identities must express a normative claim in the sense that their statement must include normative vocabulary. This is because the NAN is trying to vindicate the claim that a subset of the natural facts are also normative facts. Call that claim SUBSET. Here we are assuming that the NAN must express her identity claims in a way such that, if those claims were shown to be true, it would be shown that SUBSET is true. In order for the vindication of those identities to vindicate SUBSET, they must express claims that the non-naturalist clearly rejects. The non-naturalist accepts that there are natural facts. What she rejects is that any of those facts is also normative. The NAN and the non-naturalist might agree that true sentences containing normative vocabulary are made true by normative facts and that true sentences couched entirely in naturalistic vocabulary are made true by natural facts. For NORM=NAT to express a proposition over whose truth the NAN and the non-naturalist disagree, then, that proposition must be a normative one made true by natural facts *by* the latter's *being* normative. Importantly, for Parfit, the normativity of a claim or proposition is guaranteed by its vehicle of representation. If the vehicle for the expression of some proposition uses a normative term, that is enough, for Parfit, to guarantee that the proposition thereby expressed is normative. Third, the informativeness of the NAN's identities must not require the positing of any further, irreducibly normative properties.

We turn now from Parfit's requirements on the NAN's identity statements to his argument that no such statement could meet these requirements. As we have seen, the NAN's goal is to state an identity between some natural property, NAT, and some normative property, NORM. It might seem that such identities are easy to state. Parfit offers as his example,

> (C) an act having the property of maximizing happiness is what it is for an act to have the property of being what we ought to do.[18]

(C) is an instance of the form we have labeled NORM=NAT. Suppose some such claim is true. The fact that would make it true would be the uninteresting fact that some property—for example, the property of being what we ought to do—is identical with itself. If such sentences did no more than state such facts, they would be uninformative propositions the non-naturalist could readily accept. In order to express a substantive claim, one that the non-naturalist would deny, the NAN needs the term 'NORM' to pick out the property NORM via one of its properties. This property, that the NAN needs and hasn't identified, Parfit calls "the lost property," and he calls these concerns the *Lost Property Problem*.[19]

Holding fixed Parfit's model for explaining the informativeness of identities, the informativeness of NORM=NAT would require analogues—in the case of "water is H_2O" the aforementioned "the stuff that has the properties of quenching thirst, falling from the clouds as rain, filling lakes and rivers, etc." and "the stuff that is composed of molecules each of which contains two hydrogen atoms and one oxygen atom." "Water is H_2O" is a kind identity: its informativeness requires a difference in the properties associated with what, if the identity is correct, is a single kind. NORM=NAT is itself a property identity. So, we suggest on Parfit's behalf, the different properties required by the informativeness of that identity must be second-order properties, properties of, if the identity is correct, what is a single (first-order) property that is both normative and natural.

Here we focus not on finding a second-order property for both NORM and NAT, but only for NORM. We do this for two reasons. First, Parfit's own discussion proceeds in this way; he focuses on arguing that there could be no such property of NORM to play an appropriate role. Second, even if we grant that identities are informative only when they appeal to a property of the object of the identity, it is just false that both terms must pick out that object via some property of it. For example, we assume that Parfit would allow that 'Ben Franklin is the inventor of bifocals' is informative even though 'Ben Franklin' does not pick out Franklin via one of his properties. It suffices for 'the inventor of bifocals' to do so.[20]

Parfit then asks: what might this needed, second-order property of the property of NORM be? Sometimes Parfit assumes without argument that this missing, second-order property must itself be normative.[21] But we think his argument is best put as he expresses it later, giving it the form of a dilemma.[22] The dilemma is that this second-order property must be either a normative property or a natural one. And on either option, the resulting identity statement would not have all of the three features required of the NAN's central claims.

158

Suppose, first, that the NAN proposes that it is a normative property. To keep track of the difference between this property and NORM itself, call this second-order property of NORM *NORM2*. In this case, Parfit argues, in explaining the informativeness of NORM=NAT, the NAN posits the existence of some further, normative property, NORM2; on such a view, the informativeness of NORM=NAT would consist in its expressing the proposition that the property that has the second-order property NORM2 is NAT. However, NORM2 itself would not have been shown to be nothing over and above the natural.

This proposal would not saddle the NAN with merely one irreducibly normative property. Recall that NORM=NAT stands in for any of the NAN's central claims. The putative reduction of each normative property of order n will require positing the existence of an additional normative property of order $n+1$. If this were the only solution to Frege's puzzle available to the NAN, the work of showing that the normative is nothing over and above the natural would be in principle incompletable. Indeed, though Parfit does not himself press the point, his argument would be strengthened if we suppose, as seems plausible, that any property with an irreducibly normative property is itself irreducibly normative. If so, this strategy for explaining the informativeness of NORM=NAT would deprive the NAN of the ability of reducing *any* normative property.[23] In any case, we accept, with Parfit, that this is not a promising strategy for the NAN.

If the missing property can't be normative, it must be natural. Suppose that it is. Parfit explains how he thinks a NAN might implement such a strategy in terms of his sample statement of the form NORM=NAT: (C), above. Here, Parfit tells us that one might think that (C)'s informativeness could be explained by the informativeness of a different sentence, (Q):

> (Q) when some act would maximize happiness this act would have certain other, non-normative properties.[24]

Here is the entirety of Parfit's argument against this second strategy:

> Naturalists believe that substantive normative facts are also natural facts. Since (Q) is not a normative claim, (Q) could not state a normative fact.[25]

Recall that this is part of an overall argument to show that the NAN cannot so much as state her central identity claims in a form that would meet all of her requirements. From these compressed remarks, it is far from immediately clear why (Q)'s failure to be normative would pose a problem for the NAN. After all, the NAN who defends (C) is not claiming that (Q) is a normative claim. She is claiming that (C) is.

In the next section we will discuss how to meet Parfit's challenge. But, first, we will offer our best reconstruction of Parfit's thought. Recall Parfit's second requirement on the NAN's identities. Those identities must express a proposition that the non-naturalist must take issue with in order to establish that non-naturalism is false. Since the non-naturalist accepts that there are natural claims made true by natural facts, to be a claim at issue between them, NORM=NAT must express an uncontroversially *normative* proposition that could be shown to be about natural facts that are themselves normative.

As we have seen, Parfit assumes that a proposition's being normative could be guaranteed by the linguistic vehicle for its expression. If the sentence expressing some proposition contains a normative term, that is enough, for Parfit, to guarantee that the proposition thereby expressed is normative. By this criterion, (C) expresses a normative proposition, while (Q) does not. Recall that we are considering the proposal that the informativeness of (Q) explains the informativeness of (C). While it is unclear why, Parfit clearly thinks that this cannot be so. Here is our hypothesis: Parfit means to allow that if we learned (C) by learning (Q), this would show that (C) is informative. But he thinks that if (Q) does not state a normative fact, (C) must not as well. So then the problem would be that although (C) is informative, it cannot tell us anything normative and thus could not tell us that the normative was nothing over and above the natural.

But why should we accept that (Q)'s failure to express a normative proposition would mean that (C) fails to express one as well? There is nothing in Parfit's text that speaks to this question. However, we have a suspicion. Recall the close similarity between Parfit's solution to Frege's puzzle and Frege's own. Recall also that Frege thought that senses are semantic features of the expressions that had them *and* that sense explains the informativeness of identity statements. In other words, Frege's solution to his puzzle is a semantic one: the difference in cognitive significance between identities of the form 'a is b' and 'a is a' is explained by a difference in their semantics. If that were right, then the ability of one identity statement to communicate the same information communicable by another would be explained by their having the same semantics. Suppose Parfit follows Frege in holding that the information an identity statement is able to communicate is a feature of its semantics. In that case, if (Q) were to communicate the same information (C) can (and so explain the informativeness of (C)), this would have to be because (Q) and (C) semantically express the same proposition. But if they semantically express the same proposition and the proposition (Q) expresses is non-normative, then the proposition (C) expresses is non-normative as well. And if the proposition (C) expresses isn't normative, then (C) doesn't satisfy the second requirement on the NAN.

One reason to attribute this reconstruction to Parfit is a negative one: Parfit does not consider the sort of pragmatic response to his challenge we will urge. Yet the success of his argument, as we shall see, requires that there are no other solutions. If there were other solutions, then showing that the Fregean semantic strategy cannot be the NAN's would not be sufficient to show that the NAN couldn't explain how her identities avoid Frege's puzzle. At most, Parfit's arguments would show that the NAN requires some other strategy for explaining the informativeness of her central claims. But this is not what Parfit concludes.

Instead, Parfit takes his arguments to show that the NAN cannot so much as state her central claims in a way that meets all of her requirements. Our attribution to Parfit makes good sense of why he takes his argument to show that no NAN position could be correct. So that attribution fits with his failure to recognize alternatives to Frege's own view and makes it plain why the non-normativity of (Q) would be a problem for the NAN in a way that his own discussion does not. A lesser piece of evidence is given by his characterization of the informativeness of scientific identities. If one accepted, with Parfit, that the properties he selects as those which explain their informativeness are conceptually linked with such identities' terms, one might be inclined to further hold that those links are semantic. Since we see no other attribution that fits as well with his text and makes as good sense of his thought, we propose to make it.

If this reconstruction is correct, then, on Parfit's view, the missing (second-order) property could not be uncontroversially natural, because, were it uncontroversially natural, the information expressed by NORM in NORM=NAT could be expressed in entirely naturalistic terms. But when expressed in such terms, it wouldn't uncontroversially state a normative proposition, one whose truth the non-naturalist is committed to rejecting. So the strategy of explaining the informativeness of NORM=NAT in terms of some natural property of the property NORM would also fail to meet all of the NAN's requirements.

The assumption we have suggested that Parfit seems to need in order for the non-normativity of (Q) and sentences like it to pose a problem for the NAN is the assumption that the only way the proposition (Q) expresses could explain the informativeness of (C) is by being the same proposition (C) expresses. This would mean that (C), despite appearances, doesn't express a normative proposition, as the NAN requires. But, we shall argue, there are reasons quite independent of what is at issue between the NAN and the non-naturalist for rejecting this assumption. If we allow that (Q) semantically expresses the proposition that (C) may be used to pragmatically communicate, then we may explain the informativeness of a use of (C) with (Q), while allowing that the proposition (C) expresses in virtue of its semantics is a normative proposition for just the reason Parfit allows: it is stated using a piece of normative vocabulary—namely, NORM.

What are these reasons? They are reasons that are utterly familiar and near-universally recognized within the philosophy of language. Our advice to the NAN is, at a certain level, very simple: she should avail herself of these powerful, independent reasons to reject the assumption that NORM=NAT must be informative owing to semantic features of sentences expressing such identities. Without that assumption, as we are about to see, responding to Parfit's challenge is fairly straightforward.

Advice for the Non-Analytical Naturalist

As we've seen, one of Frege's central motivations for positing the existence of sense was precisely to account for the informativeness or cognitive significance of identity statements in semantic terms. What, he asked, accounts for the information potential of a true sentence of the form 'a is b' in contrast to 'a is a'? The answer, he suggested, is a difference in the senses associated with each of 'a' and 'b.' His proposed solution is elegant; unfortunately, Saul Kripke's famous modal arguments show that, at least for names and kind terms in English, there isn't anything that fills the job description of a Fregean sense. Kripke's arguments also suggest that such terms are devices for direct reference. In depriving us of sense, however, those arguments saddle us once again with Frege's puzzle, at least for such directly referential terms. If the meaning of 'Hesperus' and 'Phosphorus' is simply the object, Venus, to which they each refer, the proposition expressed by 'Hesperus is Phosphorus' *is* the very same as that expressed by 'Hesperus is Hesperus.' By similar reasoning, the sentences 'water is H_2O' and 'water is water' both express the same (necessary) proposition.

This means that if we accept, with Kripke, that some terms in English are devices for direct reference, we will not be able to appeal to anything like Fregean senses to provide semantic explanations of the informativeness of identity statements containing two of them. In other words, for well-motivated reasons that have nothing to do with the issue between Parfit and the NAN, we must accept extra-semantic explanations of the informativeness of some identity statements. This suggests a strategy for the NAN: look for some other, independently well-motivated, non-semantic explanation of the cognitive significance of identity statements to provide a model for explaining the informativeness of NORM=NAT in a way that satisfies all three of the NAN's requirements. That is what we propose to do here, on the NAN's behalf.[26]

No solution to Frege's puzzle currently enjoys universal acceptance. However, Robert Stalnaker has proposed one justly famous solution to that puzzle compatible with treating names, demonstratives, and kind terms as devices for direct reference. Stalnaker suggests that we treat the information potential of an identity statement of the form 'a is b' as part of the pragmatic information an assertion of such a sentence may communicate. His idea is to make that suggestion plausible by offering a broadly Gricean, possible-worlds framework in which to represent the effect an assertion has on a conversation. For the sake of concreteness, we here sketch how the NAN might rebut Parfit's Triviality Objection by borrowing the tools Stalnaker's solution makes available. However, it should be kept in mind that there are other solutions to Frege's puzzle that the NAN might explore.

Stalnaker suggests we represent the effect of an assertion on a conversation in terms of its ability to alter the set of conversational presuppositions (the 'common ground') that participants share. Those presuppositions may be represented by the set of propositions that participants jointly treat as true for the purposes of the conversation (and are known to jointly treat as true). In a framework in which propositions get represented as sets of possible worlds, a conversation's common ground will induce a context set, the set of worlds at which each of the propositions in the common ground is true. We may think of the worlds in the context set as presumptive candidates for actuality. The aim of an assertion, then, is to update the context set. If accepted by the other participants, the effect of an assertion is to throw out the worlds in the context set that are incompatible with the content of that assertion. In this way, the acceptance of an assertion into the conversational record allows participants to become more opinionated about which worlds are presumptive candidates for actuality.

To do its job, an assertion requires that the conversational contexts must meet several pragmatic constraints. Two of Stalnaker's constraints are important for our purposes here. The first is that the proposition expressed by an assertion must be true at some, but not all, of the worlds in the context set. It is easy to see why contexts must meet this constraint for an assertion to be capable of doing its job; on the one hand, if the proposition expressed is true throughout the worlds in the context, it cannot do its job of narrowing the context set. Crucially for our purposes, this will be true of assertions with trivial or uninformative contents, like 'water is water.' On the other hand, if an assertion were false at every world in the context set, its acceptance would have the effect of throwing all of the worlds out in that set, so that there would be no world left as a candidate for actuality.[27]

Stalnaker's second principle requires that the same proposition be expressed by an assertion relative to each world in the context set. To see why this is required, consider a (very simple) context in which this requirement is not met. We are sitting in a classroom with a door open. Out in the hallway, someone we can hear, but not see, says,

(G) "I just bought a copy of John Gibbons' new book."

From the voice, we know that the speaker must have been either Allison or Clare. Since we are each presuming this and know that each other is presuming this, the mere utterance of that sentence allows us to throw out all of the worlds in the context set in which someone else used the sentence. But how should we narrow the context set in terms of what was *asserted* in that utterance? Our problem is that the context set does not settle what was asserted by that utterance because it still contains two importantly different sets of worlds, worlds in which Clare is speaking and worlds in which Allison is. Relative to the worlds in which Clare is the speaker, what is said is that Clare has bought Gibbons' book. Relative to the worlds in which Allison is, what is said is that Allison has bought the book. Suppose that, knowing both women are truthful, we are willing to accept that utterance, whether said by Allison or Clare. How should we update the context? Do we throw out the worlds in which Allison hasn't bought the book or those in which Clare hasn't? Since we don't know which of two propositions was expressed, acceptance of the speaker's assertion cannot have its usual effect of throwing out the worlds in the context set incompatible with its truth.

These two independently motivated constraints on contexts allow for a diagnosis of the source of the puzzle posed by sentences expressing *a posteriori* necessities, such as 'water is H_2O,' and suggest a solution. Our best semantic theory of kind terms tells us that assertive uses of scientific identity statements, such as 'water is H_2O,' will violate our first constraint on contexts, either by being true in every world in any context set (when they are true) or by being false throughout (when they are false). This means that assertions of such identities are unable to do their characteristic job *in virtue of their semantics*. Of course, assertions may be informative in ways not owing to their semantics. Stalnaker suggests that we look to the pragmatic information communicated to explain how the assertions of identities can do their characteristic job.

First, let's see how Stalnaker's proposal works for the scientific identities many Non-Analytical Naturalists have suggested are analogous to their own favored identities and then consider how that proposal might help such naturalists block Parfit's conclusion. In Stalnaker's framework, which proposition is pragmatically communicated in the cases of concern is defined on a context set: that is, different context sets will determine different propositions. So, to see how Stalnaker's proposal works, we will need to consider a specific context of utterance. Suppose the context is like this: a group of scientists are working to discover the chemical composition of water by examining the composition of a sample they have in their lab. Prior to the results of that analysis, they each assume that their sample is indeed a sample of water and that the analysis of that sample will reveal that it is made up of molecules with one of two different structures, H_2O or XYZ. Ella is the scientist who has just completed her analysis of the sample. Excitedly, she tells her colleagues,

(W) "It's settled! Water is H_2O!"

How should we understand the information communicated by her second assertion? To determine this in Stalnaker's framework, we first identify the set of propositions jointly presupposed by the participants in the conversation. These include that the kind instantiated in the sample is water and that its composition is not of some kind other than XYZ or H_2O. This gives us the common ground for this conversation, from which we may derive its context set, the set of worlds at which each of these presuppositions is true. Prior to her assertion, (W), participants are unopinionated about which of the two molecular structures is instantiated in their sample. To represent this, we need some worlds in the context set in which the kind instantiated in the sample is H_2O and some in which it is XYZ. Simplifying, let our context set include one representative of each world; let i = the world in which the sample is made up of H_2O and j = the world in which it is made up of XYZ. Since in every world in the context set, water is presumed to be whatever kind is instantiated in the sample, that will be so in both i and j. We may then represent Ella's utterance by its corresponding propositional concept, defined on this context set. An utterance's propositional concept is a function from contexts to propositions. Here we represent the propositional concept associated with Ella's second assertion in a two-dimensional framework that takes each world, i and j, in the context set both as a determiner of content and as a world of evaluation.

ADVICE FOR NON-ANALYTIC NATURALISTS

	Worlds in their role as circumstances of evaluation:	
Worlds in their	i	j
role as determiners i	T	T
of content: j	F	F

Worlds along the vertical axis represent the role worlds in the context set play as determiners of what is said. On the assumption that the world of the context is world i, what is expressed by 'water is H_2O' is that the stuff in the samples, H_2O, is H_2O. That proposition is true at both i and at j, so we write 'T' for 'true' underneath i and j along the horizontal axis, which represents the role a world plays in its contribution to what is true, given what is said. On the assumption that the world of the context is world j, in contrast, what is expressed by 'water is H_2O' is that the stuff in the samples, XYZ, is H_2O. Since that proposition is false at both i and j, we write 'F' for 'false' next to j along the vertical and underneath i and j along the horizontal.

This use of the two-dimensional matrix, above, allows us to clearly represent how this context fails to meet either of our two requirements on contexts. First, Stalnaker's second constraint is violated, as we have different propositions expressed relative to different worlds in the context set. If the world of the context is world i, then what is said by 'water is H_2O' is that H_2O is H_2O, while if the world of the context is j, what is said is that XYZ is H_2O. Second, even if it were evident to participants which of those two propositions Ella has expressed, his first constraint would be violated, since the effect of accepting what is asserted in that case would either be to throw out all or none of the worlds in the context set. Stalnaker's proposed solution is to focus on a third proposition our matrix represents, the diagonal proposition—roughly, that what is said by the sentence 'water is H_2O' in w is true at w. This is a proposition that is true at i and false at j. So it is true at some, but not all, of the worlds in the context set. Moreover, that proposition is available to be communicated by Ella's assertion, whether the world of the context is i or j. To see this, suppose the world of the context is i. In that case, *that what is said in w is true in w* is a proposition that is true at i and false at j. Likewise, if the world of the context is j, it is still the case *that what is said in w is true in w* is a proposition that is true at i and false at j. So we have now identified a proposition, the diagonal proposition, that is available to be communicated, that is constant with respect to which world is the world of the context, and is true at some, but not all, of the worlds in the context set. The information that Ella's interlocutors are able to acquire from Ella's assertion, then, is the information that she has expressed a truth. For this to be so, j cannot be the world of the context. So her assertion is able to have its essential effect of reducing the worlds in the context set by allowing her interlocutors to rule out that they are in j.

Of course, Stalnaker's strategy is not merely applicable to this example; it is a general strategy for explaining the informativeness of *a posteriori*, metaphysical necessities, a task anyone who accepts Millianism about names and kind terms must accept. As Parfit notes, many Non-Analytical Naturalists propose to model the informativeness of their central claims, of the form NORM=NAT, on that of scientific identities, such as "water is H_2O." How might we employ Stalnaker's strategy to help the Non-Analytical Naturalist respond to Parfit's Triviality Objection? Here we will provide a schematic sketch, but, first, it is important to note that the property used to pick out water in the above example, being the stuff in the lab sample, is an inessential, *a posteriori* property of water and so would figure in no analysis of our concept of water.[28] This means that, on the Stalnakerian model, the informativeness of an assertion of a sentence of the form NORM=NAT will depend upon which, likely inessential, *a posteriori* features of NORM are used by interlocutors to pick it out in specific contexts.

First, imagine a context in which a set of interlocutors agree that each in some set of actions, A_1's act at time t_1 ... and A_n's act at t_n, share the property NORM (we might think of these as sample instantiations of NORM, much like the sample liquid in the above scientific example is a water sample). One candidate for a second-order property of NORM, NORM2, would be 'being the property that A_1's act at time t_1 ... and A_n's act at t_n have in common,' where 'A_1's act at time t_1 ... and A_n's act at t_n' is read *de dicto*, so that in some worlds of evaluation those individuals performed acts at the relevant times other than the ones they actually did. In some of those worlds, NORM wouldn't have the property of being a property those acts had in common. In other words, NORM2 is an accidental property of NORM; it is a property that NORM has actually, that it needn't have counterfactually. In this way, relying on NORM2 to pick out NORM in a context of utterance of NORM=NAT is analogous to our scientist's relying upon the contingent fact that the sample in her lab is (and is generally acknowledged to be) a water sample to pick out water in the context of her utterance. Our Non-Analytical Naturalist would pick out NORM in the envisioned context via a property clearly, but contingently, had by the set of acts performed at a certain times by certain individuals.

To illustrate this thought with a more concrete example that gives a different interpretation of the two-dimensional diagram, above, suppose Nykki and Teresa are in a context in which it is uncontroversial that NORM has the property of being the property A_1's act at time t_1 ... and A_n's act at t_n. Assume, for concreteness, that the normative property in question is rightness in an action. Like in the water case, in which the scientists have ruled out that it is some liquid other than water in their sample, Nykki and Teresa have ruled out that it is some property other than being right that is the property the actions in question have in common. This means that these actions share the property of rightness in every world, here simplified to *i* and *j*, in the context set.

Suppose also, like in the water case, they have ruled out all candidates for that property other than two: the property of *being so as to maximize value* and the property of *being an act such that, in performing that act, the agent of the act was able to simultaneously will that her maxim become a law of nature*. Let *i* be our sample of a world in which the property the acts in question have in common is the value-maximizing one, and *j*, our sample of a world in which it is maxim-universalizability.

Reasoning together, Teresa and Nykki realize that some of their sample right actions do not have universalizable maxims. Expressing their discovery, Teresa says,

(N) "It's settled then! Rightness in action = being so as to maximize value!"

The informational impact of her utterance is to rule out that they are in world j, a world in which (N) expresses the necessarily false proposition that an act's maxim universalizability = its maximizing value.

This is but one way a NAN might try to implement a Stalnakerian strategy. A second possible candidate for the needed property, NORM2, would be given by the property of being the property denoted by 'NORM'. Here we would need an account of what makes something the denotation of some term, but whatever that account is, it is going to be contingent that NORM is the property that 'NORM' denotes. So there will be contexts in which the proposition communicated by NORM=NAT is that what is said by NORM=NAT in w is true at w, where what is said in w will be the proposition that *the property denoted by 'NORM' in w IS NAT*. Speakers, prior to the assertion of NORM=NAT will be unopinionated about whether the property denoted by 'NORM' is NAT or some other property. So there will be some worlds in which the property denoted by 'NORM' is NAT and some in which it is some other property (or none). This means that, audience members will be able to use the assertion of NORM=NAT to rule out that the world of the context is a world in which there is some property other than NAT denoted by 'NORM'.

In each of our two cases, an assertion of NORM=NAT will be able to have its essential effect of ruling out some, but not all, worlds in the context set. This ability of an assertion to rule out some, but not all, worlds in a context set is its information potential. So, an assertion of NORM=NAT would be informative in either of the two kinds of context just sketched. True, its informativeness wouldn't be explained by its semantics. But, if we accept that names and kind terms are devices for direct reference, we are already committed to giving a non-semantic explanation of the informativeness of some true identity statements.

Conclusion

The conclusion of Parfit's Triviality Objection is not merely that no Non-Analytical Naturalist position is true. Rather it is that the NAN cannot so much as state her position in a way that meets the requirements for being a candidate for an informative truth.

Our argument in reply to Parfit therefore does not need to offer grounds for thinking a Non-Analytical Naturalist position true. Here we take no stand on the nature of normative properties. For all we have said, non-naturalism is true. Neither do we take any stand on how identity statements of the form 'a is b' are able to communicate information in a context of utterance. For all we have said,

Stalnaker's strategy fails. Here we have the fairly modest aim of showing how the NAN might state her view in such a way that it meets all the requirements Parfit holds such a position must meet to be so much as a candidate for a true NAN position. We do this by showing how a Non-Analytical Naturalist might extend Stalnaker's strategy for explaining the informativeness of *a posteriori*, metaphysically necessary identities to explain the informativeness of their identities of the form NORM=NAT. This suffices to meet Parfit's challenge and rebut his Triviality Objection.

However, although Stalnaker's strategy for explaining the informativeness of identities containing two devices for direct reference is well-motivated, it may not be your favorite such strategy. If so, we invite you to consider extending your favorite such strategy to explaining the informativeness of claims of the form NORM=NAT, and you will have your own response to Parfit on behalf of the NAN.

Indeed, that there are other strategies for explaining the informativeness of identity statements in a non-Fregean semantic framework means that our sketch shows something a bit stronger: ruling out all candidate NAN positions relying upon the sort of reasoning Parfit relies upon in stating his Triviality Objection requires showing not just how the above Stalnakerian strategy for explaining the informativeness of statements like NORM=NAT fails, but that no plausible strategy for solving Frege's puzzle that the NAN might help herself to could serve all of her purposes.[29] It is not true, then, that the NAN has no way of stating her central claim compatible with meeting Parfit's requirements; indeed, she has a number of ways of doing so.[30]

Notes

1 It should be said that Parfit argues for a "Non-Metaphysical Cognitivism" in which positive normative claims are "in the strongest sense, true, but these truths have no positive ontological implications" (OWM 2, p. 479). Mathematical truths are offered by way of comparison.
2 OWM 2, p. 341.
3 OWM 2, p. 356.
4 Parfit claims that philosophers such as Rawls, Brandt, Falk, and Williams are best interpreted as not intending their claims about reasons to be substantive claims about the ordinary normative concept of what we have good reason to do. Rather, Parfit claims, such philosophers are best understood as offering tautologous claims of the form that if you have an informed desire for X then you have an informed desire for X. Such claims on Parfit's behalf are perhaps not mere idle trash talk but rather, we suspect Parfit thinks, partly the consequence of the NAN framework. Such philosophers did not, on Parfit's view, just happen to fail to state substantive naturalistic accounts of this or that type of normativity. Rather, it may be that on Parfit's view, the very nature of the NAN view makes it non-accidental that proponents will be unable to state substantive (rather than tautologous) normative claims.
5 OWM 2, p. 344. Officially, Parfit's Triviality Objection is an objection only against what Parfit calls "soft NAN" views that allow that claims that natural properties are identical to normative properties can be informative and not trivial. In Parfit's terminology, Hard Naturalists deny this. We claim that the Triviality Objection does not rule out all Soft Naturalist positions and so do not need to consider the Hard Naturalist

position to make our case that the Triviality Objection does not rule out all NAN positions. Since we are focused only on the case of the soft NAN, when we use the term 'NAN' we will mean only the soft NAN.

6 OWM 2, p. 266. Frank Jackson, in Jackson (2003), p. 558, maintains that ethical sentences "are a priori equivalent to and analyzable in terms of nonmoral ones."

7 OWM 2, p. 295, italics added. Allan Gibbard (2006, p. 323), for example, writes that

> normative concepts are distinct from naturalistic concepts: on this score, Moore was right. But normative and naturalistic concepts signify properties of the same kinds: indeed a normative and a naturalist concept might signify the very same property. What's distinctively normative, then, are not properties but concepts.

We think most contemporary naturalists about the normative would count themselves as NANs.

8 OWM 2, p. 325.
9 See, for example, Railton (1989), especially p. 157. See also Brink (1989) and Boyd (1988).
10 To be genuinely normative, in the sense that Parfit intends, it must be the case that there are genuine reasons to do or avoid that which has normative status. So, for example, if morality were not itself genuinely reason-giving, then morality would not be normative in the "reason-implying" sense Parfit is discussing. He helpfully distinguishes this sense of being normative from the "rule-implying sense." Something is normative in this latter sense "when these facts are about what is correct or incorrect, or allowed or disallowed, by some rule or requirement in some practice or institution" regardless of whether there are genuine reasons to do what is correct in that sense (OWM 2, p. 308).
11 OWM 2, p. 299.
12 For a discussion of ontological emergentism, see O'Connor and Wong (2012), §3.
13 OWM 2, p. 341.
14 With regards to fussing over some details, it is widely accepted among metaphysicians of the mind that the truth of a properly formulated constitution claim could establish, of some higher-level property, that its instantiations are not over and above those of some lower-level ones. Taking a page out of such a metaphysician's book, the NAN could defend her view without defending any claim that is an identity claim.
15 While we are accepting that an explanatory tracking claim between the normative and the natural does not rule out Non-Reductive Cognitivism, we are not yet persuaded of Parfit's stronger claim that showing that such an explanatory tracking claim were true "would not support Moral Naturalism" (OWM 2, p. 299). Although non-naturalist views might be compatible with accepting such a claim, it could nonetheless be that the naturalist could provide the best explanation for why that explanatory tracking claim held.
16 OWM 2, p. 335.
17 OWM 2, p. 336, our emphasis.
18 Various wordings across OWM 2, §§93–5.
19 OWM 2, p. 345.
20 Parfit could hold that 'Ben Franklin' picks out Franklin by his property of being Franklin, but that would seem to require positing haecceities. Since a better argument achieves the same goal without controversial assumptions than one that relies on them, we are attributing to Parfit a view that requires fewer controversial assumptions by attributing to him one that does not require haecceities. Parfit himself does seem profligate in the properties that he tolerates. He tells us that "[a]s I use the concept of a *property*, any information about such acts could be stated as the claim these acts would have some property" (OWM 1, p. 348).

21 *OWM* 2, p. 345.
22 *OWM* 2, pp. 354–6.
23 *OWM* 2, p. 345. It might seem here that Parfit's conclusion is too strong. Why can't a normative property invoked to explain the informativeness of one identity be in turn reduced in an identity that invokes the normative property reduced in the first? The answer is that the current proposal requires that explaining the informativeness of an identity requires invoking a property of a different, higher order than the one being reduced. Let n be the level of the property being reduced. To be informative, the reductive identity would invoke a property of the property at level n, i.e. an $n+1$ property. So that reduced property, at level n, cannot then be invoked to explain the informativeness of reduction of the property at level $n+1$. What is required, on this proposal, is that the latter identity invoke a further property, at level $n+2$, of the property at level $n+1$. No property at level n could be a property of a property at level $n+1$.
24 *OWM* 2, p. 354.
25 *OWM* 2, p. 354.
26 Other non-analytical views of normative properties may benefit from this advice—for example, Geoff Sayre-McCord's moral-kinds account of moral terms, which purports to be metaphysically non-committal on the question of naturalism (Sayre-McCord 1997). Taking our advice would be a way to guarantee that this view is compatible with metaphysical naturalism. Nicholas Sturgeon's non-reductive naturalism may also benefit, in so far as it aims to be compatible with the truth of non-analytical, reductive naturalism. See Sturgeon (1986 and 1988).
27 Stalnaker (1999).
28 By *a posteriori property* we mean only that knowledge of that property's possession is *a posteriori*.
29 Various strategies of this sort have been defended—for example, Perry (2012) and Salmon (1983); see also Soames (2005).
30 Thanks to Matti Eklund for comments on an earlier draft of this chapter, to our audience at The Ohio State University for discussion, and to three helpful referees for this volume.

References

Boyd, Richard (1988) 'How to Be a Moral Realist', in *Essays on Moral Realism*, Geoff Sayre-McCord (ed.) (Ithaca, NY: Cornell University Press), pp. 187–228.

Brink, David (1989) *Moral Realism and the Foundations of Ethics* (New York: Cambridge University Press).

Gibbard, Allan (2006), 'Normative Properties', in *Metaethics after Moore*, Terry Horgan and Mark Timmons (eds) (Oxford: Oxford University Press), pp. 319–38.

Jackson, Frank (2003) 'Cognitivism, A Priori Deduction, and Moore', *Ethics* 113, pp. 557–75.

O'Connor, Timothy and Wong, Hong Yu (2012) 'Emergent Properties', in *The Stanford Encyclopedia of Philosophy* (Spring 2012 edition), Edward N. Zalta (ed.): http://plato.stanford.edu/archives/spr2012/entries/properties-emergent/.

Parfit, Derek (2011) *On What Matters* (Oxford: Oxford University Press), vols 1 and 2.

Perry, John (2012) *Reference and Reflexivity*, 2nd edition (Stanford: CLSI Publications).

Railton, Peter (1989) 'Naturalism and Prescriptivity', *Social Philosophy and Policy* 7, pp. 151–74.

Salmon, Nathan (1983) *Frege's Puzzle: Content, Cognition and Communication* (Cambridge, MA: MIT Press).

Sayre-McCord, Geoff (1997) '"Good" on Twin Earth', *Philosophical Issues* 8, pp. 267–92.

Soames, Scott (2005) 'Naming and Asserting', in *Semantics vs. Pragmatics*, Zoltan Szabo (ed.) (Oxford: Oxford University Press), pp. 356–82.

Stalnaker, Robert (1999) 'Assertion', in his *Context and Content: Essays on Intentionality in Speech and Thought* (Oxford: Oxford University Press), pp. 78–95.

Sturgeon, Nicholas (1986) 'Harman on Moral Explanations of Natural Facts', *Southern Journal of Philosophy* 24, pp. 69–78.

Sturgeon, Nicholas (1988) 'Moral Explanations', in *Essays on Moral Realism*, Geoff Sayre-McCord (ed.) (Ithaca, NY: Cornell University Press), pp. 229–55.

9
CONTINGENCY AND CONSTRUCTIVISM

Julia Driver

Derek Parfit and I share the same worries about anti-realist views of morality. They are at least *prima facie* disturbing. I would *like* it to be the case that nihilism is false. Nihilism is so worrisome, however, precisely because it is a view that holds our moral practices up to a rigorous, naturalistic scrutiny. The sort of moral-norm 'exceptionalism' non-natural realist views are committed to seems, in this light, a sort of wishful thinking. However, the non-naturalist will often respond by pointing to the truths of mathematics—surely, there is nothing mysterious about mathematics, and yet some of the same metaphysical concerns can arise. Mathematical nihilism seems completely unwarranted, so, by analogy, we can make the same claim for morality. However, unlike Parfit, I do not believe that the best alternative to nihilism is non-naturalism. I will not in this chapter be criticizing non-naturalism head on, but, rather, trying to defend an alternative against the worry that Parfit raises about what it is to 'matter.'

On my view the most sensible approach to understanding morality will fit well with a naturalistic understanding of the world and our place within the world. My approach to this understanding of morality is, very broadly, Humean. Our reasons for acting are underwritten by the way we are, either as individuals or members of a class of sympathetic beings. In *On What Matters*, Derek Parfit takes great pains to argue against the Humean view of morality and moral reasons, though the view presented as Humean takes Hume to be a mere formalist when it comes to reasons. There is a sense in which this is true and a sense in which it is not true. Hume was a formalist in the sense that Sharon Street describes, since Hume does believe that what counts as a reason is understood as contingent upon evaluative starting points.[1] However, one can also read Hume as committed to norms that are universal among human beings—indeed, many of the critical practices he discusses would not be possible without this view. Thus, I would like to suggest another way to understand the Humean project as positing substantive reasons given by substantive norms for action that are not contingent on individual idiosyncrasies.[2] The more substantive forms of constructivism were not adequately discussed in *On What Matters*.[3] I take it that this family of approaches to understanding moral reasons includes constitutivism, which in some versions treats the reasons as extractable from basic norms of agency.[4] This approach is anti-realist in one sense and not in another. There are moral truths, and truth makers, though those are established either via idealized responses or via holding certain normative commitments to be fundamental to the task of agency itself. Historically, within the Humean tradition, the first of these approaches has dominated, but I think that the Humean can also approach the problem via the norms that are constitutive of agency in human beings.

However, a very significant problem for this family of Humean approaches is that it seems to hold moral norms and their authority *contingent* on features of human nature—perhaps what human beings typically, or characteristically, desire or value, for example. This contingency makes the view seem as though it holds the content of norms to be objectionably arbitrary.[5] The focus of this chapter is to argue that contingency does not lead to vicious arbitrariness. Contingent norms still matter and still render our lives subject to the critical practices that are crucial to mattering. In arguing the latter I discuss why contingency is not as worrisome as some suppose.

Reasons that matter

Parfit believes that a version of reasons externalism is true, and that I have reason to avoid pain independently of any basic or fundamental desires that I may have to experience pain. The attractiveness of this view stems from an unwillingness to accept a more subjective alternative, one frequently labeled *reasons internalism*. On such a view if what someone has reason to do is tied to her basic desires, then it could well turn out that she could have reason to perform any number of highly imprudent or immoral acts. And that strikes many as highly counter-intuitive. In contrast, on *reasons externalism* our reasons to act are not reducible to our desires, and our reasons bear no necessary relation to facts about what motivates us, such as our desires.[6]

Some argue that reasons internalism has serious advantages over reasons externalism. For example, it gives us a way to know the content of reasons—what counts as a reason.[7] How do I know that I have a reason to avoid pain, independent of my desire to avoid pain? This is true, though the externalist could here respond that on the more plausible versions of reasons internalism there is also room to question how one knows one's reasons, given that they are understood in relation to *basic* desires and not derivative ones. For example, Mary may desire to go to medical school on the false belief that that is the most productive career for her to pursue. This would be a mistake, since it turns out that her desire to be productive would be best fulfilled by becoming a foreign-aid worker. Here, she is mistaken not about her basic desire but about how best to fulfill it. There might be cases, though, in which someone is actually mistaken about even a basic desire.

At least, there is a portion of moral phenomenology that attests to this. Consider Mary again. Mary believes that her most basic desire is the desire to be productive, and she works very hard in medical school, working long hours. After a few years her life appears to be empty, and she has the sense of 'discovering' that, maybe, productivity wasn't what she really desired all along. Her real desire was to live a life in which she achieved personal fulfillment, which includes productivity but in conjunction with work she considers personally meaningful. In light of this discovery, she decides to become a foreign-aid worker. The phenomenology of 'discovering' what she really wants and, thus, what she really has reason to do can support either the internalist or externalist position, depending on how the view is developed. On the one hand, if it seems as though one is discovering reasons that seem untethered from one's actual desires, then the externalist view is supported. However, the internalist, who is free to idealize, can hold that Mary simply 'discovered' what she really desires, something more basic than the simple desire to be productive. This is something that, in principle, is recoverable from her psychology, even if it is not something that was apparent to her.

However, the externalist has the advantage of seeming to adhere best to other facets of our moral phenomenology and to our intuitions that people have reason not to do certain things—such as actions that are immoral—regardless of their actual *or* idealized desires. We can call this the *categoricity* intuition. This is closely related, though not identical to, the *externality* intuition: moral authority comes from without, not within. It exerts a kind of external pressure on the moral agent. We need to separate these two because they point to different concerns. The categoricity intuition is specific to the relation of reasons to desire (or, more broadly, affect or attitude). The externality intuition is not specific to desire, though desires are some of the 'internal' psychological states that make up our character. But beliefs are as well. And simply in virtue of *believing* that something is wrong, I don't have a reason not to do it. This is because one might hold, for example, that the values that underlie reasons for action—that give agents reasons for action—exist independently of those agents. This latter claim can be spelled out in a variety of strengths. If Mary thinks that she ought to kill someone because that person has parked in her parking spot, then she is wrong and she has no reason to kill the person in the parking spot. Her belief does not reflect normative *facts* that obtain regardless of *any* of the agent's actual psychological states.

Parfit vigorously argues for a view in which some things matter in the reason-implying sense. This involves, crucially, the existence of irreducibly normative truths, since normativity is not reducible to the natural (thus non-naturalism). He explicitly connects this to the view that some things matter.[8] Further, these irreducibly normative truths are of a certain sort—they are attitude-independent. What they track is not connected to any agent's psychology. Commitment to these sorts of irreducibly normative truths also rules out noncognitivism. There are many occasions in which Parfit holds that this is the only kind of mattering that matters. Only with this do we get genuine reasons of the sort appealed to in moral evaluation and justification. Further, moral truths are necessary: if it is true that, for example, torturing people for fun is wrong, it is true in all possible worlds. Parfit is certainly not alone in having this view about moral truth. This view at first seems to be supported by the *experience* of imaginative resistance: that is the phenomenon of balking at the consideration of fictions that depict perverse values as the true ones. This seems puzzling, since we don't balk at considering more mundane, non-normative, merely physical impossibilities—such as talking mice and invisibility-inducing rings.[9] One commonly discussed case is *Death*, a story of how Jack and Jill were killed by a person named Craig because they were blocking traffic while arguing. What gives rise to imaginative resistance is the claim within the story that "Craig did the right thing, because Jack and Jill should have taken their argument somewhere else where they wouldn't get in anyone's way."[10] We balk at this, unable to go along with the fiction. One explanation of why we balk in moral cases is that such stories set up impossible worlds, ones that are inconceivable. They are impossible because not only is it not right to kill someone for the fun of it, it *cannot* be right to kill someone for the fun of it—and 'cannot' is understood in the strongest sense. Just as there is no possible world in which 2+2=5, there is no possible world in which killing for fun is right.[11] Just as we would experience resistance in imagining a world in which 2+2=5, so we resist imagining a world in which torturing kittens for fun is the right thing to do. I do not share this view of what accounts for imaginative resistance. For one thing, there is some unclarity in how we are to understand 'resistance' here. Certainly, it is true that I can tell a story about a round square and people will go along with it, after a fashion, even if they are struck by the absurdity.[12] However, if you examine how they are approaching the parts of the story, they will be editing out the inconsistencies. They do not think of the protagonist as round and a square at the same time. However, it is *also* true that another account of what is going on with imaginative resistance in ethics has to do with our unwillingness to go against our deep moral commitments—this unwillingness is a matter of desire.[13] This is actually the view that I favor. Thus, a person who rejects non-naturalism can take this route in accounting for the experience of imaginative resistance. Still, the non-naturalist remains free to appeal to the sense that moral truth just cannot be otherwise in her account of why non-naturalism is so intuitively powerful, and why the alternatives seem lacking when it comes to this feature of moral phenomenology. Thus, this feature of Parfit's non-naturalism appeals to a very powerful aspect of our moral phenomenology—moral truths do not 'just happen to be' true, they must be true, just as 2+2 must equal 4. This is a significant theoretical advantage for non-naturalism. However, I hope to show at the end of this chapter that finding comfort in necessity is relying on an illusion. Necessity does not provide a reassuring bedrock.[14]

Some constructivists accept versions of reasons internalism because norms are 'constructed' and reasons derived from an agent's *own* practical point of view. There are caveats. For example, Sharon Street holds that even though our reasons are attitude-dependent we need to be more expansive on what we consider an attitude—it can't be mere desire, for example. Instead, the relevant attitude is that of valuing. Street's view is a kind of *formal* Humean constructivism:

> *Humean* versions of metaethical constructivism . . . deny that substantive moral conclusions are entailed from within the standpoint of normative judgment as such. Instead, these views claim, the substantive content of a given agent's reasons is a function of his or her particular, contingently given, evaluative starting points . . . that substance must ultimately be supplied by the particular set of values with which one finds oneself alive as an agent—such that had one come alive with an entirely different set of evaluative attitudes . . . one's reasons would have been . . . entirely different.[15]

Her strategy is to come to terms with the contingency involved by challenging the Kantian constructivist alternative to the Humean view.[16] It might seem that the Kantian has an advantage since on that view morality follows from 'pure practical reason.' And, indeed, this seems important to retaining categoricity. But Street argues correctly that, in effect, there are grades of categoricity, and even the formal constructivist can account for some categoricity—that is, one might think one ought to keep one's promise even if there is a part of one that doesn't want to. Still, that I ought to keep my promise appeals to some feature of me as a valuing agent, on Street's view. My response to the contingency worry will be somewhat different from Street's. I think she is right, but I also think it isn't the full story.

One advantage of going the constructive/constitutive route is that one can thread the needle and capture in one's account those features of both internalism and externalism that are intuitively appealing. My strategy is to argue for a view which is Humean, but from which we can extract norms that are substantive in the sense of not being contingent on some *idiosyncratic* features of an agent's psychological make-up but nevertheless *are* contingent on the practical point of view of social creatures. Like the Kantian constructivist, the substantive Humean constructivist will seek to extract a commitment to substantive norms—certain reasons for action that obtain for particular agents—from a particular standpoint, that of the evaluator.

Substantive Humean Constructivism (SHC)

In this section I very briefly sketch a form of Humean constructivism that is substantive in the sense that it holds that certain reasons that apply to all social beings are extractable from the practical point of view of such beings—specifically, that feature of the practical point of view involved in evaluating. This kind of 'substance' is in contrast to what is meant when constructivism is used to discuss first-order normative views; thus, there is a contrast between substantive normative constructivism and substantive metaethical constructivism. One could develop a

Humean version of both of these, but I am concerned with the latter. The Kantian version, however, seeks to derive substantive norms. A Humean could attempt a similar strategy, although the starting points would be different. Hume believed that morality is something that, in some way, is based on features of human nature—in particular, our capacity for sympathy, which he optimistically believed was common to all human beings. The relevant practical point of view, then, is that of a being who is moved by certain considerations, such as the well-being of others.[17] This approach, however, is subject to several problems. The most worrisome are the circularity problem and the contingency problem.

The circularity problem arises in the following way. Human beings, on Hume's view, are practical reasoners committed to norms of sympathy. We might argue that it is a feature of human beings that, as they move through the world as social beings, they are guided by certain considerations, such as the consideration that the well-being of another provides one with at least some reason to act. It may be that we can make this case by positing a kind of psychological necessity to this sort of normative commitment, one that is an essential part, or constitutive of, what we consider recognizably moral behavior. However, the worry is building in a commitment to a norm that *approves of* concern for the well-being of others—arguably, simply building morality into the picture rather than explaining it, even if we take pains to give a very naturalistic case for the *commitment* to such a norm and such a commitment as being reasons-providing.[18] In this way, those who argue for an account of reasons that is purely formal in structure and neutral in content seem to have an advantage in avoiding this problem. But therein lies another worry: we are left with exactly the sort of view that Parfit finds objectionable—and for very compelling reasons. Such a view requires that one hold that agents can have reasons to perform deeply immoral or imprudent actions. Any constructivist strategy that tries to avoid this risks circularity at least. Others have written about this problem for constructivism, and I will not go over that material in this chapter.[19] I do believe, however, that the circularity problem can be countered by noting that the starting points in the construction are to be construed naturalistically. However, in this chapter my focus is on a different worry about this approach: the *contingency* worry.

Constructivists regard value, and the reasons we have for acting, as in some way attitude-dependent. The constructivism I will focus on here is restricted to moral reasons. For constructivism more generally, a judgment that one has (*pro tanto*) reason to act is true, or true that one realizes a value in so acting, "if and only if (and because) it is the judgment anyone capable of following the norms of reasoning would make, on the basis of faultless reasoning, in conditions of optimal reflection."[20] Different varieties can be spelled out according to different ways of cashing out the relevant contingency. On the view that I favor we appeal to features of human nature, such as our capacity to sympathetically engage with others, which underlie norms of concern for others. Thus, our reasons are derived from our attitudes but in a 'corrected' way. I have reason to care for others because *anyone* who makes judgments from the corrected perspective—in Hume's case, that is the general point of view—concurs or approves. Of course, there are other ways the construction can proceed. For example, Michael Smith, in developing a form of constitutivism, has argued very persuasively that the standard Humean account of the ideal agent needs to be supplemented.[21] The standard Humean view is that the agent is one who possesses the capacity to know the world around her and the capacity to realize her desires. But these can pull against each other, so the ideal agent also needs desires that are coherence-inducing. These in turn provide grounds for arguing that the ideal constitutivist agent will

> desire not to interfere with the exercise of the knowledge-acquisition and desire-realization capacities of not just herself in the present and the future, but of anyone whose possession and exercise of their knowledge-acquisition and desire-realization capacities is dependent on what she does.[22]

Since coherence is a formal desideratum of the ideal agent, it does not seem circular to add coherence-inducing desires to the mix. Challenging this would involve committing oneself to the implausible view that an agent could have reason to be incoherent, maybe in virtue of having some perverse final or basic desire to be incoherent. But, unlike the final desire to suffer, the final desire for incoherence clearly conflicts with the epistemic element in Smith's model of the ideal agent. The really tricky part in this argument has to do with the move from a commitment to not interfere and help when it comes to the self—and when it comes to others. Smith holds that a failure to endorse this move on the part of the ideal agent would be *ad hoc*, and that such an agent is committed to the move via a symmetry argument.

Of course, this model goes beyond what Hume himself at least *believed* himself committed to. When we make judgments of virtue and vice we are not picking up on anything out there in the world. However, he also held that this made no practical difference, because our sentiments, and the findings of our sentiments, are very real to us, and serve to regulate our behavior. Another part of this account is that our sentiments cannot regulate—and, thus, underlie our critical practices—just willy-nilly. Successful regulation requires correction. It is the general view of the action or character trait that is relevant to its status as virtuous or vicious. One reason the view is attractive is that it offers a way to get true quasi-universal claims about what someone has reason to do, morally, without the metaphysical baggage of realism.

At least a substantial part of what we do as valuers is evaluate—that is, apply criteria based on our values in deciding what to do, what to approve of, etc. The valuing standpoint is the practical point of view all agents, as agents, must adopt. For example, Peter Railton outlines the way in which animals develop an *evaluative landscape* as they move through the world, one that allows them to be highly efficient foragers.[23] The same holds for more than food and shelter. As we move through the social landscape we also generate and are moved by evaluations regarding our social interactions. These evaluations reflect our attitudes, what we desire and have need of.

Not all reasons are *immediately derivable* from our attitudes. Again, most sentimentalists recommend either an affective filter or a standard to correct affect itself, depending on the type of deficit in the agent/evaluator's attitudes. There are two ways we can see this at work in Hume. One way is via the general point of view: when we appropriately make judgments of virtue it is from the general point of view. This is the point of view that abstracts away from an individual's idiosyncratic responses, or idiosyncratic features of the agent's psychology. Though sympathetically engaging with others is a core feature of human beings, it is in need of correction by a standard that we all have reason to accept. The other way is by appeal to features that are crucial to moral agency, or any kind of normative agency. Those features have to do with our applying evaluations to our mental states and the mental states of others. There is pressure not only for intra-subjective coherence but for intersubjective coherence as well. These combine to give a constructivist account of norms that is not as purely formal as Street's, though neither will it get everything that Parfit, and other non-naturalists, want out of a metaethics.

In his arguments for the need for such correction Hume does not make the claim that we need correction in order to match objective facts. Rather, he argues that we need the standard in order to be able to effectively communicate with each other and, seemingly, differently situated versions of ourselves:

> tho' sympathy be much fainter than our concern for ourselves, and a sympathy with persons remote from us much fainter than that with persons near and contiguous; yet we neglect all these differences in our calm judgments concerning the characters of men. Besides, that we ourselves often change our situation in this particular, we every day meet with persons, who are in a different situation from ourselves, and who cou'd never converse with us on any reasonable terms, were we to remain constantly in that situation and point of view, which is peculiar to us. The intercourse of sentiments, therefore, in society and conversation, makes us form some general inalterable standard, by which we may approve or disapprove of characters and manners. And tho' the *heart* does not always take part with those general notions, or regulate its love and hatred by them, yet are they sufficient for discourse, and serve all our purposes in company, in the pulpit, on the theatre, and in the schools.[24]

This argument has been criticized as insufficient for motivating a corrective standard.[25] I think that those criticisms are correct. However, I also think that what Hume says in this passage is very useful in motivating the general externalist intuition. We move through the world as beings sensitive to value or bits of the world that we take to be valuable, and this in part involves moving through the world as social beings, interacting with others. That involves evaluating our actions and the actions of others—in our own case, for the earlier purpose of self-regulation, in the case of others, to try to have some impact on their attitudes and behavior, or, more indirectly, the attitudes and behavior of an audience. These are what are referred to as 'critical' practices. The last line of the passage indicates an openness to an external standard and, thus, external reasons of a sort—that is, external to the idiosyncratic responses of any given individual. Samantha may have no desire to give to Oxfam and yet sincerely recognize that she has a reason to do so. Alan may see that Samantha has no desire to give to Oxfam and yet also hold, correctly, that she has a reason to do so.

Hume isn't merely saying that this is how we go about making moral judgments. When we make moral judgments we *ought* to correct for idiosyncrasies of our psychology. We can view this as a kind of intelligibility requirement. As social beings communicating with each other on moral matters we have a strong interest in being intelligible to each other. But there is no appeal, here, to creatures utterly different from human beings, such as non-social creatures with no real interest in mutual intelligibility. Moral norms do not bind such creatures. For this reason, the view fails to capture the moral phenomenology that helps us see why Parfit's realist view is so attractive: if it is true that torturing kittens for fun is wrong, it is of necessity wrong—this means that not only is it wrong in all possible worlds, but for all possible intelligent beings it is universally wrong.

One response involves drawing an analogy between Hume's epistemology and his account of morality. We could, for example, draw an analogy between Hume's response to *practical* skepticism and his account of normative commitments in morality. Hume is famous for having appealed to common sense in his practical epistemology: one leaves by the door not by the window! In the same way, practically speaking, there is a kind of psychological necessity attached to the norms that guide moral behavior.[26] Those who allow themselves to be guided by norms, or to act on reasons, that are not reflective of the general point of view will find themselves in a similar place to those who leave by the window.

But it isn't simply that they will be socially dysfunctional. Hume also regards self-regulation as accompanied by a kind of self-reflection that is important to our *understanding of ourselves* as socially productive. We care about what others think of us, but we also care about an inward sense of dignity:

> who can think any advantages of fortune a sufficient compensation for the least breach of *social* virtues, when he considers that not only his character with regard to others, but also his peace and inward satisfaction depend upon his strict observance of them; and that a mind will never be able to bear its own survey, that has been wanting in its part to mankind and society?[27]

On the sketched alternative, what we have a reason to do is not always a function of what *our* individual desires are. In social contexts, what we have reason to do will also in some cases be a function of what we desire *given a corrected perspective*, but a corrected perspective that we have good reason to endorse. In particular, to follow Hume's considerations, the corrected perspective is the perspective that allows for meaningful communication between different individuals in such a way that critical practices are supported rather than undermined. This allows for interesting mixed cases of endorsement and criticism, of the sort that Hume discusses: "as when the fortifications of a city belonging to an enemy are esteem'd beautiful on account of their strength, th'o we cou'd wish they were entirely destroy'd." [28]

A general has a good reason to hate his courageous enemy as well as a good reason to admire him, and it is the very same reason! But viewing it as a reason to admire acknowledges the 'externality' and 'categoricity,' intuitions about some reasons. Further, engaging in the sort of reflection the general engages in—or having the reason counterfactually pass a corrected test—renders that reason non-arbitrary even if contingent. Properly reflecting on the quality of one's own mental states and the reasons those states seem responsive, too, and then endorsing the states/reasons means that one has 'good' reason to act. Consider the case of the perfectly coherent Caligula. On Parfit's view, Caligula has no reason to harm others, even though that is what he desires or values fundamentally, and in a way that is coherent with the rest of his fundamental desires and values. On Street's view, we cannot say this. On SHC, we can say that Caligula has no reason to harm others, even though that is what he wants to do, since the desire cannot withstand reflective endorsement of the right sort, from the general point of view. In a world of creatures who are socially and sympathetically engaged with each other it is still true that, from the general point of view, killing for fun is disapproved of.

I admit this position can only go so far in accounting for moral phenomenology. It says nothing about reasons that non-social rational beings might be subject to. It doesn't fully solve the reasons-relativism problem. But, again, it may simply be the case that the problem cannot be solved with any plausible alternative. We can regret that, just as we might regret that we cannot come up with a libertarian account of freedom that makes any sense. But that may just be where we are.

The contingency worry and SHC

How would this, albeit sketchily presented, alternative get out of the contingency worry? The contingency worry has two manifestations. The first is that contingency seems to conflict with our moral phenomenology. The second is that the sort of contingency referenced seems to undermine authority by providing a basis for 'debunking' arguments. Here I will focus on the first worry, as I believe Parfit has himself provided good reasons for not worrying much about debunking.[29]

Two contrasts with 'contingent' are relevant. In logic 'contingent' is usually contrasted with 'necessary.' Thus, a merely contingent truth is not a necessary truth. First, a merely contingent truth is a proposition that is not true 'in all possible worlds.' Another way to understand the contingency worry for SHC is via the contrast between 'contingent' and 'arbitrary.' A choice one makes, for example, may be contingent on what one wants, but it does not follow that the choice is arbitrary, since (in that case) what one wants is a good reason for making the choice. If one asks why one chooses one way rather than the other then in some contexts, 'that's what I wanted' is a perfectly good reason; it gives a perfectly good accounting of my choice.

Parfit believes that irreducible normative truths are necessary:

> Fundamental normative truths are not about how the world happens to be.
>
> In any possible world pain would in itself be bad, and *prima facie* to be relieved rather than perpetuated.[30]

As I mentioned in the opening of the chapter, there is no doubt that, at least when we initially think about core moral commitments, this seems true. Again, this is a significant theoretical advantage of the sort of account Parfit puts forward. Those who disagree with the necessity claim are faced with the option of trying to develop an alternative that is forced to sacrifice this appeal to moral phenomenology.

However, it is also possible to hold that viewing moral truths as necessary doesn't end the need for further explanation. It doesn't reduce the mystery of moral normativity. We want an account of the claims and what *makes* them true. The non-naturalist stops the account with appeals to necessity and claims about our intuitive grasp of these truths. Analogies with mathematics abound. But tautologies are necessarily true, and empty. Of course Parfit does not think that moral truths are tautologies. But even a necessity claim that is not empty does not save one from the charge of arbitrariness. Appeals to mathematics do not help. There are some mathematical truths that are necessary and that are also true 'by accident.' Alan Baker defines mathematical accidents as follows: "A universal, true mathematical statement is *accidental* if it lacks a unified, non-disjunctive proof."[31] The idea is that in cases where the proof of a claim is purely disjunctive, there is no real explanation provided as to why the claim is true—so it is true accidentally. Putative examples include the Goldbach Conjecture, the claim that all even numbers greater than two are expressible as the sum of two primes. Support for the claim is provided through "many billions of examples."[32] If true, it is necessarily true but also inexplicably true. In mathematics as well, explanation seems important to having a satisfactory understanding of the truths of mathematics.[33]

Consider, for example, logical fatalism: there is exactly one possible world. Given logical fatalism, all truths are necessary truths. It then follows that if 'pain is bad' is true, it is necessarily true, yet this doesn't settle the uneasiness or worry. We can still ask for a richer explanation of why pain is bad. So if necessity is used to try to stop further inquiry, to make such inquiry irrelevant, it doesn't work.

Another example: suppose that Bob, a meat eater, thinks one day "Well, I could have been a cow" and this causes him to start thinking more benevolently about cows, so that he eventually swears off eating cows altogether. Then, after reading Kripke, he comes to be convinced that he could not have been a cow after all. He comes to realize that he is necessarily a human being. This doesn't show that the counter-logical 'what if' he entertained does not raise challenges. Indeed, it would be quite odd for him to then go back and say, well, since I could not have been an animal after all, the suffering of animals doesn't matter. The metaethical analogy is this: there is the thought that we could have been otherwise—perhaps giant insects, or lizards, who evolved so as to have utterly different emotional attachments—and, thus, morality could have been otherwise as well. If we then come to realize that 'no, we could not have been otherwise,' and morality could not have been otherwise either, the challenge raised by the counter-logical conditional is not thereby extinguished.[34]

There may be some slide between viewing something as necessary and viewing it as 'essential'—so if pain is necessarily bad, then it is part of pain's essence that it is bad. If it is pain's essence that it is bad, that blocks the quest for a further accounting. But Kit Fine argues that there are some necessary properties that are not essential properties. For example, being a member of the singleton set PARFIT and being Derek Parfit. Derek Parfit is essentially Derek Parfit (he is identical to himself), and he is also identical to being a member of PARFIT. The latter is a necessary property but not essential to being Derek Parfit.[35]

So if we look to necessity (rather than contingency) to ground our confidence, we may not be looking for the right sort of thing. The non-naturalist agrees with the error theorist that the grounding cannot be natural properties. But if the view is that non-natural properties are needed to anchor these necessary truths, the explanation is unsatisfying. This is the worry that many have about all non-natural accounts. We have gotten rid of supernatural agents in accounting for normativity, only to rely on another hidden, occult realm. This seems to be the same picture that the non-naturalist paints. It is necessarily and inexplicably true that causing suffering is bad. Why is this not a kind of arbitrariness? Parfit does not himself believe in a separate realm of the non-natural. He is a quietist about the ontology of morality, defending a view he terms "Non-Metaphysical Cognitivism":

> [t]here are some claims that are irreducibly normative in the reason-involving sense, and are in the strongest sense true. But these truths have no ontological implications. For such claims to be true, these reason-involving properties need not exist either as natural properties in the spatio-temporal world, or in some non-spatio-temporal part of reality.[36]

But this makes his view all the more mysterious. The appeal to an analogy with the necessary truths of mathematics is used to help the view with intuitive plausibility.[37] However, the analogy can only go so far—existence in a non-ontological sense, whether in mathematics or practical philosophy, is still mysterious.[38]

Further, suppose that it were the case that 'pain is bad' is not necessary. What would really be lost? The content of norms may be contingent in a very general way on features of human nature, without the contents of those norms being arbitrary. But what is it for something to be arbitrary? One way to understand it would be to hold that, for example, the content of a norm is arbitrary when the content doesn't reflect *real* value but, rather, reflects something that is idiosyncratic in some way. A person who makes an arbitrary moral choice, for example, will make such a choice for no *good* reason, not guided by genuine value but guided by, perhaps, a mere like or dislike. But on this understanding it looks like the externalist must be right—holding the authority of reasons to be contingent on desire does seem to make them arbitrary in this way. But what is up for grabs, so to speak, has to do with how we understand *real* or *genuine* value. That a person likes one thing over another and has no other reason for choosing it doesn't mean that the person's choice did not reflect actual value. It simply doesn't reflect a reaction that is universal. When Chloe chooses vanilla over chocolate ice cream she is making that choice solely on the basis of her liking vanilla and not liking chocolate. Thus, there is another sense of 'arbitrary' in which this choice is *not* arbitrary, though certainly her choice is dependent on some contingent feature of *her*, and what is really valuable *for her*. That Roger disagrees (in a purely practical way) and chooses chocolate over vanilla because he likes chocolate and doesn't like vanilla does not in any way imply criticism of Chloe's choice is warranted. The arbitrary is contingent, but the contingent is not necessarily arbitrary. In the case of Chloe and Roger it is not arbitrary because we believe that the fact that Chloe loves vanilla ice cream over all others is a good reason for her to choose vanilla ice cream. And Parfit would agree in this particular case. What is in question are the more fundamental normative considerations: for example, can good *moral* reason be contingent in a way that is not arbitrary? And that, I argue, depends upon the level of contingency. A form of constructivism that bases norms on features of our nature as social beings, and strives for as much universality as possible, will not make the authority of moral norms depend upon the either the desires or the will of an individual. Though I cannot argue for it here, even though Kantian constructivism will have certain theoretical advantages over SHC, attributing the authority of norms to willing is not one of those advantages. Insofar as 'willing' a norm has any intuitive pull as regards authority, it will rest on the supposition that we will all be similarly bound by rational norms—that the willings of rational beings converge.

Hume himself sought to avoid this worry by holding that sympathy was universal as a contingent matter of fact—that is, it just happens to be universal in humans, though the scope of its operations in the psychology of each human being varies greatly from person to person. But appeal to a contingent universal is not as satisfactory as we would like. And here I depart from the actual Hume, from the way Hume actually developed his theory, to a way he could have developed it that I think would address this worry better. Don't appeal *merely* to a corrected human response (in this case, one of sympathy) as providing the truth maker for a moral claim. Rather, also look at the commitments we have as *moral agents and evaluators* in need of a standard to regulate our interactions, including our critical practices, and derive universal norms in that way. This won't solve the contingency worry completely, but it will go a long way towards mitigating it, and it will defend the view from what I think is the much more troubling worry that the view is somehow arbitrary.

Parfit's worry is that if it is the case that moral and certain prudential reasons work like this, there will be no way to criticize a person who intrinsically desires to suffer horribly where the satisfaction of that desire does not interfere with the satisfaction of other, stronger, desires. That desire would be sufficient to give her a reason, if reasons depend on desire—which, of course, is a contingent feature of that particular person. Ice-cream flavor is one thing, but no one has a reason to suffer horribly, even those who desire to suffer horribly.

Here the difference between contingent and idiosyncratic is important. Contingency comes into the story at different levels. None of the early sentimentalists were troubled by the fact that a person might have odd and perverse desires. These odd, perverse desires could indeed be criticized—in Hume's case from 'the general point of view.' This is why Kant's famous case of the person who feels no sympathy for others and yet still manages to act properly towards them out of respect for moral duty is no problem for a Humean sentimentalist account of reasons.[39] Idiosyncratic responses are not a problem, where we understand 'idiosyncratic' relative to an *individual*. Even if we correct for individual differences, the corrected response approach has a problem when we think of the idiosyncrasy at the level of *species*. It seems that if we think there are reasons to hold agents who are members of other species accountable, then this standard makes our reasons too relativistic.[40] This might be solved by going to a higher level of corrective response—say, what some ideal social creature would find pleasing from the general point of view, or something along those lines. Of course, the ultimate in corrective standards would be Smith's 'ideal' observer.

However, I grant that there remains an issue with relativism. There may be rational beings who lack any capacity for sympathy at all. We need not even postulate strange, alien beings. Perhaps extreme psychopaths are like this, for example. Further, we can consider an expansion on Parfit's example: imagine an entire species of creatures who desire to suffer. Is there nothing we can say to them that would constitute a legitimate criticism? As I mentioned earlier, however, there is a way to mitigate the worry about this sort of relativism, because we need not give up on many of our critical practices when faced with these sorts of case. Hume's distinction between appraisability and accountability, noted earlier, comes into play. True, we may not get all we want, but we get most of what we want as well as a good explanation for why we cannot get all we want.

Consider an analogy with positions on free will. Compatibilism is often taken to be a kind of compromise view: it doesn't get us everything we want, but it is widely seen to get us all we can reasonably expect. The problem is similar. What we want in accounting for the authority of morality, for the truth of some moral claims, may not be possible. It is reasonable to lament that but less reasonable to pursue the alternative that leaves the phenomenon mysterious. Libertarians are in this position. There is free will, and free will is not compatible with determinism, so despite what our best understanding of the world around us tells us, some of our choices are not determined—except purely and wholly by the self in some way that marks it off from the rest of nature. In Parfit's case we have a kind of moral phenomenology that renders moral truth somehow necessary—universal in a very, very deep sense. Yet we cannot account for this naturalistically; therefore, non-naturalism provides the right answer.

What the nihilists have right is a questioning of the phenomenology itself. However, one need not go as far as the nihilists, anymore than one needs to be a hard determinist in rejecting libertarianism. The question of whether or not a particular action is free and whether or not a person is acting freely is answered at least in part by reference to that person's desires. What it is to be acting freely just is to be (in some sense) acting on one's desires, without external force or coercion. Can a similar move be made in accounting for what it is to act rightly, or well, or what is it to have a reason to act in a certain way? We can reject some of the phenomenology—the type of categoricity, let's say, that nihilists such as Richard Joyce make so much of—and keep *externality*—and resist holding moral reasons to be idiosyncratic.[41] Humean reasons externalism, based on SHC, is external in one sense, not in another. It would only meet some of Parfit's desiderata for the best theory. But Parfit's desiderata are too demanding. SHC will get us all we need for 'mattering.'[42]

Notes

1 Street (2010).
2 Though I will not be arguing this here, one can pursue the same strategy and avoid any appeal to basic norms altogether, simply holding this for reasons, or view norms as parasitic on reasons. Nothing in the present argument hangs on this.
3 Parfit does endorse a form of *normative* constructivism, it seems to me, when endorsing the Scanlonian view in OWM 1. There has been some discussion on how exactly to demarcate the normative from the metaethical forms, a topic too large for me to develop here. To be clear, my worry is to determine the truth conditions for moral claims, something I take to be a classic metaethical concern.
4 There are clearly differences between many types of constructivism and constitutivism, but the common element that concerns me here is the shared project of accounting for moral truth on the basis of the qualities we have as agents and evaluators.
5 It is one advantage of Kantian constructivism that it at least seems to avoid this particular problem by tying normative commitments to pure rational commitments.
6 There are a variety of different ways to spell out the view. Brink holds that *reasons internalism* is the claim that holds "that it is *a priori* that the recognition of moral facts itself necessarily provides the agent with reason to perform the moral action." See Brink (1984), p. 113. *Reasons externalism* denies this. Full reasons externalism is the view that normative reasons are facts that do not depend in any way on features of human beings.
7 Finlay (2006).
8 OWM 2, pp. 464ff.
9 The literature on imaginative resistance is vast. See Gendler (2000) and Weatherson (2004).
10 This is Brian Weatherson's case, discussed in Weatherson (2004).

11 I discuss Weatherson's case and imaginative resistance in more detail in Driver (2008).
12 Driver (2008).
13 Gendler (2000).
14 I am not sure what Parfit's settled view on this matter is. In *Reasons and Persons*, in discussing death and regretting the impossible, he writes that we can "regret truths even when it is logically impossible that these truths be false" (*RP*, p. 175). This *seems* to indicate that he may believe that necessity carries little or no weight in how reassured we should be about a claim. However, the non-natural metaethical view articulated in *On What Matters* is strongly supported by intuitions regarding the necessity of moral truths.
15 Street (2010), p. 370.
16 Street (2012).
17 This is a very quick gloss on Hume on sympathy. In fact, his views on sympathy are quite complex and seem to differ between the *Treatise* and the *Enquiry*.
18 Aaron James (2007) addresses the circularity worry for constructivism about practical reasons in general.
19 James (2007). I am hopeful that the circularity worry can be avoided by appealing to conservative starting points in the process of construction.
20 James (2007), p. 302.
21 Smith (2013).
22 Smith (2013), p. 24.
23 Railton (2014).
24 Hume (2007), p. 385. (T 3.3.3.)
25 Cohon (1997).
26 Driver (2008).
27 Hume (2007), p. 395.
28 Hume (2007), p. 375.
29 OWM 2, pp. 511–42.
30 OWM 1, p. 489.
31 Baker (MS). See also Lange (2010) and Sorensen (MS).
32 Baker (MS).
33 Indeed, *contra* what Parfit seems to believe about mathematics, Justin Clarke-Doane argues that it is in fact "intelligible to imagine the mathematical truths being different." See Clarke-Doane (2012), p. 315.
34 For more discussion of this interesting issue see Nolan (1997).
35 Fine (1994).
36 OWM 2, p. 486.
37 OWM 2, pp. 479–80.
38 Mendola (2014), pp. 98–9.
39 Though it might be for motivation. Before reaching this conclusion we would need to consider what a sentimentalist would say about the motivating force of second-order desires.
40 Some empirical work on testing intuitions about relativism seems to indicate that most people don't share this worry. See Sarkissian *et al.* (2011).
41 Joyce (2001).
42 An earlier version of this chapter was presented at a workshop on Normativity, Reasons, and Agency at the University of Kent in June 2014. I would like to thank members of the audience for their extremely helpful comments, Simon Kirchin in particular. I would also like to thank Connie Rosati and David Sobel for helpful discussions of an earlier draft. Some of the material in this chapter was also discussed in a blog post on PEA Soup, October 28, 2013 (http://peasoup.typepad.com/peasoup/2013/10/featured-philosopher-julia-driver-part-two.html), and I thank the participants of the discussion for their very helpful feedback.

References

Baker, Alan (MS) 'Mathematical Accidents and the End of Explanation'.
Brink, David (1984) 'Moral Realism and the Sceptical Arguments from Disagreement and Queerness', *Australasian Journal of Philosophy* 62, pp. 112–25.
Clarke-Doane, Justin (2012) 'Morality and Mathematics: the Evolutionary Challenge', *Ethics* 122, pp. 313–40.
Cohon, Rachel (1997) 'The Common Point of View in Hume's Ethics', *Philosophy and Phenomenological Research* 57, pp. 827–50.
Driver, Julia (2008) 'Imaginative Resistance and Psychological Necessity', *Social Philosophy and Policy* 25, pp. 301–13.
Fine, Kit (1994) 'Essence and Modality: The Second Philosophical Perspectives Lecture', *Philosophical Perspectives* 8, pp. 1–16.
Finlay, Stephen (2006) 'The Reasons That Matter', *Australasian Journal of Philosophy* 84, pp. 1–20.
Gendler, Tamar (2000) 'The Puzzle of Imaginative Resistance', *Journal of Philosophy* 97, pp. 55–81.
Hume, David (2007/1739–40) *A Treatise of Human Nature*, David Fate Norton and Mary J. Norton (eds) (Oxford: Oxford University Press).
James, Aaron (2007) 'Constructivism about Practical Reasons', *Philosophy and Phenomenological Research* 74, pp. 302–25.
Joyce, Richard (2001) *The Myth of Morality* (Cambridge: Cambridge University Press).
Lange, Marc (2010) 'What Are Mathematical Coincidences (and Why Does It Matter)?', *Mind* 119, pp. 307–40.
Mendola, Joseph (2014) *Human Interests: Or Ethics for Physicalists* (Oxford: Oxford University Press).
Nolan, Daniel (1997) 'Impossible Worlds: A Modest Approach', *Notre Dame Journal of Formal Logic* 38, pp. 535–72.
Parfit, Derek (1984) *Reasons and Persons* (Oxford: Oxford University Press).
Parfit, Derek (2011) *On What Matters* (Oxford: Oxford University Press), vols 1 and 2.
Railton, Peter (2014) 'The Affective Dog and Its Rational Tale: Intuition and Attunement', *Ethics* 124, pp. 813–59.
Sarkissian, Hagop, Park, John, Tien, David, Wright, Jennifer and Knobe, Joshua (2011) 'Folk Moral Relativism', *Mind and Language* 26, pp. 482–505.
Smith, Michael (2013) 'A Constitutivist Theory of Reasons: Its Promise and Parts', *Law, Ethics, and Philosophy* 1, pp. 9–30.
Sorensen, Roy (MS) 'Mathematical Coincidences'.
Street, Sharon (2010) 'What Is Constructivism in Ethics and Metaethics', *Philosophy Compass* 5, pp. 363–84.
Street, Sharon (2012) 'Coming to Terms with Contingency: Humean Constructivism about Practical Reason', in *Constructivism in Practical Philosophy*, James Lenman and Yonatan Shemmer (eds) (Oxford: Oxford University Press), pp. 40–59.
Weatherson, Brian (2004) 'Morality, Fiction, and Possibility', *Philosophers' Imprint* 4, pp. 1–27.

10
RESPONSES[1]

Derek Parfit

1 Response to Simon Kirchin

Simon Kirchin's wide-ranging and thought-provoking chapter describes and discusses several of my moral and metaethical claims. Rather than trying to write a unified response, I shall discuss Kirchin's claims under several headings.

Incommensurability

Kirchin writes that

> value incommensurability is both seemingly a real phenomenon and ... makes trouble for Parfit.... If Parfit had thought in a more detailed fashion about the phenomena of indeterminacy and imprecision, he may have been led to realize that value is complex and admits of incommensurability of a sort.
>
> (17 and 24)

These remarks puzzle me. Some normative questions are, I claimed, indeterminate in the sense that these questions have no answer. I also claimed that, when we ask about the relative of value of things that are qualitatively different, the answers are often imprecise. This *imprecision* is what Kirchin calls *incommensurability*. In these cases, when neither of two things is better than the other, these things would be imprecisely equally good. It would then be true that, if one of these things became better, these things might still be only imprecisely equally good.

Our awareness of such imprecision ought to affect our reasoning and our conclusions. In such cases, for example, the fact that B is not worse than A does not imply that B is at least as good as A. Though *at least as good as* is a transitive relation, *not worse than* is not transitive. If C is at least as good as B, which is at least as good as A, C must be at least as good as A. But if C is merely not worse than B, which is not worse than A, C *might* be worse than A. There are other important implications. People often assume that, if X is in one way better than Y, and in no way worse than Y, X must be better than Y all things considered. That would be true only when *being not worse than* implies the precise relation *being at least as good as*. If X is in one way better than Y, and in other ways X and Y are imprecisely equal, we cannot conclude that X must be better than Y all things considered.

Since I made these claims about indeterminacy and imprecision, I don't know why Kirchin believes that I failed to realize that we ought to make such claims.

At one point Kirchin acknowledges that I made such claims. Kirchin writes:

> he thinks that his comments about incomparability and imprecision are such that they undercut many or all of Wolf's criticisms, despite what I have just said. But, in that case, he owes us a detailed explanation to that effect.
>
> (17)

He also writes:

> Parfit could challenge some of what I have said here. Perhaps his small passages in §121 can be built up to show that he has a more nuanced view of the guidance of action than I have saddled him with. But, again, we require detail of this more complicated picture.
>
> (19)

What Kirchin calls my "small passages" do amount to only seven pages. But in these pages I believe that I go further than most other philosophers in claiming that truths about relative value are often indeterminate or imprecise.

The singular sense of 'best'

Kirchin also asks why I use a 'singular' sense of the word 'best', and he suggests that it would be better to use 'best' in some other, non-singular sense. Our use of 'best' is in one sense non-singular when we deny that there is any single thing that is best, since there are two or more things that are equal-best, or are not worse than any of the other things. I often use 'best' in this weakly non-singular sense.

I cannot think of any other coherent non-singular sense of 'best'. For such a sense to be more strongly *non-singular*, this sense would have to imply that two or more things are not only *not worse* than anything else – which would merely put these things in the *single* class of such best things – but also that each of these things is *better* than everything else. For X and Y to be in this sense non-singularly best, it would have to be true both that X is better all-things-considered than Y and that Y is better all-things-considered than X. No such claim could be true.

RESPONSES

The Triple Theory

In defending what I call the *Triple Theory*, I claim that

(A) when Kant's Formula of Universal Law is revised in two ways, as it needs to be, this formula succeeds, but only because, as I also argue, this revised formula supports Rule Consequentialism.

I also claim that

(B) Scanlon's Contractualist Formula should be revised in certain ways, and would then also support Rule Consequentialism.

Discussing these claims, Kirchin writes:

Are we content to jettison so much of what is part and parcel of three familiar normative ethical theories simply to provide guidance in a fairly simplified and unified way?

(25–6)

When I discuss Kant's Formula of Universal Law, I do suggest that we should give up one part of Kant's view. Kant's formula, I claimed, should not appeal to maxims in the wide sense that covers policies. Whether our acts are wrong, in Kant's sense of being contrary to duty, cannot depend on the policies on which we are acting. There are many possible policies acting on which is sometimes but not always wrong. One example is the Egoist's maxim 'do whatever is best for me'. I imagine someone who acts on this maxim when he keeps his promises and pays his debts, intending to preserve his reputation, and when he saves a drowning child, hoping to get some reward. Such acts, though having no moral worth, would not be wrong in the sense of being what Kant calls *contrary to duty*. I also suggest that Kant's formula should appeal, not to what *each* of us could rationally will, but to what *all* of us could rationally will. Kant seems to have assumed that this revision would make no difference.

If we drop Kant's appeal to maxims in the sense that covers policies, we are, as Kirchin says, jettisoning one of the familiar parts of Kant's moral view. But we are not abandoning Kant's view. We jettison something when we throw this thing away so that we can save the more valuable things that are left. We jettison a ship's cargo to save the passengers and the crew. Many Kantians have regretfully concluded that Kant's Formula of Universal Law cannot be made to work. I argue that, with these two revisions, Kant's formula *can* be made to work.

When I discuss Scanlon's version of Contractualism, I argue that Scanlon ought to give up two of his claims about what would be reasonable grounds for rejecting some moral principle. Scanlon claims that we cannot reasonably reject some principle by appealing to the numbers of people who would bear burdens if this principle were followed. Suppose, for example, that some principle implies that doctors ought to give one person twenty more years of life rather than giving to each of a thousand other people five more years of life. These thousand people, I argue, could reasonably reject this principle by claiming that they together would fail to be given not a mere twenty years of life but a total of 5,000 years of life. These people would together have a stronger moral claim.

I also argue that, in some cases, we could reasonably reject some principle by appealing not to the burdens that would be imposed on us or others but by the ways in which, if this principle were followed, things would go much worse in the impartial-reason-implying sense. One example is a case in which, if we chose one of two energy policies, we would greatly lower the quality of life in future centuries. We might know that our choice of this policy would not be worse for any of the people who would later live because, if we had chosen the other policy, these particular people would never have existed. It would have been other people who would have later lived and had this higher quality of life. I argued that, if Scanlon allowed us to appeal in these special cases to claims about what would make things go much worse, Scanlon could keep his main claim that, in other cases, we could reasonably reject principles only by appealing to the burdens that these principles would impose on us and others.

Kirchin's remarks imply that, when I argued that Scanlon ought to revise his view in these ways, I was jettisoning claims that are part and parcel of our moral thinking. That is not so. I was defending the widely accepted claims that it matters morally how many people receive benefits and burdens, and that it may matter morally which of two outcomes would be worse in the impartial-reason-implying sense. It is Scanlon, I argued, who ought not to jettison these widely accepted parts our moral thinking.

Kirchin also writes:

> The Triple Theory in its present form does not work because there is at least one perspective, a particular Kantian view, that is missing from what Parfit has given us.
>
> (25)

I don't know why Kirchin believes that the Triple Theory "does not work", because this theory does not include a particular Kantian view. The Triple Theory isn't intended to include all Kantian views. When I defend the Kantian part of the Triple Theory, in Parts Three and Five of *On What Matters*, I am discussing only Kant's Formula of Universal Law. I discuss some of Kant's other formulas and beliefs in Part Two and Appendices (F) to (I).

When Kirchin claims that the Triple Theory "does not work", he may instead mean that the Triple Theory permits some acts that most of us rightly believe to be wrong or condemns some acts that we rightly believe to be permissible.

But this objection to the Triple Theory isn't an objection to what I wrote. Though I claimed that we have strong reasons to accept this theory, I did not claim that we ought to. I also claimed that, if this theory's implications conflicted too often with our intuitions, we could justifiably reject this theory.

Actual consent

Kirchin repeats Susan Wolf's claim that, in discussing Kant's views, I ignore the importance of actual consent. That is not so. I wrote:

> Wolf objects that, by interpreting Kant in this way, I abandon the Kantian idea of respect for autonomy, which often condemns treating people in ways to which they do not *actually* consent. But I do not abandon this idea. Many acts, I claim, are wrong, even if people could rationally consent to them, because these people do not in fact give their consent. To cover such acts, I suggest, we could plausibly appeal to
>
> > the Rights Principle: Everyone has rights not to be treated in certain ways without their actual consent.[2]

These claims do not ignore the importance of actual consent.

Kirchin also repeats Wolf's objection that my arguments about the Kantian Formula commit me to rejecting principles that protect our autonomy. Kirchin does not, however, comment on the five pages in my Section 66 in which I respond to this objection. I shall not summarize these pages here.

Undefended assumptions

Kirchin writes:

> Parfit may not believe everything that Wolf or I load him with. But that requires correction from him, and if he does believe anything here he owes readers a defence. Further, such a defence has urgency *for Parfit* given that OWM is built upon the premise that seemingly conflicting theories can and should be seen as having more in common than we thought. In order to advance the Triple Theory we require a defence of the assumptions that allow it – or any other similar, unifying theory – to be advanced.
>
> (20)

I am puzzled by Kirchin's suggestion that I ought to defend the assumptions to which the Triple Theory appeals. I defend these assumptions in at least seventeen of my chapters, which together amount to several hundred pages. Kirchin's claim should at most be that my attempts to defend these assumptions fail. When Kirchin discusses the objections to my view that are stated by Wolf and Wood, he similarly writes, "part of my aim is to encourage Parfit to say something in his defence" (10). I wrote two chapters in response to these objections.

Conflicting moral theories

Kirchin quotes a passage in which I write:

> it would be a tragedy if there was no *single true morality*. And conflicting moralities could not all be true.[3]

He remarks:

> If one views a normative ethic as, in part, a description of what is of value – that is, what values exist – then it could easily be the case that different kinds of ethical theory could all be true, *contra* Parfit's second sentence in the quotation.
>
> (19)

I agree that *different* ethical theories might all be true. My claim was about *conflicting* theories. Two theories conflict when they make or imply claims which are contradictory, so that these theories cannot both be true.

Kirchin also writes that "a moral vision that embraces conflict . . . may itself be morally important" (26). Kirchin's point here may be not that contradictory claims might both be true, but that, if people have different, conflicting theories, our attempts to resolve disagreements between such theories may get us closer to the truth. I would accept this important, Millian claim.

Moral methodology

When Kirchin discusses my assumptions about what he calls *moral methodology*, he partly endorses Wolf's objection that, rather than considering moral principles at a general level, I ought instead to appeal to our intuitive beliefs about particular cases. Kirchin later partly endorses Allen Wood's objection that, rather than appealing to our intuitive beliefs about particular cases, I ought instead to consider moral principles at a general level. These objections cannot both be justified. It can't be true both that our moral thinking ought to be about particular cases rather than general principles and that our moral thinking ought to be about general principles rather than about particular cases. Kirchin might claim that we ought to think about morality in only one of these ways. But he does not tell us which way we ought to use. I believe that we ought to think about morality in both these ways.

When Kirchin discusses Wood's comments on my view, he repeats Wood's thought that, if we think about certain particular cases, such as those that are called *trolley problems*, this method leads us to the Consequentialist assumption that "the chief bearers of value are states of affairs" (21).[4] In Kirchin's words, "Other considerations, such as 'circumstantial rights, claims and entitlements', which people have in real-life situations, are 'ignored or stipulated away'" (21). These claims seem to me inaccurate. Of the people who appeal to trolley problems and other such cases, most use such cases to argue *against* Consequentialist assumptions. That is how such cases are used by, for example, by Philippa Foot, Judith Thomson, Frances Kamm and Warren Quinn. These people appeal to such cases in order to defend various non-Consequentialist beliefs about people's rights and entitlements, and to defend distinctions between killing and failing to save and between killing people as a means and as a foreseen side effect. Thomson's original trolley problem did challenge the view that the negative duty not to kill always has priority over the positive duty to save people's lives. But Thomson's aim was in part to show that this challenge to widely accepted non-Consequentialist moral beliefs could be restricted to a few unusual cases.

Kirchin's chapter contains many other interesting and important claims, most of which I accept. My aim here has only been to respond to some of Kirchin's objections to what I wrote.

2 Response to David Copp

Near the start of his very helpful chapter, David Copp writes:

> If Derek Parfit is correct . . . the naturalist's project is deeply misguided. Indeed, he makes the astonishing claim that normative naturalism is "close to nihilism" . . . He holds that if normative naturalists are correct that there are no "irreducibly normative facts," then normativity is "an illusion."
>
> (28)

There are, I believe, some normative naturalists whose views are close to nihilism. These people claim that, because all facts are natural facts, there are no irreducibly normative non-natural facts. If there were no such facts, nothing would matter, since we would have no reason to care about anything. But Copp's version of Naturalism is not, I am glad to learn, of this kind.

Copp describes properties and facts as *natural* if they are of a kind that would be "'countenanced' in . . . 'a scientifically constrained view of what exists'" (31). These natural facts about the world are also, I would add, empirical in the sense that we might have empirical evidence for or against our belief in them. There are some other facts that are not in these senses natural and empirical, such as logical, mathematical and modal facts.

Copp also distinguishes two conceptions of facts, which he calls *worldly* and *propositional*. Some examples of worldly facts are facts about concrete objects and their causally efficacious properties. On a wider and more finely grained propositional conception, facts are true propositions. To illustrate this distinction, Copp compares the trivial fact that

(A) water is water,

with the significant scientific discovery that

(B) water is H_2O. (34)

Copp claims that, though (A) and (B) state the same worldly fact, these claims state different propositional facts. As this example shows, some propositional facts may be more important than less finely grained worldly facts.

When Copp discusses normative naturalism, he writes:

> On the worldly conception of a fact, the naturalist claims that normative facts are natural facts. On the propositional conception, however, the naturalist can agree that normative facts are *not* natural facts. This may be confusing, but it is an important point.
>
> (34)

This point is indeed important, since it shows that we should distinguish between two significantly different versions of normative naturalism. Some naturalists claim that all normative facts are worldly facts which are natural in the sense that we could have empirical evidence for or against our beliefs in such facts. Copp's view is not of this kind, since he believes that there are some *non-natural* normative facts. Copp's view partly overlaps with the views of those whom I earlier called *Non-Metaphysical Non-Naturalists* and now call *Non-Realist Cognitivists*.[5] These people believe that there are some reason-implying normative truths that are not in this sense natural or empirical. These truths are in these ways like logical, mathematical and modal truths. Such truths are not empirically discoverable facts about the natural world, and they are not metaphysical in the sense that they have no weighty ontological implications. On this view, for example, mathematicians need not fear that arithmetic might all be false because there aren't any numbers. When Copp writes that "normative facts are *not* natural facts" (34), these seem to be the kinds of fact that he has in mind.

To illustrate his view, Copp supposes that

(C) acts are wrong if and only if they undermine general welfare.

Copp then compares the claims that

> (D) some action will undermine the general welfare,

and that

> (E) this act will be wrong.

On Copp's view, if (C) were true, (D) and (E) would state the same worldly fact. When some act would undermine general welfare, Copp writes, there would be

> no extra or additional *worldly* normative fact such as the fact that this action will be wrong.
>
> (41)

But (D) and (E), Copp writes, would state different propositional facts, and the non-natural normative propositional fact that is stated by (E) would be different from the natural fact stated by (D).

We can now turn to properties. Some people use the word 'property' in a robust, ontologically weighty sense, which refers to causally efficacious features of concrete objects in the natural world, such as heat or mass. In another philosophical sense, two concepts refer to the same property if these concepts are *necessarily co-extensive*, because they apply to all and only the same things. One example are the concepts expressed by the phrases

> being the only even prime number

and

> being the positive square root of 4.

Since these concepts both necessarily apply only to the number 2, they refer to the same property in this necessarily co-extensional sense. We can also use the word 'property' in a wider, finer-grained sense. Any claim about something can be restated as a claim about this thing's properties. Instead of saying that the Sun is hot and that some proof is valid, we can say that the Sun has the property of being hot, and that this proof has the property of being valid. Since this use of the word 'property' adds nothing to the content of our claims, such properties are sometimes called *pleonastic*, and claims about such properties have no ontological implications. Though this use of the word 'property' merely restates some claim, it can help us to draw some important distinctions. We can say that, though the two arithmetical concepts that I have just mentioned refer to the same property in the necessarily co-extensional sense, these concepts refer to different properties in the wider, more fine-grained pleonastic sense. Being the only even prime number is not in this sense the same as being, or *what it is* to be, the positive square root of 4.

When Copp supposes that

(C) acts are wrong if and only if they undermine general welfare,

he writes that, on this view,

[w]rongness is not some property in addition to the property of undermining the general welfare.

(41)

When Copp claims that there is only one property here, he seems to be using the phrase "the same property" in the necessarily co-extensional sense. If Copp also used this phrase in the wider pleonastic sense, he could claim that the concepts *wrong* and *undermining general welfare*, though they refer to the same property in the co-extensional sense, refer to different properties in the finer-grained pleonastic sense.

Copp does not make this second claim. Though he distinguishes between worldly facts and the more fine-grained propositional facts, Copp rejects my similar distinction between the necessarily co-extensional sense of the word 'property' and the finer-grained pleonastic sense.[6] Since Copp rejects this conception of a property, he might reject my claim that the property of being the only even prime number is in this sense different from the property of being the positive square root of 4. Copp might also claim that, though some proofs are valid, these proofs do not have the property of being valid, since there is no such property. Such objections to this use of the word 'property' seem to me mistaken. As I have said, this sense of the word 'property' merely restates some claim in a way that adds nothing to the content of this claim. Since this sense adds nothing, if we claim that there are some non-natural normative *facts*, we have no need to add that there are some non-natural *properties*. The important question is only whether there are some non-natural normative facts. As we have seen, Copp claims that there *are* some such facts.

Copp makes some claims which may seem to deny that there are any such facts. For example, Copp writes that naturalists like him

agree that the normative and the *non-normative* are importantly different, but they deny that the normative and the *natural* are importantly different since they hold that normative properties and facts *are* natural.

(28)

This last phrase may seem to imply that there are no non-natural normative facts. But that is not what Copp means. Copp writes elsewhere:

> [i]n this chapter, unless I indicate otherwise, I will be using 'fact' in the worldly sense, to refer to states of affairs. But in some contexts the propositional conception will be at issue.
>
> (34)

In the sentence that I have just quoted, Copp does not indicate otherwise, so this sentence does not contradict his claim that, in the propositional sense, there *are* some non-natural normative facts.

As well as claiming that there are such facts, Copp claims that we need to think about these facts. He writes:

> if we did not have the normative concepts, we would be unable to have such beliefs as that torture is wrong . . . even though, as we are assuming for present purposes, the property of undermining the general welfare *is* the property of wrongness . . . a person could believe that torture undermines the general welfare without believing that torture is wrong . . . This would be a cognitive loss.
>
> (39)

> Moreover, if we lacked this concept, we could not have a policy of avoiding wrongdoing. Even if we saw how to avoid undermining the general welfare, we might not understand that this is how to avoid wrongdoing. These would be significant losses.
>
> (41)

Return to the passage in which Copp writes:

> [i]f Derek Parfit is correct . . . the naturalist's project is deeply misguided. Indeed, he makes the astonishing claim that normative naturalism is "close to nihilism" . . . He holds that if normative naturalists are correct that there are no "irreducibly normative facts," then normativity is "an illusion."
>
> (28)

Since Copp believes that there are some non-natural irreducibly normative facts, I don't regard Copp's view as deeply misguided. When I made what Copp calls my "astonishing claim", I was using the phrase 'Normative Naturalist' to refer only to people who believe that there are *no* non-natural normative facts. Nor do I believe that, on Copp's view, normativity is an illusion. Copp believes that there are some non-natural normative facts which are not what Copp calls worldly facts and which have no weighty ontological implications. This view overlaps with the Non-Metaphysical Non-Natural View accepted by Nagel,

Scanlon, me and others, which I now call *Non-Realist Cognitivism*. Copp and I seem to have developed our views in ways that resolve what used to be our main metaethical disagreement. That is, to me at least, a very welcome fact.

3 Response to Julia Markovits

In much of her impressive chapter, Julia Markovits defends what I call *Subjectivism about reasons*. On this view, all practical reasons are given by facts about how we might fulfill either our actual present desires or the desires that we would now have after informed deliberation. I claim that, as Markovits writes:

> Subjectivism . . . has deeply implausible as well as deeply troubling consequences.
> (55)

One such implication, she writes, is that, if our desires were "sufficiently weird" (55), we would have no reason to choose to avoid future agony. But this is not my main objection to Subjectivism. As Markovits also writes, what I claim to be most implausible is the Subjectivist belief that

> (A) we can have no reasons for desiring anything or having certain aims.
> (55)

Suppose we remember what it was like to be in agony, by being burnt or whipped. I wrote:

> According to Subjectivists, what we remember gives us no reason to want to avoid having such intense pain again. If we ask 'Why not?', Subjectivists have, I believe, no good reply.[7]

This objection does not apply only to imagined cases in which someone weirdly has no desire to avoid future agony. Even if everyone *has* this desire, we can ask Subjectivists why they believe that facts about what it is like to be in agony can't give us any *reason* to have this desire.

Markovits does not directly answer this question. She suggests an indirect answer when she writes:

> Subjectivism does not entail that we can have no reasons for our desires . . . Desires are candidates for the same sort of justification *coherentists about justification* take beliefs to have: desires are justified when they are part of a coherent web of desire.
> (73)

These claims imply that

> (B) we would have a reason to have some desire when our having this desire would make our set of desires more coherent.

Though we can justify some of our *beliefs* in this coherentist way, no such claim applies to our desires. Our beliefs are incoherent when they conflict, so that these beliefs cannot all be true. Our desires can be incoherent, or conflict, only in the quite different sense that we cannot fulfill all of these desires. But such conflicts do not show that these desires are not justified. If we wanted both to save one person's life and to save someone else from going blind, but we would not be able to fulfill both of these desires, that would not make this pair of desires in any way irrational, or less than fully rational. As Markovits points out, our desires may also fail to cohere in the weaker sense that we care about several things for their own sake, and these desires cannot be given some unifying explanation, such as the explanation that hedonists give. But we should not assume that, for our desires to be justified, we must be able to give them some such unifying explanation. We can rationally care about several distinctively different things.

We can next compare these claims:

> (C) Our reason to want to avoid future agony is given by the fact that, if we were later in agony, we would be having sensations that we intensely dislike.
>
> (D) Our reason to want to avoid future agony is given by the fact that our having this desire would make our set of desires more coherent.

If Markovits believed that (C) was true, she would appeal to (C) rather than to (D). There are some other people who would be unable to appeal to (C). When these people claim that we have a reason to act in some way, these people *mean* that, after informed deliberation, we would be motivated to act in this way. I understand why these people believe that facts about what it is like to be in agony could not give us a reason to want to avoid future agony. As these people could rightly claim, the fact that we would be motivated to act in some way isn't a *reason* to be motivated to act in this way. But Markovits often claims that she uses the phrase 'a reason' in the purely normative sense which we cannot helpfully define by using other words, but which we can also express with the phrase 'a fact that counts in favour'. I don't know why Markovits believes that what it is like to be in agony can't count in favour of wanting to avoid future agony.

Markovits refers to my "worry that Subjectivism entails a bleak and nihilistic picture of the normative world" (56). This worry is, I believe, justified.

If not even facts about agony could give us any reason to want to avoid future agony, we could have no such reason to care about other things. As we might more briefly say, if even agony doesn't matter, nothing matters. Markovits writes:

> if we accept Subjectivism, Parfit argues, *then nothing matters*.
>
> (71)

and, earlier,

> [a]ccording to the Subjectivist, things *matter*, ultimately, *because they matter to us* . . . According to the Objectivist, by contrast, things *matter to us*, when we are reasoning well, *because they matter*.
>
> (58)

As Markovits here rightly claims, Subjectivists believe that some things matter in the *psychological* sense that we care about these things. Objectivists believe that some things matter in the *normative* sense that we have reasons to care about these things. When Nihilists claim that nothing matters, they are not claiming that no one cares about anything. That psychological claim is clearly false. Nihilists mean that, as Subjectivism implies, no one has any reason to care about anything.

Markovits discusses and defends two versions of Subjectivism. In her elegant formulation, some Subjectivists discuss *which* reasons there are, and others discuss *what* reasons are. I shall first consider Markovits' claims about this second, meta-ethical question.

Describing the metaethical debate between those whom she calls *Subjectivists* and *Objectivists*, Markovits writes:

> What they disagree about is what is involved in some fact's *counting in favor of* an action.
>
> (57)

Markovits appeals to claims about what she calls our "idealized desires". These are the desires that we have, or would have, after some process of informed deliberation. Markovits states her view in different ways. Subjectivists, she writes, claim to give

> the right account of what *grounds* reasons for action – of what *makes* some consideration count in favor of acting.[8]

On what we can call this *Grounding Version* of Markovits' view, or

GVM: when some fact shows how some act might fulfil some present idealized desire, this property of this fact makes this fact count in favour of this act.

Markovits also writes:

> Subjectivism . . . aims to provide an informative account of what property a certain property is *identical to*: in this case, the property of being a reason . . . . *what it is* for a fact to count in favor of an action is for that fact to show how the action would help fulfill some idealized desire.
>
> (57)

According to this *Identity Version* of Markovits' view, or

IVM: when some fact shows how some act might fulfil some present idealized desire, that is *the same as* this fact's counting in favour of this act. Showing how some act might fulfil such a desire is *what it is* for some fact to count in favour of this act.

Markovits may assume that we don't have to choose between these versions of her view, since we can accept both GVM and IVM. According to this Combined Version of her view, or

CVM: when some fact shows how some act might fulfil some present idealized desire, this property of this fact both *makes* this fact count in favour of this act and *is the same as* this fact's counting in favour of this act.

Markovits compares her view with the scientific discoveries that water is H_2O and that heat is molecular kinetic energy. Markovits might compare CVM with the fact that

H: when the molecules in some object move energetically, that both *makes* this object hot and is *the same as* this object's being hot. Having such energy is what it is to be hot.

The similarity of these claims may seem to support this version of Markovits' view. But when we look more closely, I believe, we can find that this analogy fails and in a way that counts against this view.

We can first note that, when H claims that having molecular kinetic energy *makes* an object hot, this relation of *non-causal making* here implies *being the same as*. So we can drop this use of 'makes' and shorten H to

H2: having molecular kinetic energy is the same as being hot.

We can similarly shorten CVM to

> CVM2: when some fact shows how some act might fulfil some present idealized desire, this property of this fact is the same as this fact's counting in favour of this act.

Though these claims seem similar, *being hot* is not relevantly like *counting in favour*. In the sense that is relevant here, 'being hot' means

> having the property that has certain effects, such as causing us to feel certain sensations, melting solids, turning liquids into gases, etc.

Scientists discovered that

> H3: when the molecules in some object move energetically, that is the same as this object's having the property that has these effects.

The property *that has* certain effects is not the same as the property *of having* these effects. We can claim that

> the Sun's brightness is the property *that makes* the Moon shine,

but we should not claim that

> the Sun's brightness is the property *of making* the Moon shine.

Being what makes the Moon shine isn't the same as *making* the Moon shine. As we might more fully say:

> the Sun's brightness is the property that has the different property of being the property that makes the Moon shine.

We can similarly claim that

> molecular kinetic energy is the property *that has* certain effects,

but we should not claim that

> molecular kinetic energy is the property *of having* certain effects.

Having molecules that move energetically isn't the same as causing us to feel certain sensations, or melting solids, or turning liquids into gases, etc. We can add:

> nor is molecular kinetic energy the same as these effects.

Return now to the property of *counting in favour*. We can similarly claim that

> the property *that makes* some fact count in favour of some act isn't the same as the property *of making* this fact count in favour of this act.

We can add:

> nor is this property the same as the property of *counting in favour* of this act.

As these remarks imply, Markovits might be able to defend the Grounding Version of her view, but she could not defend the Identity Version. Markovits might claim

> GVM2: when some fact shows how some act might fulfil some present idealized desire, this property of this fact may be the property *that makes* this fact count in favour of this act. But this property could not be the same as the property *of making* this fact count in favour of this act. Nor could this property be the same as the property of *being made* to count in favour of this act, or the property of *counting in favour* of this act.

As she could more briefly say:

> showing how some act might fulfil such a desire couldn't be the same as counting in favour of this act.

Though I believe that these properties couldn't be the same, it is worth pointing out that if – impossibly – they were the same, Markovits' view could not give us any positive substantive normative information. Suppose – impossibly – that

> (E) showing how some act might fulfil such a desire is the same as counting in favour of this act.

Markovits could not then claim that

> (F) when some fact shows how some act might fulfil some present idealized desire, that would give this fact the different normative property of counting in favour of this act.

On this version of Markovits' view, there would be *no* such *different* property. Her view would tell us only that

> (G) when some fact shows how some act might fulfil such a desire, this fact would have the property of showing how this act might fulfil such a desire.

This would be what Markovits herself calls a bleak reductive view.

Markovits might reply that scientists made a significant discovery when they realized that

> (H) when some object has molecular kinetic energy, that is the same as this object's being hot.

This claim is significant even though it does not imply that when some object has molecular kinetic energy, that gives it the *different* property of being hot. (H) does not merely tell us that

> (I) when some object has molecular kinetic energy, this object has molecular kinetic energy.

Markovits might similarly claim that

> (J) when some fact shows how some act might fulfil some present idealized desire, this property of this fact is the same as the property that makes this fact count in favour of this act.

Even if these properties were the same, Markovits might say, (J)'s truth would give us important normative information. (J) would not merely tell us the trivial truth that when some fact has the property of showing how some act might fulfil such a desire, this fact would have this property.

This appeal to this scientific analogy may seem to answer my objection. Other normative naturalists have made similar claims, whose plausibility helps to explain how such views have been defended by some of the best moral philosophers. But as before, I believe, this analogy fails. We should agree that if (J) were true, this claim would give us important normative information. But (J) states the non-reductive Grounding Version of Markovits' view. We could restate (J) as

> GVM3: when some fact shows how some act might fulfil some present idealized desire, this property of this fact is the same as the property that makes this fact have the different, normative property of counting in favour of this act.

I have mainly been discussing the reductive, Identity Version of Markovits' view. This view claims that

> (K) when some fact shows how some act might fulfil such a desire, this property is the same as the property of counting in favour of this act.

This claim, I have argued, could not possibly be true. Showing how some act might fulfil some desire couldn't be the same as counting in favour of this act.

But if – impossibly – (K) were true, (K) could not give us positive substantive normative information. Unlike GVM3, (K) could not tell us how some fact's explanatory property makes this fact have the different, normative property of counting in favor of some act. (K) denies that there is any such different property.

As these remarks imply, when normative naturalists appeal to scientific analogies, such as the discovery that heat is molecular kinetic energy, they can make various true claims which seem to support their view. Though these analogies, I believe, fail, this fact is far from being obvious. These analogies fail in a fairly subtle, particular way. When we discuss the reductive version of Markovits' view, we must distinguish between the property *that makes* some fact count in favour of some act and the property *of making* some fact count in favor of some act. This distinction is easy to miss. That is why Markovits writes both that her Subjectivism gives

> the right account . . . of what *makes* some consideration count in favor of acting,[9]

and that her view gives

> an informative account of what property a certain property is *identical to* . . . [or of] *what it is* for a fact to count in favor of an action.
> (57)

These claims, I have argued, cannot both be true, and Markovits ought to accept the first, non-reductive version of her view. Markovits should claim that when some fact shows how some act might fulfil some present idealized desire, that makes this fact have the different, normative property of counting in favour of this act.

If Markovits accepted this version of her view, that would enable her to strengthen her view, by dropping some of her other claims. Markovits writes that she accepts my worry about some "*reductive-naturalist* versions of Subjectivism . . . [which] equate normative-reasons facts with purely psychological facts about our motivational dispositions" (72). One example is the view that

> (L) if we would be motivated to act in some way after informed deliberation, that is the same as our having a reason to act in this way.

Facts about such reasons are not normative, since they are merely facts about what would motivate us. Markovits defends the different view that

> (M) if we would be motivated to act in some way after informed and procedurally rational deliberation, that is the same as our having a reason to act in this way.

For our deliberation to be *procedurally rational*, we must meet certain normative standards, such as those of vividly imagining the effects of different acts, avoiding bias and wishful thinking and so on. Markovits claims that because this use of the phrase 'procedurally rational' is normative, her (M) is unlike the reductive view stated by (L), since (M) is a normative claim.

When I earlier discussed views of the kind that are stated by (M), I argued that these views are not relevantly normative. If we appealed to (M), we could make normative claims about which kinds of deliberation are procedurally rational. But these would not be normative claims about what we had reasons to want or reasons to do. As Markovits notes, the view that she states with (M) appeals to what Rawls calls *pure procedural justification*. On such views, there are no independent normative truths about what we have reasons to want or reasons to do. Our process of deliberation could be fully procedurally rational whatever we end up wanting or being motivated to do.

Of the Subjectivists who defend views like (M), some claim that when they say that

(1) we have some practical reason,

they mean that

(2) after informed and procedurally rational deliberation, we would be motivated to act in some way.

If this is what we mean by the phrase 'a reason', we could restate (M) as

(N) if we would be motivated to act in some way after informed and procedurally rational deliberation, this fact would make it true that, after such a process of deliberation, we would be motivated to act in this way.

Though (N) uses the normative phrase 'procedurally rational', (N) is not a significant normative claim. Everyone could agree that (N) is trivially true.

Markovits, however, does not use the phrase 'a reason' in the sense defined by (2). She uses the purely normative concept of a reason that we can also express with the phrase 'a fact that counts in favour'. So Markovits could claim instead that

(O) if we would be motivated to act in some way after such a process of deliberation, this fact would have the different, purely normative property of giving us a reason to act in this way.

This claim *is* relevantly normative. (O) is one of the non-reductive Subjectivist Normative views that I discuss in OWM §§2, 3 and 4. But if (O) is our only claim about which facts give us reasons, as these Subjectivists claim, this view implies that we have no reasons to be *motivated* in certain ways. To repeat my example, these views imply that

> (P) what it is like to be in agony gives us no reason to want to avoid future agony.

If Markovits accepted only the Subjectivist view stated by (O), she could not deny that her view implied (P).

Since Markovits uses the purely normative concept of a reason, she could cease to be a Subjectivist, and she could reject both (O) and (P). Markovits could claim that we do have such a reason to want to avoid future agony.

In several passages, Markovits comes close to accepting this different, Non-Subjectivist view. She also, I believe, conflates two different views. If Markovits distinguished these views, she and I might be able to resolve not only our meta-ethical disagreements but also our normative disagreements.

Markovits makes several excellent points about my list of ten ways in which I claim that some of us are led to accept Subjectivism about reasons, though that is not really what we believe. When I gave this list, I failed to state one other way in which we can be led astray. We may forget that Subjectivist views about reasons appeal to facts that are about only our *present* actual or hypothetical desires or other motivational states. I failed to repeat this claim because I assumed that I had made this claim sufficiently often in earlier sections of my book. But I see now that, if Markovits was mainly considering my descriptions of these ten ways in which we might be mistakenly led to accept Subjectivism, it would be easy for her to misunderstand my claims. If that is how she was led to reject my claims, her view may be closer to mine than she believes.

After describing these ten ways, I later wrote:

> It might next be claimed that my predictable future desire not to be in agony gives me a desire-based reason now to want to avoid this future agony. But this claim cannot be made by those who accept subjective theories of the kind that we are considering. These people do not claim, and given their other assumptions they could not claim, that facts about our *future* desires give us reasons.
>
> Some other theories make that claim. A value-based objective theory about *reasons* might be combined with a desire-based subjective

theory about *well-being*. On such a view, even if we don't now care about our future well-being, we have reasons to care, and we ought to care. These reasons are value-based in the sense that they are provided by the facts that would make various future events good or bad for us. But if our future well-being would in part consist, as this view claims, in the fulfilment of some of our future desires, these *value-based* reasons would be reasons to act in ways that would cause these future *desires* to be fulfilled.[10]

When Markovits discusses these theories about well-being, she writes:

> [a]ccording to such views, the fulfillment of our present desires is in itself good for us.
>
> (68)

These theories of well-being do not claim only that the fulfilment of our *present* desires is in itself good for us. As I have said, these theories give as much weight to our *future* desires. Markovits continues:

> Parfit says that it follows from these views that we have *value-based, object-given* reasons to fulfill our desires rather than *desire-based, subject-given* reasons to do as we desire. But it is very unclear what this difference comes to.
>
> (68)

The distinction I intended is, I believe, clear. These Objectivists about reasons claim that we have reasons to do what would be best for ourselves in our whole life. If these Objectivists accept some desire-fulfilment of well-being, they claim that we have reasons to do what would best fulfil our future desires, to which we ought to give as much weight as we give to our present desires. We have such reasons to do now what would fulfil these future desires, whether or not we now care about the fulfilment of these desires. On these theories, for example, our future agony will be bad for us because of the strength of the desires that we shall later have not to be in this conscious state. That is why we all have reasons to want to avoid all future agony and to do what would avoid this agony if we can. These Subjectivists, in contrast, deny that we have any such reasons. These people believe that all of our reasons are given by facts that are about only our *present* desires or other motivational states. When applied to most people, these two views have very different implications.

Markovits also writes:

> [d]efenders of a desire-fulfillment view of well-being have already embraced the subjectivist thought that things matter *for* us, ultimately,

because they matter *to* us. So there is something odd about accepting such a view of well-being while rejecting Subjectivism.

(68)

Similar remarks apply. There would be nothing odd in both accepting a desire-fulfilment theory of well-being and rejecting Subjectivism about reasons. We may believe that we have strong reasons to care about, and promote, our future well-being. We would then reject the Subjectivist view that we have no such reasons, since our reasons are all given by facts about what matters to us now, or our *present* desires.

Markovits rightly criticizes theories which claim that our well-being does not depend at all on what matters to us. She then writes:

> if Objectivists embrace, instead, a conception of our good that is more beholden to our desires, such as a desire-fulfillment or a preference-hedonist view, Objectivism begins to look suspiciously like a less well-motivated version of Subjectivism.
>
> (71)

Similar remarks apply. When I discussed Objectivist theories about reasons, I supposed that these theories would often appeal to what I call *hedonic reasons*. One example is our reason to want to avoid future agony. In the three passages that I have just quoted, Markovits seems to be closer to accepting, not the Subjectivist view about reasons against which I argued, but an Objectivist view which appeals to some desire-fulfilment or preference-hedonistic view about well-being. If that is Markovits' view, as these and other passages suggest, we have resolved our main disagreements. Given the subtlety and plausibility of many of Markovits' claims, that would be good news for me – and, I hope, for Markovits as well.

4 Response to Philip Stratton-Lake

I am convinced by all of the arguments, and I accept all of the claims, in Philip Stratton-Lake's wonderfully precise and helpful chapter.

5 and 6 Responses to David McNaughton and Piers Rawling and to Kieran Setiya

Given the similarities between some of the main claims and arguments in Kieran Setiya's chapter and in the chapter jointly written by David McNaughton and Piers Rawling, I shall discuss these chapters together.

These chapters both discuss two kinds of reason. Some reasons I call *deontic* in the sense that these reasons are provided by the fact that some act is morally wrong.

All other reasons I call *non-deontic*. Our reasons to act in some way are *decisive* when they are stronger than any conflicting reasons, so that, if we know the relevant reason-giving facts, we ought rationally to act in this way.

In their rich and interesting chapter, McNaughton and Rawling claim that

(A) there are no deontic reasons.

On this view, though we have various reasons not to act in ways that are wrong, the wrongness of these acts does not give us a further reason. In their words, "wrongness, if it were an extra reason, would be superfluous". Claims about wrongness merely add "idle cogs to the moral machinery" (116).

McNaughton and Rawling believe that my view conflicts with theirs. There may be no such disagreement. McNaughton and Rawling quote my remark that

> when certain acts would be wrong . . . we *can* claim that the wrongness of these acts gives us further, independent reasons not to act in these ways.[11]

But this quotation is incomplete. We can make this claim, I wrote, if we are using the word 'wrong' in one of several senses. When we claim that some act is wrong, we may mean that we have decisive moral reasons not to act in this way. We are then using 'wrong' in what I call the *decisive-moral-reason* sense. McNaughton and Rawling seem to use 'wrong' only in this sense. I claim myself that, if this is what we mean by 'wrong', we should deny that an act's wrongness gives us a further reason not to act in this way. The fact that we have these decisive moral reasons cannot, by itself, give us a further reason.

We can also use 'wrong', I claimed, in several other senses. There are several definable senses. When we call some act wrong, we might mean, for example, that this act is blameworthy, or unjustifiable to others, or that this act gives the agent reasons to feel remorse, and gives other people reasons for indignation or resentment. We might instead use 'wrong' in an indefinable sense, which we might also express with the words 'impermissible' or 'mustn't-be-done'. In the sentence that McNaughton and Rawling quote above, I wrote:

> when certain acts would be wrong *in these other senses*, we can claim that the wrongness of these acts gives us further, independent reasons not to act in these ways.[12]

We have such further reasons, I believe, not to act in ways that are blameworthy, or unjustifiable to others, or ways that give us reasons for remorse and give others reasons for indignation. These reasons may often not be as strong as the reasons given by the facts that would make some act wrong – such as the suffering that this act would cause. But that does not show that an act's being blameworthy and unjustifiable to others give us no further reasons. Similar claims apply to the indefinable sense of 'wrong'. We shouldn't assume that, when some act is impermissible, or mustn't-be-done, that this fact cannot give us any further reason not to act in this way. Since McNaughton and Rawling do not discuss my claims about these other senses of 'wrong', I can hope that they would accept these claims. This disagreement would then be resolved.

McNaughton and Rawling also write:

> Parfit, then, 'double-counts': the moral reasons against an immoral act contribute twice, once in their role as reasons against the act and once in their role as contributors to the act's moral wrongness, which then itself gets counted as a further independent reason against the act.
>
> (114)

When we use the word 'wrong' in these other senses, the facts that we believe to make acts wrong don't count twice in an objectionable way. These facts may have two implications, but that is no objection. We can defensibly believe that certain facts about some act both give us moral reasons not to act in this way, and make this act blameworthy, unjustifiable to others, and something that mustn't-be-done, thereby giving us further reasons not to act in this way.

I shall now turn to Setiya's elegant, subtle and thought-provoking chapter. According to a view that Setiya calls

> *Wrong-Making Reasons*: whenever some act would be wrong, the nonmoral facts that would make this act wrong would also give us decisive reasons not to act in this way.

> Such reasons I call *non-deontic*.

If this view were true, Setiya suggests, moral theories and moral beliefs would have little practical importance. In deciding what we ought rationally to do, we would seldom need to know that some act would be wrong. It would be enough to know the nonmoral facts that would make this act wrong, since these facts would by themselves give us decisive reasons not to act in this way. As we have seen, McNaughton and Rawling make similar claims.

Setiya does not commit himself to the truth of Wrong-Making Reasons, but he gives what he calls a "tentative defense" (125) of this view. According to what Setiya calls

> *Moral Rationalism:* we always have decisive reasons not to act wrongly.

According to

> *Deontic Reasons*: whenever some act would be wrong, this moral fact would give us a decisive deontic reason not to act in this way.

On Setiya's suggested argument:

> Moral Rationalism is true.
>
> If Wrong-Making Reasons were not true, it would be Deontic Reasons that made Moral Rationalism true.
>
> If Deontic Reasons is true, Wrong-Making Reasons is true.

Therefore

> Wrong-Making Reasons is true.

In a fuller statement:

> (1) We always have decisive reasons not to act wrongly.
>
> (2) If the nonmoral facts that would make some act wrong did not give us decisive non-deontic reasons not to act in this way, it would be this act's wrongness that gave us such reasons.
>
> (3) If an act's wrongness gave us such decisive deontic reasons, the nonmoral facts that made this act wrong would also give us decisive non-deontic reasons.

Therefore

> (4) The nonmoral facts that make some act wrong always give us decisive non-deontic reasons not to act in this way.

Premise (3), I believe, is false. When certain facts make some act wrong, these nonmoral facts may often give us decisive non-deontic reasons. One example is the fact that some act would give us some slight benefit in a way that would kill some innocent person. This fact would give us a decisive reason all by itself. But some other wrong-making facts may not by themselves give us such decisive non-deontic reasons. It may be true that

> (5) some nonmoral facts give us decisive reasons only when, and because, these facts make some act wrong, thereby giving us a decisive deontic reason not to act in this way.

To illustrate these claims, I discussed two familiar imagined cases. In the case that I called

> *Tunnel*, a driverless, runaway train is headed for a tunnel in which it would kill five people. As a bystander, you could save these people's lives by switching the points on the track, thereby redirecting this train on to another track and into another tunnel. As you know, I am in this other tunnel, so this redirected train would kill me.[13]

In what I called

> *Bridge*, the train is headed for the five, but there is no other track and tunnel. I am on a bridge above the track. Your only way to save the five would be to open, by remote control, the trap-door on which I am standing, so that I would fall on to the track. The train would then hit and kill me in a way that triggered its automatic brake, thereby stopping the train before it killed the five.[14]

In both these cases, you could save the five other people only in a way that would also kill me. You would have a strong non-deontic reason not to act in a way that would kill me. But this reason might not by itself be decisive, since it might be outweighed by your non-deontic reason to save the other five people's lives. There is a moral difference, many people believe, between these cases. In *Tunnel*, you could save the five in a way that would kill me only as a foreseen side effect. This act, many people believe, would not be wrong, so you would have sufficient reasons to save the five by redirecting the runaway train in a way that would also kill me. In *Bridge*, you would save the five only by killing me, not as a *side effect*, but as a *means* of stopping the train. This fact, many people believe, would make this act wrong, and this act's wrongness would give you a decisive deontic reason not to act in this way.

According to Setiya's premise (3), if some act's wrongness would give us decisive deontic reasons not to act in this way, the facts that made this act wrong would also give us decisive non-deontic reasons not to act in this way. *Tunnel* and *Bridge*, we may believe, provide a counterexample to this claim. Though many people would believe that, in *Bridge*, your act would be wrong, some other people reject that view. These people believe that *Bridge* is relevantly like *Tunnel*. On this view, in both cases, you could permissibly save five people's lives in a way that would also kill me, and it would make no moral difference whether you would be killing me as a foreseen side effect or as a means. Since both acts would cause four fewer people to die, you would have sufficient reasons to act in both these ways.

Many of us would reject this second view, since we believe that your act would be morally justified only in *Tunnel*. We may then believe that

> (6) the fact that you would be killing me as a means, in *Bridge*, does not by itself give you a decisive non-deontic reason not to act in this way. This fact gives you a decisive reason only indirectly, by making this act wrong, thereby giving you a decisive deontic reason not to act

in this way. If this fact did not make this act wrong, this case would be relevantly like *Tunnel*, since you would have sufficient reasons to save the other five people's lives in a way that would also kill me.

If (6) is true, we could reject Setiya's claim that

(3) if an act's wrongness gave us such decisive deontic reasons, the facts that made this act wrong would also give us decisive non-deontic reasons.

We might claim instead that

(5) some facts give us decisive reasons only because these facts make some act wrong.

This objection to Setiya's argument does not depend on the view that there is a moral difference between *Bridge* and *Tunnel*. Some of us would reject (6). We should admit, however, that in other cases claims like (6) might be true. Since such claims might be true, Setiya's argument does not show that (5) cannot be true.

In considering this argument, we should also remember that the phrase 'morally wrong' can be used in different senses. When we call some act wrong in what I called the decisive-moral-reason sense, we mean that we have decisive moral reasons not to act in this way. Though these are *moral* reasons, they are not *deontic* reasons, since these reasons are given by the facts that *make* some act wrong, not by the fact *that* this act is wrong. If this is what we mean by 'wrong', I claimed, the fact that some act would be wrong would be the fact that we had these decisive reasons, and our having these decisive reasons would not give us a further reason not to act in this way. That would support Setiya's premise (3).

If we use 'wrong' only in the decisive-moral-reason sense, we may accept Setiya's premise (3). But if we use the other senses, I believe we can reject (3) and defensibly believe (5). One example is provided, I suggest, by the comparison between *Tunnel* and *Bridge*. People who believe that your act would be wrong in *Bridge* may believe not that you have decisive moral reasons not to kill me as a means, but that killing someone as a means is impermissible, and mustn't-be-done.

Setiya makes some other claims which may seem to support premise (3). He writes:

> assuming deontic reasons, a practically rational agent who knows the non-deontic facts that make an action wrong will conclude that the action is wrong and thus refrain from doing it . . . if knowledge of certain facts would prevent a practically rational agent from performing an action, those facts provide decisive reason not to act in that way. It follows that we must accept Wrong-Making Reasons.

(131)

RESPONSES

These claims do not, I believe, support (3), which is part of Setiya's argument for (4), the belief which he calls *Wrong-Making Reasons*. If some act's wrongness would give us a decisive deontic reason, Setiya's practically rational agent who concludes that some act is wrong might refrain from acting in this way because he recognizes this deontic reason. That may be true even if the nonmoral facts that make this act wrong do not, by themselves, give this person a decisive non-deontic reason. These wrong-making facts might give this person a decisive reason only by making this act wrong.

Setiya earlier wrote:

> If right and wrong have rational authority, a fully rational agent must recognize that an act is wrong when he knows the facts that make it wrong, and he must act on this belief, or he must act directly on the relevant facts. Either way, an agent who is not decisively moved by knowledge of wrong-making facts is less than ideally rational. It follows, through the connection between reasons and rationality, that the facts that make an action wrong provide decisive reasons against it.[15]

When Setiya makes these claims, his view is closer to mine. Setiya here recognizes that, when some rational agent refrains from doing what he believes to be wrong, there are two ways in which this may be true. This agent may be acting directly on the relevant wrong-making facts, because he believes that these facts give him decisive non-deontic reasons. But he may instead be acting on his belief that this act is wrong, because he believes that this act's wrongness gives him a decisive deontic reason. Since Setiya recognizes that this agent might be moved in this second way, he should not claim that it *follows* that the facts which make acts wrong always by themselves provide decisive reasons not to act in these ways. If Setiya's fully rational agent is moved not to act in some way by his belief that this act is wrong, he may also believe that the wrong-making facts give him a decisive reason, not by themselves, but only indirectly, by making this act wrong. This argument for Wrong-Making Reasons therefore fails.

Setiya also thinks

> (7) Unless he is moved by the facts that make an act wrong without needing to form deontic beliefs, we should conclude that he is not ideally rational.

But Setiya cannot, I believe, appeal to (7). If any ideally rational agent would be moved by his belief in some wrong-making facts without needing to form the belief that some act is wrong, that would have to be because it was true that

217

(4) the nonmoral facts that make some act wrong would always give us decisive non-deontic reasons not to act in this way.

But Setiya's argument cannot assume (4) – or Wrong-Making Reasons – since (4) is what this argument is intended to show. We may instead believe that

(5) there are some nonmoral facts that give us decisive reasons only when, and because, these facts make some act wrong, thereby giving us a decisive deontic reason not to act in this way.

Setiya claims that if some agent is ideally rational, this person would be moved by his beliefs in the wrong-making facts without needing to form the belief that this act is wrong. If that were true, this would have to be because these wrong-making facts would by themselves give this person a decisive non-deontic reason. But this ideally rational person may instead believe that some nonmoral facts give us decisive reasons only by making some act wrong. If that were true, this person's beliefs in these nonmoral facts might not move this person to act unless he forms the deontic belief that this act is wrong.

Though Setiya mentions my appeal to (5), he gives no argument against this claim.[16] As I note, (5) is in one way hard to assess. When discussing *Bridge*, we might believe that

(8) if it would not be wrong for you to save the other five people's lives by killing me, you would have sufficient reasons to save these people's lives in this way.

We may find it hard, however, to assess (8), since this claim appeals to a counterfactual whose antecedent, we may believe, could not possibly be true. If we cannot imagine how this fact might fail to make this act wrong, we may find it hard to decide whether, if this fact did *not* make this act wrong, this fact would nonetheless give us a decisive reason. But there are some plausible arguments against the view that this act is wrong. When we consider these arguments, we may be able to imagine ceasing to believe that this act is wrong, and we may therefore be able to judge whether we would nonetheless have a decisive non-deontic reason. That is how it helps to compare *Bridge* with *Tunnel*. We may believe that in *Tunnel* it would not be wrong for you to save five people's lives in a way that you know would also kill me. This may help us to suppose that it would also not be wrong for you in *Bridge* to save five people's lives in a way that you know would also kill me. We may then conclude that if you have a decisive reason not to kill me in *Bridge*, this reason is given by the fact that killing me as a means would be wrong, in the sense of being impermissible, or something that mustn't-be-done.

There are other such examples. Consider, for example, the view that using artificial birth control is wrong. Even if the artificiality of birth control did not make such acts wrong, few people believe that this artificiality would give us decisive *non*-deontic reasons not to act in this way. Similar claims apply to voluntary euthanasia or assisting suicide. We can plausibly believe that if we had decisive reasons not to act in these ways, that would be true only because these acts are wrong.

Moral Rationalism, I conclude, does not imply Wrong-Making Reasons. There are three ways in which Moral Rationalism might be true. When it is true that

(B) we have decisive reasons not to act wrongly,

these reasons might be provided either

(C) only by this act's wrongness,

or

(D) by this act's wrongness together with the facts that make this act wrong,

or

(E) only by the nonmoral facts that make this act wrong.

Setiya's argument does not show that only (E) could be true.

I conclude that, even if Moral Rationalism is true and Deontic Reasons is true, these claims do not imply Wrong-Making Reasons. We can plausibly believe that to know whether we have decisive reasons not to act in some way we may sometimes need to know whether this act would be wrong.

Similar remarks apply to the claim that

(A) there are no deontic reasons,

which is implied by (E). When McNaughton and Rawling defend (A), they seem to use the word 'wrong' in the decisive-moral-reason sense. They might agree that if we use 'wrong' in various other senses, as many people do, we can defensibly believe that an act's wrongness may give us at least some further reason not to act in this way. McNaughton and Rawling might defend (A) by appealing to Setiya's argument for (E). But this argument, I have claimed, does not succeed.

In other parts of their chapters, Setiya, McNaughton and Rawling discuss my claims about the revised Formula of Universal Law. According to one version of what I called this

> *Kantian Contractualist Formula*: everyone ought to follow the principles whose universal acceptance everyone could rationally will, or choose.[17]

What we could rationally choose, in the sense that is relevant here, is what we would have sufficient reasons to choose. This Kantian Formula succeeds, I argued, because it supports Rule Consequentialism.

According to Setiya's Wrong-Making Reasons,

> (4) the nonmoral facts that make some act wrong would always give us decisive non-deontic reasons not to act in this way.

After giving the argument for (4) that I have just been discussing, Setiya writes:

> Although it does not refute the Kantian formula, this line of thought casts doubt on its power to guide and illuminate practice... [I]f we accept Wrong-Making Reasons, what we have to learn from Kantian Contractualism is not of practical value. What then is the point of the Kantian project?
>
> (129)

He also writes:

> On any account, the use of Kantian Contractualism assumes a delicate balance of known and unknown normative facts. I have argued that we almost never satisfy these constraints and that the Kantian formula is practically inert. Even if I am wrong, why fixate on this epistemic state? Why address someone who knows all there is to know about non-deontic reasons, including ones that bear on the treatment of others, but is oddly blind to deontic facts? There is nothing to prevent us from doing this, but why expect to learn valuable truths?
>
> (133)

When Setiya writes that "we almost never satisfy these constraints", he means that we almost never know about our non-deontic reasons to act in certain ways without also knowing whether these acts would be wrong. That might be true but is irrelevant here. Setiya is discussing what I call the *Deontic Beliefs Restriction*. On a rough statement of the Kantian Contractualist Formula, which is one version of Kant's Formula of Universal Law, everyone ought to follow the principles whose universal acceptance everyone could rationally will, or choose. According to the Deontic Beliefs Restriction, or

> DBR: when we ask which are the principles whose universal acceptance everyone could rationally choose, we should not appeal to our beliefs about which acts are wrong.

There would be no point in claiming both that

> (1) certain acts are wrong because we could not rationally choose that we all accept principles that permit such acts,

and that

> (2) we could not rationally choose that we all accept such principles because such acts are wrong.

These claims would go round in a circle, getting us nowhere. We can call this the *Circularity Argument* for the Deontic Beliefs Restriction.

When we apply the Kantian Contractualist Formula, in ways that follow this restriction, it is not because we have no knowledge about which acts are wrong. We believe that we have some knowledge, but we apply this formula to help us to decide whether these beliefs are justified and to answer questions when we are undecided about whether certain acts would be wrong. Though we don't appeal to facts about wrongness, that is not because we are *oddly blind* to these deontic facts but because appealing to these facts would make the Kantian Contractualist Formula vacuously circular. As I remarked, Kant follows this Deontic Beliefs Restriction. When Kant claims that his false promiser could not rationally will that his maxim be a universal law, he does not defend this claim by arguing that this man couldn't rationally will that people act in a way that was wrong.

Setiya also writes:

> What state of knowledge does the Kantian project address? . . . It assumes that we have knowledge of impartial reasons. But it does not assume . . . that we know what is right and wrong. Why focus our attention here?
>
> (132–3)

> Why is this state of limited knowledge—knowledge of impartial but not deontic reasons —an urgent target of ethical thought? Why not assume less knowledge and set a more ambitious challenge? Why not confront the normative skeptic? Or if that seems hopeless, why not aim for much less? A modest project would begin with those who know what to do, and why to do it, and defend their claim to know.
>
> (133)

Even to achieve this more modest aim, we would have to follow the Deontic Beliefs Restriction. When we defend our claim to know that certain acts are wrong, it would not help to appeal to the claim that these acts are wrong. Setiya's arguments do not, I conclude, show the pointlessness or unimportance of the Kantian project.

McNaughton and Rawling make some partly similar claims. They discuss what they call *deontological constraints*. According to one such constraint, it would be wrong to kill one person as a means of saving the lives of only a few other people. This claim states a constraint against *killing as a means*. We can follow Judith Jarvis Thomson's helpful terminological suggestion that when we *violate* some constraint, our act is wrong, but that when we *infringe* some constraint, this claim leaves it open whether our act is wrong. On this view, we are sometimes morally justified in infringing some constraint. One example might be the claim that we could justifiably kill one person as a means, if our act would save as many as a million or a thousand other people's lives.

If we believe that some act violates some such constraint, this belief is about the wrongness of such acts. According to one such constraint, it is wrong to harm some people as a means of saving others from greater harm. According to the Deontic Beliefs Restriction, when we apply the Kantian Formula, by asking which are the principles that everyone would have sufficient reasons to choose, we cannot appeal to our beliefs about the wrongness of acts that would violate such constraints.

In discussing these claims, I distinguished between two kinds of reason. Deontic reasons are given by the fact that some act is wrong. All other reasons are non-deontic. These other reasons include the reasons that are given by the facts which make some act wrong. Some of these reasons may be given by facts that give us what Ross called *prima facie* duties. Since these may not be actual duties, we can regard them as facts about some act that would make some act wrong unless this fact is morally outweighed by some other fact which justifies this act. If some act would be the breaking of a promise, for example, that would make this act *prima facie* wrong, but this act might be justified if we would have to break some promise to save some stranger whose life is threatened. Our reasons not to break promises are often called deontological, but they are not in my sense *deontic*, since we can have these deontological moral reasons not to act in some way even when these reasons are outweighed, so that the act in question is not wrong.

When McNaughton and Rawling discuss my claim that, when we apply the Kantian Contractualist Formula, we ought to follow the Deontic Belief Restriction, they suppose what they earlier question, which is that an act's wrongness might give us a further reason. They then write:

> If wrongness is an independent reason, why can't we dig in our heels and say that someone's impartial reasons are decisively outweighed by the wrongness of an act those reasons endorse?

(107)

They also write:

> Parfit apparently sees the fact that some act would violate a constraint as a *deontic* reason against it – akin to the fact that it is wrong. And, as we

saw in the previous paragraph, deontic reasons, in Parfit's view, are out of bounds at this point in the argument.

(107)

They also write: "A constraint is a *prohibition* against harming people, even in pursuit of good ends" (103–4). A constraint so understood is the claim that some act is wrong, so our reason not to violate this constraint isn't merely *akin* to the reason given by the fact that this act is wrong. This reason would be given by the fact that this act is wrong.

McNaughton and Rawling say that they won't discuss my argument for the Deontic Beliefs Restriction. The Circularity Argument, given above, seems to me decisive. If we could appeal to our beliefs about the wrongness of act in deciding whether everyone could rationally choose that everyone accepts some moral principle, we could not also appeal to the Kantian Formula to help us to decide which acts are wrong.

In the remarks quoted above, McNaughton and Rawling might use 'violate' to mean 'infringe'. They might then be asking why we can't appeal to the reasons which are given by the fact that some act has some property which makes acts *prima facie* wrong, such as the property of being the breaking of a promise. The reason given by the fact that some act is *prima facie* wrong may seem to be *akin* to the deontic reason given by the fact that some act *is* wrong.

This is a good question, which I should have mentioned and answered. I would say that, in applying the Kantian Formula, we would be entitled to appeal to the nonmoral fact which makes some act *prima facie* wrong, as long as we don't appeal to this fact in a way that appeals to its *prima facie wrongness*. We might claim, for example, that we could all rationally choose that everyone accepts some principle that requires us not to break promises without some good reason. We might then appeal to our reasons not to break promises, such as those given by the need for cooperation, for confidence about what others will do, etc. My Deontic Beliefs Restriction claims only that if we claim that everyone could rationally choose that we all accept some principle that requires us to keep most promises, we can't appeal to the further belief that breaking promises is wrong.

McNaughton and Rawling then ask what view I accept about these moral constraints. They write that if Parfit

> endorses neither constraints nor quasi-constraints. . . his ultimate view is far removed from both Kantianism and rule consequentialism as they are commonly understood.[18]

They also write:

> Parfit, however, seeks to reconcile the two theories – so does he opt for constraints (forcing the rule consequentialist into the Kantian

mould), quasi-constraints (forcing the Kantian into the rule
consequentialist mould), or neither? We are not sure.

(106)

I don't do either, nor do I need to. These claims misunderstand my argument that the Kantian Contractualist Formula implies Rule Consequentialism. In asking whether everyone would have sufficient reasons to choose some moral principle, setting aside deontic reasons, I don't need either to endorse or to reject constraints or quasi-constraints.

When McNaughton and Rawling state (in the quotation just now) that my "ultimate view is far removed" from Kantianism and Rule Consequentialism, they misunderstand me. I don't attempt to defend or even state any such ultimate moral view. I merely try to make some progress in answering certain questions. In Parts Three and Five of *On What Matters*, I defend the view that if Kant's Formula of Universal Law is revised in two ways, which I believe to be needed, this Kantian Contractualist Formula implies Rule Consequentialism. My view isn't 'far removed' from Kantianism and Rule Consequentialism, since this view is about the relation between these other views. In defending this view, I can leave it open which constraints or quasi-contrasts would be supported by this Kantian Formula and by Rule Consequentialism.

I have been discussing only the questions or objections that McNaughton and Rawling ask or present when discussing my claims. McNaughton and Rawling make several other plausible and interesting claims in the rest of their chapter, most of which I accept. Since these claims are not about my view, I shall not discuss them here.

7 Response to Douglas W. Portmore

In his impressive, rigorously argued chapter, Douglas Portmore criticizes some of my claims about Rule Consequentialism. According to one version of this view, which I called

> UFRC: everyone ought to follow the rules whose being followed by everyone would make things go best.[19]

We *follow* some rule when we succeed in doing what this rule requires us to do. According to what I called

> the Ideal World Objection: this version of Rule Consequentialism requires us to follow such ideal rules even when we know that, because some other people are not following these rules, our acts would have very bad effects.[20]

RESPONSES

To illustrate this objection, Portmore imagines

> *The Unsolved Climate Case*: if everyone (or even just nearly everyone) makes the significant sacrifices required to drastically reduce their carbon footprints, then the climate disaster that will otherwise ensue in the next century will be averted. Unfortunately, no one is making, nor is anyone going to make, these sacrifices.
>
> (141)

When applied to this example, Portmore writes, UFRC requires us to make these sacrifices, which would be bad for ourselves and our families, even though, because no one else will act in this way, these sacrifices would be "completely pointless, doing absolutely no good whatsoever" (147).

This Ideal World Objection can, I wrote, be answered. These Rule Consequentialists could appeal to

> R1: Follow the rules whose being followed by everyone would make things go best, unless some other people have not followed these rules, in which case do whatever, given the acts of others, would make things go best.[21]

I claimed that

> (A) this is one of the ideal rules, since everyone's following R1 would make things go best. So UFRC does *not* require us to follow those ideal rules whose being followed by only some people would have very bad effects.[22]

Portmore denies that Rule Consequentialists could appeal to rules like R1. He writes:

> It might be thought that the ideal (or optimific) code would include a rule saying that one is required to bear the burdens of doing one's part in some possible cooperative venture only if one's doing so would not be pointless due to the unwillingness of others to do their parts. But even if the ideal code would include such a rule in certain possible worlds, it would not include such a rule in the possible world that I am imagining, which is one in which climate disaster would ensue if everyone (or nearly everyone) were to follow (or even accept) such a principle.
>
> (141–2)

This objection to (A) does not, I believe, succeed. There are two ways in which, in Portmore's *Unsolved Climate Case*, everyone might follow R1. That would be true if everyone made the significant sacrifices that would together prevent the climate disaster. Portmore tells us to suppose that this won't happen, since no one will make these sacrifices. If that is true, however, everyone would again be following R1. If no one makes these sacrifices, everyone would be doing what, given the acts of others, would make things go best. So if these Rule Consequentialists appeal to R1, their view would not require anyone to make these pointless sacrifices, which would do no good. On this version of Rule Consequentialism, we would be acting rightly either if we all make these sacrifices or if no one does.

It might be objected that in Portmore's imagined case, Rule Consequentialists *ought* to require everyone to make these sacrifices, since that is the only way in which we could prevent the climate disaster. But Portmore would not make this claim. R1 permits us not to make these sacrifices only when, and because, these sacrifices would do no good. Portmore does not believe that Rule Consequentialists ought to require such pointless sacrifices. His main objection is, precisely, that UFRC must require these sacrifices even when they would do *no* good. I have argued that, as (A) claims, that is not true.

In the passage quoted above, Portmore claims that this Ideal World Objection also applies to those Rule Consequentialists who appeal to the effects, not of our *following* but of our *accepting* certain rules. According to one such view, which I called

> UARC: Everyone ought to follow the rules whose acceptance by everyone would make things go best.[23]

One such rule might be

> R2: follow the rules whose being accepted by everyone would make things go best, unless some other people have not accepted or followed these rules, in which case do whatever, given the acts of others, would make things go best.

Portmore's objection assumes that in his imagined case, climate disaster would ensue if everyone accepted R2. As before, that is not true. If everyone accepted R2, there are two ways in which everyone might follow R2. That would be true either if everyone made these sacrifices, thereby preventing the climate disaster, or if no one made these sacrifices, which would be pointless since, given the acts of others, these sacrifices would do no good. I conclude that, as I claimed, these Rule Consequentialists can answer what I called the Ideal World Objection.

As I wrote, however, there are other objections to these versions of Rule Consequentialism. Consider

R3: Follow the rules whose being followed by everyone would make things go best, unless some other people have not followed these rules, in which case do whatever you like.[24]

According to UFRC, this is another ideal rule, since if everyone followed R3, things would go best. In asking whether this rule would be ideal, we ignore what would happen if some people did not follow this rule. In the real world, we would nearly always know that some people have not followed the ideal rules. So, in permitting us to follow R3, UFRC nearly always permits the rest of us to do whatever we like. That is clearly an unacceptable conclusion. According to what I called this

> *New Ideal World Objection*: Once a few people have failed to follow the ideal rules, UFRC implies that none of our possible acts would be wrong.[25]

Similar remarks apply to UARC, which appeals to the rules whose being *accepted* by everyone would make things go best.

To answer this objection, I claimed, Rule Consequentialists should ask what would happen if various rules were followed or accepted, not only by *everyone* but also by other numbers of people. Some of these rules should take conditional forms, telling us to act in different ways, depending either on what other people are doing or on what, on the evidence, we can rationally expect other people to do. When judged in these ways, rules like R3 would clearly not be ideal, since whenever some rule has been followed not by everyone but only by some people, R3 permits us to do whatever we like.

According to one such revised version of Rule Consequentialism, which Portmore calls

> PFRC: everyone ought to follow the rules whose being followed, not only by everyone but by any other number of people, would make things go best.

These more complicated rules would tell us to act in the ways that would make things go best given the number or proportion of people who are following these rules. According to the similar

> PARC: everyone ought to follow the rules whose being *accepted* by different numbers of people would make things go best.

Such claims tell us which acts are right in what I called the *fact-relative* sense. These theories ought to make different claims about what we ought to do in the *evidence-relative* or *belief-relative* senses. These senses of 'ought' are more important than the fact-relative sense, both when we are deciding how to act and when we ask which acts are blameworthy. One such rule might be

> R4: do whatever, on the available evidence about what others are doing, would be most likely to make things go best.

When Portmore considers what he believes to be the best versions of such views, he writes:

> If the expected value of a code is to be calculated in terms of subjective probabilities, then there is no way for maximizing-expectation-rate PFRC to avoid implying that agents will be required to make pointless sacrifices in certain more fully specified versions of *The Unsolved Climate Case*. After all, if the comparative value of a world in which climate disaster ensues is low enough and/or the subjective probability that nearly everyone will follow a code requiring significant sacrifices is high enough, then the ideal code—that is, the code with the highest expected value—will require agents to make significant sacrifices. . . even though, as a matter of fact, there is. . . no objective chance that anyone will be making these sacrifices.
>
> (144)

As Portmore here points out, this version of Rule Consequentialism may require us to make significant sacrifices when the evidence available to us makes it likely that these acts would make things go best, even when these acts would in fact do no good. But this feature of these views is not, as Portmore assumes, a strong objection to them. We can similarly claim, for example, that what doctors ought to do, in the evidence-relative sense, is to treat their patients in the ways that, on the evidence available, are much the most likely to save these people's lives. It is no objection to this claim that there are some cases in which, because the evidence is misleading, such treatment would in fact kill some patients. Portmore's objection to this version of Rule Consequentialism therefore fails.

Portmore claims that similar objections apply to other versions of PFRC and PARC. He writes:

> rule consequentialism requires us to make significant sacrifices even when doing so is completely pointless, doing absolutely no good whatsoever.
>
> (147)

These objections assume that no version of Rule Consequentialism could appeal to some rule like

R5: do not make sacrifices when these acts would be completely pointless, doing absolutely no good whatever.

Such rules, Portmore claims, could not be optimific, since there are bound to be some cases in which, if we believe that we are morally permitted not to make such pointless sacrifices, the effects would be very bad.

As before, I believe this objection fails. Several versions of Rule Consequentialism could appeal to R5 or to other similar rules. These views would never imply that we ought in the *fact*-relative sense to make such pointless sacrifices. These views might imply that such acts are morally required in the *evidence*-relative sense even when, because the available evidence is misleading, these acts would do no good. But that is no objection to these views.

I did not try to decide which versions of Rule Consequentialism would best answer the New Ideal World Objection, since that question was irrelevant to my main claims. Portmore writes that all possible versions of PFRC and PARC would be open to 'devastating objections'. Rather than describe these objections, Portmore refers to an article by Kevin Tobia. This article concludes:

> In this paper I have sought to explain a new way in which Rule Utilitarian theories can handle problems of partial acceptance.
> I contend that current forms of Rule Utilitarianism, namely Fixed Rate, Variable Rate, and Optimum Rate Rule Utilitarianism, can be improved upon by taking into consideration the likelihood that given acceptance levels will actually obtain.

Discussing his proposal, Tobia writes that "there are three main foreseeable objections . . . but I believe none critically damages this theory".[26] These claims do not describe a devastating objection to Tobia's suggested version of Rule Utilitarianism.

Portmore concludes:

> We have seen that rule consequentialism sometimes requires us to act in ways that we lack sufficient reason to act. This presents a dilemma for Parfit. Parfit should concede either that rule consequentialism (and, hence, Triple Theory, which entails it) is false, despite the putatively strong reasons that he believes we have for accepting it, or that morality doesn't have the importance he seems to attribute to it given that it has been undermined by his own substantive account of morality.
>
> (149)

Portmore's ingenious arguments do not, I have claimed, show the Triple Theory to be false. But Portmore makes several original claims, which may help us to decide what one part of the Triple Theory ought to claim about some important kinds of case.

8 Response to J.L. Dowell and David Sobel

Those whom I call *Soft Naturalists* believe that, though there are no irreducibly normative properties or truths, we need to make some irreducibly normative claims, since such claims, when they are true, can help us to make good decisions and to act well. Soft Naturalism, I argued, cannot be true. Consider, for example, the Utilitarian belief that

(A) when some act would maximize happiness, this act is what we ought to do.

This view, I wrote, can take two forms. Non-Naturalists like Sidgwick claim that

(B) when some act would maximize happiness, this fact would make this act have the different property of being what we ought to do.

Utilitarian Naturalists reject (B), claiming instead that

(C) when some act would maximize happiness, this property of this act is the same as the property of being what we ought to do.

We can argue:

(1) (A) is a substantive normative claim, which would, if it were true, state a positive substantive normative fact.

(2) If, impossibly, (C) were true, (A) could not state such a fact.

Therefore

Soft Naturalism is not true.

I called this *the Triviality Objection*.

In their impressive chapter, J.L. Dowell and David Sobel describe their main aim as that of showing how Non-Analytical Naturalists, whom they call *NANs*, could answer my Triviality Objection. They write:

Parfit's Triviality Objection purports to show that NANs are unable to do so much as state informative identities between the normative and the natural . . .

(153)

This remark misdescribes my objection. I did not argue that Naturalists would be unable even to state identity claims like (C), nor did I argue that if, impossibly, such claims were true, they would not be informative but would be trivial. I wrote that, if (C) were true, this truth would be far from trivial. (C) would give us substantive normative information. But this information would be *negative*. We would learn that, when acts would maximize happiness, this fact could not give these acts the *different*, normative property of being what we ought to do, since (C) implies that there is *no* such different property. If we learnt that there is no such different property, what we learnt could not, as Soft Naturalists claim, help us to make good decisions, and to act well. In a phrase that I often use to sum up this Triviality Objection, claims like (C) could not give us any '*positive* substantive normative information'. Perhaps because Dowell and Sobel never use or mention this often repeated phrase, they do not discuss my Triviality Objection.

There is one passage in which Dowell and Sobel come closest to discussing my objection. When I argued that claims like (C) could not give us positive substantive normative information, I considered the suggestion that (C) might be claimed to imply that

> (Q) when some act would maximize happiness, this act would have certain other non-normative properties.[27]

Dowell and Sobel comment:

> Here is the entirety of Parfit's argument against this second strategy:
>
>> Naturalists believe that substantive normative facts are also natural facts. Since (Q) is not a normative claim, (Q) could not state a normative fact.
>
> Recall that this is part of an overall argument to show that the NAN cannot so much as state her central identity claims in a form that would meet all of her requirements. From these compressed remarks, it is far from immediately clear why (Q)'s failure to be normative would pose a problem for the NAN. After all, the NAN who defends (C) is not claiming that (Q) is a normative claim. She is claiming that (C) is.
>
> (159)

As before, these remarks misdescribe my view. I did not argue that according to these Soft Naturalists *claim (Q)* is normative. As Dowell and Sobel point out, these Naturalists believe that *claim (C)* is normative. I argued that, to defend their view that (C)'s truth would give us positive substantive normative information, these Naturalists cannot appeal to the fact that (C) implies some other non-normative claim, such as the claim stated by (Q). If (C) implied some other, non-normative claim, that could not help to show that (C) might indirectly give us positive substantive normative information. What Dowell and Sobel call "this second strategy" therefore fails to answer this argument against Soft Naturalism.

I should admit, however, that Dowell and Sobel's misunderstanding of my argument may be partly my fault. After discussing other possible answers to this objection, I wrote that this objection "shows that Naturalism cannot be true".[28] I should have again included the word "Soft", since, as I pointed out myself, the Triviality Objection could not show that what I called *Hard* Naturalism cannot be true.

In the rest of their chapter, Dowell and Sobel make several interesting claims about the informativeness of some statements about the identity of some property and of various ways in which there can be non-semantic explanations of the cognitive significance of some identity statements. But none of these claims apply to my Triviality Objection against Soft Naturalism. Nor, I believe, do these claims support objections to any of my other claims.

9 Response to Julia Driver

In her agreeably humane and sensible chapter, Julia Driver writes that she is not criticizing my defence of the view that there are some irreducibly normative truths, such as the truth that some things matter in a reason-implying sense. Driver aims instead to describe and defend a view according to which there are moral truths without the mysterious underpinnings of non-naturalism. On these views, she holds, "things still matter as much as anything can be said to 'matter'".[29]

These claims imply that nothing can be said to 'matter' in what I call the *purely normative reason-implying sense*. Driver may believe that nothing can be said to matter in this sense because the belief in normative non-natural truths would commit us to mysterious ontological claims. She suggests that, on my view, "We have gotten rid of supernatural agents in accounting for normativity, only to rely on another hidden, occult realm" (183). In my Chapter 31 and Appendix J, I discuss this widely accepted objection. I argue that some non-empirically discoverable truths, such as logical, mathematical and modal truths, and purely normative truths, have no weighty mysterious ontological implications. These truths do not imply that there is any such hidden, occult realm. Since Driver does not discuss my arguments, I don't know why she rejects them, so I cannot try to reply.

Driver makes some suggestions about how these arguments fail. Driver writes: "Analogies with mathematics abound. But tautologies are necessarily true, and empty". Mathematics does not, I believe, consist of empty tautologies. "Appeals to mathematics do not help", Driver also writes, since some of these mathematical truths, though necessary, are "accidental" in the sense that they lack "a unified non-disjunctive proof". If some mathematical truths lack such a proof, that does not, I believe, make these truths "accidental" in some damaging sense. Driver adds that, in such cases, "there is no real explanation provided as to why the claim is true" (all from 182). These remarks seem to imply that even if Non-Naturalists could justifiably claim that normative truths had the same status as these logical and mathematical truths, that would achieve little. If we can justify such claims, that would, I believe, achieve a great deal. When we consider the most fundamental truths of these kinds, we should expect there to be no further explanations of why these claims are true. We may be unable to explain why no statement or proposition could be both wholly true and wholly false, or why two plus two must equal four, and could not possibly equal three or five. But this inability does not, I believe, cast serious doubt on our belief in these truths. If some normative truths have the same kind of truth as such logical and mathematical truths, that would be enough to show that some things can be said to matter in the sense that we have purely normative reasons to care about these things.

Driver briefly discusses some of the truths that I claim to be fundamental and not to be explicable in other terms. One example is the truth that pain is bad in the reason-implying sense that we all have reasons to want to avoid or prevent future pain. If we can't explain why it is bad to be in agony, Driver suggests, this claim involves "a kind of arbitrariness" (183). The badness of pain, Driver suggests, consists only in how we respond to pain. She also discusses my view that some moral truths

> are necessary: if it is true that, for example, torturing people for fun is wrong, it is true in all possible worlds . . . [But] finding comfort in necessity is relying on an illusion. Necessity does not provide a reassuring bedrock.
>
> (175)

I wasn't trying to find such a bedrock. I made such claims because I don't see how torturing people for fun could fail to be wrong.

Driver's aim, she writes, is not to criticize my non-naturalist view but to defend a naturalist view that she calls *Substantive Humean Constructivism*. "Substantive forms of constructivism", Driver writes, "were not adequately discussed in *On What Matters*" (173). That is true. I made no attempt to discuss these forms of Humean Constructivism, partly because I know too little about them. I shall, however, end by repeating some remarks about Hume. Driver doubts my belief that we all have reasons to want to avoid future agony. As I also claimed, however, Hume believed that we have such reasons. It is true that, in a much quoted passage, Hume writes:

> 'Tis as little contrary to reason to prefer even my own acknowledged lesser good to my greater, and have a more ardent affection for the former than the latter.[30]

But Hume seems here to be using the word 'reason' to refer to the mental abilities that lead us to form true beliefs. Hume may mean that such preferences cannot be false. Hume did not discuss whether we have reasons to have desires of the kind that Driver calls *external* and I call *object-given* and *value-based*. But Hume writes:

> So little are men govern'd by *reason* in their sentiments and opinions, that they always judge more of objects by comparison than from their *intrinsic worth* and *value*.[31]

He also writes that we mistakenly "desire objects more according to their situation than their intrinsic value".[32] When Hume talks of our preferring our own acknowledged lesser good to our greater good, he seems to be referring to our tendency to prefer lesser goods in the near future to greater goods that would be more remote. Discussing this *bias towards the near*, Hume writes:

> There is no quality in human nature which causes more fatal errors in our conduct.[33]

That is a very strong criticism. As these and other remarks show, Hume believed that when we prefer such lesser goods, we are failing to be *governed by reason*. Such preferences are in this sense contrary to reason. We are preferring what we have no reasons to prefer and strong reasons not to prefer. When Hume claims, in the passage quoted above, that such preferences are *not* contrary to reason, he is forgetting, or misstating, some of his normative beliefs. We should distinguish between Hume's *stated* view and his *real* view.[34]

Notes

1. All page references in the main text are to this volume.
2. OWM 2, p. 143.
3. OWM 2, p. 155.
4. OWM 2, pp. 66–70. Wood says that Kant's Formula of Humanity tells us "that the fundamental bearers of value are not states of affairs at all, but persons and the humanity or rational nature in persons" (OWM 2, p. 68).
5. OWM 3, §38.
6. In his n. 14.
7. OWM 1, p. 82.
8. Markovits used this phrase in the first submitted version of her chapter. Though she does not use this phrase in the revised, printed version of her chapter, my comments about this phrase do not, I believe, misstate her view. If Markovits intended to drop this version of her view, one of my aims is to argue that this would be a mistake.
9. Again, from the original version of her chapter.
10. OWM 1, p. 74.
11. OWM 1, p. 173.
12. OWM 1, p. 173, emphasis added.

13 OWM 1, p. 218.
14 OWM 1, p. 218.
15 Setiya (2011), p. 1287.
16 He does, however, consider my response. Setiya suggests that, to answer his argument for the practical irrelevance of moral theories, we might revise our definition of 'deontic reason', so that this phrase covers reasons that are provided by the nonmoral facts that make acts wrong.

This response, he suggests, would achieve little. I agree. Setiya also writes:

> There are hints of this in Parfit's book, as when he suggests that features of an act that make it wrong "might give you a decisive reason not to act in this way" but "only by making this act wrong." He goes on to say: "[this] decisive reason would have to be deontic" and that "[you] would not have decisive non-deontic reason not to act in this way". . . . These remarks can be interpreted in two ways. On one reading, Parfit adopts the broad definition according to which non-deontic facts that count as reasons because they make acts wrong are themselves deontic reasons. On the second reading, he claims that they "give us" deontic reasons, which consist in deontic facts, since they make such facts obtain.
>
> (n. 32)

Setiya's second reading is correct. When I claimed that, in some cases, this decisive reason might have to be deontic, I did not use that phrase to cover non-deontic reasons. After giving this correct reading, Setiya adds nothing. He gives no argument against (5).

17 In various places, but see OWM 1, p. 342.
18 In a previous draft.
19 OWM 1, p. 405.
20 I discuss this objection in OWM 1, §45.
21 OWM 1, p. 317.
22 OWM 1, p. 317.
23 OWM 1, pp. 377–419.
24 OWM 1, p. 317, where, confusingly, I call this principle R2.
25 OWM 1, p. 316 where I state this objection in a form which applies to Kant's Formula of Universal Law.
26 Tobia (2013), p. 651.
27 OWM 2, p. 354.
28 OWM 2, p. 356.
29 From the original version of her chapter.
30 Hume (2007), *Treatise*, Book II, Part III, Section III.
31 Hume (2007), Book II, Part II, Section VIII.
32 Hume (2007), Book III, Part II, Section VII.
33 Hume (2007), Book III, Part II, Section VII.
34 Hume's beliefs about such reasons are well discussed in Wiggins (2006).

References

Hume, David (2007/1739–40) *A Treatise of Human Nature*, David Fate Norton and Mary J. Norton (eds) (Oxford: Oxford University Press).

Parfit, Derek (2011) *On What Matters* (Oxford: Oxford University Press), vols 1 and 2.

Parfit, Derek (2017) *On What Matters* (Oxford: Oxford University Press), vol. 3.
Setiya, Kieran (2011) 'Review of *On What Matters*', *Mind* 120, pp. 1281–8.
Tobia, Kevin (2013) 'Rule Consequentialism and the Problem of Partial Acceptance', *Ethical Theory and Moral Practice* 16, pp. 643–52.
Wiggins, David (2006) *Ethics: Twelve Lectures on the Philosophy of Morality* (Cambridge: Cambridge University Press).

INDEX

autonomy 11–14, 60, 67, 110, 193

Baker, Alan 182
Bayesianism 112
best, notion of 13–14, 16–17, 102, 106, 190
Brandt, Richard B. 168 n. 4
Bridge 107, 116, 127–8, 215–19
Brink, David 186 n. 6
buck-passing 7, 82–95; defined 82–3; buck-passing facts 86–7

Chang, Ruth 77 n. 12
circularity argument (for deontic beliefs restriction) 221–3
circularity problem 177
consent 11–13, 17, 193
consequentialism 2–3, 21, 24, 102–3, 105, 117–18 n. 18, 118 n. 20
constraints (deontic) 7, 72, 102–7, 222–4
contingency 8, 172–88
contractualism 3, 10, 11, 191; Kantian contractualism 8, 106–7, 123–34, 220
Copp, David 6–7, 195–200

Darwall, Stephen 108–11
Davidson, Donald 96–7
Dowell, J. L. and Sobel, David 8, 230–2
Driver, Julia 8, 232–4

egoist 102, 117–18 n. 18, 191
Ella the scientist 164–5

facts, conception of 34–5, 37–8, 41, 96, 154, 159, 195–200, 230–1
Falk, W. D. 168 n. 4

free will 185–6
Frege, Gottlob 51 n. 49, 156–7, 159, 160–1, 162, 168

Gibbard, Allan 50 n. 27, 51 n. 45, 169 n. 7
Golden Rule 133 n. 2

hedonism 68–9, 102, 201, 211
Hume, David / Humeanism 61, 65, 89, 108, 172–3
Humean Constructivism 176–86

identity statements 8, 31, 153, 156–62, 164, 167–8, 203–6, 231–2
imaginative resistance 175
incommensurability 14–20, 24–5, 26, 189–90

Jackson, Frank 169 n. 6
Joyce, Richard 186

Kantian constructivism 108–9, 176–7, 184, 185
Kantian Contractualism 13, 106–7, 123–34, 219–24
Kantianism 2–4, 11–12, 20, 21, 25, 57–8, 72, 74–5, 105–6, 192, 193; Formula of Universal Law 3–4, 124, 191, 192, 224, 234 n. 4
King, Jeffrey 34
Kirchin, Simon 6, 189–95
Kolmogorov's axioms 113
Korsgaard, Christine 109
Kripke, Saul 162, 183

Lifeboat 126
lost-property problem 158

INDEX

A Midsummer Night's Dream 78–9 n. 38
McDowell, John 29
Mackie, J. L. 29
McNaughton, David and Rawling, Piers 7, 211–13, 219, 222–4
Markovits, Julia 7, 200–11
Means 12
methodology 4, 6, 20–5, 194–5
moral rationalism 130–1, 213–4, 219

Nagel, Thomas 199
naturalist (normative) realism 5, 6–7, 28, 30–5, 76 n. 8, 76 n. 10, 177, 196–9, 206, 207, 230–2; Hard Naturalism 30, 168–9 n. 5, 232; non-analytic naturalism 5, 8, 31, 32, 35, 42–4, 153–71; reductivist naturalism 30–1, 35, 42, 72, 207; Soft Naturalism and Soft Naturalist's Dilemma 28, 29–30, 36–8, 47–9, 168–9 n. 5; 230–2; Triviality Objection 5, 8, 153, 162, 166, 167
nihilism 5, 28, 30, 36, 37–8, 48, 55, 72, 172, 186, 195, 199, 201–2
noncognitivism 5, 6, 174
non-naturalist (normative) realism 5, 6, 7, 28–9, 31–4, 38, 41, 44, 48, 72, 153–4, 155, 157, 158, 160, 161, 172, 174, 175, 182, 183, 186, 195–9, 232–3
normative ethics 3, 6, 9–10, 14, 16, 18–19, 21, 24–6, 191, 194
normativity 6, 28, 32, 33–4, 38, 43, 54, 61, 73, 157, 174, 182, 195, 199, 232; normative concepts 2, 6–7, 29–31, 35–41, 43–9, 76 n. 10, 97, 98, 154, 168 n. 4, 169 n. 7, 199, 208–9; normative properties 5, 28–9, 31–4, 35, 37, 40–1, 46, 48, 155–9, 166, 167, 198, 205–7, 230–1

objectivist theories of reasons 1–2, 7, 11, 54–81, 99, 103, 111, 124, 127, 132, 202, 209–11; contrasted with subjectivist theories 56–8

Perry, John 46
Portmore, Douglas 8, 224–30
Prichard, H. A. 111–12

Railton, Peter 67, 155, 178–9
Rawls, John 66, 79 n. 45, 114, 117 n. 17, 168 n. 4, 208
reading Spinoza's *Ethics* (whilst eating strawberries, for example) 4

reasons 1–2, 5, 7, 28, 33–4, 54, 82, 83, 96–122, 123–4; additivity/non-additivity of 84–91; desire-based views of *see* subjectivist theories of reasons; fundamental conception of 58, 82; internalism / externalism 5, 7, 108, 173–4, 175, 180; motivating reasons 54, 59, 62–5, 70, 108, 210; value-based views of *see* objectivist theories of reasons
Reasons and Persons 1, 9, 69, 70, 187 n. 14
Ross, W. D. 97, 99, 103, 117 n. 17, 119 n. 29, 222
Rule Consequentialism 3, 8, 10, 13, 54, 105–7, 125, 135–52, 191, 220, 223–4, 224–30; collapse into act consequentialism 105, 150 n. 1; Ideal World Objection 224–6, 229; PARC 143, 146, 227–9; PFRC 143–6, 227–9; UARC 143, 145–6, 226–7; UFRC 141–6, 224, 225–7

Sayre-McCord, Geoff 170 n. 26
Scanlon, T. M. 1, 4, 7, 58, 77 n. 12, 79 n. 40, 109, 120 n. 77; and buck-passing 82–3, 87; Scanlonian contractualism 3, 10, 133 n. 9, 191–2
Scheffler, Samuel 2
Schroeder, Mark 7, 85–90, 94
securability cases 138–40
Setiya, Kieran 8, 62, 211, 213–21
Sidgwick, Henry 5, 20, 21, 23, 78 n. 35, 118 n. 20, 155, 230
Smith, Michael 51 n. 42, 72–4, 79 n. 45, 178, 185
Stalnaker, Robert 154, 162–8
Stratton-Lake, Philip 7, 211
Street, Sharon 79–80 n. 50, 172, 175–6, 179, 181
Sturgeon, Nicholas 50 n. 17, 170 n. 26
subjectivist theories of reasons 1, 2, 5, 7, 11–12, 54–81, 132, 173, 200–11; contrasted with objectivist theories 56–8
sympathy 177, 179, 184–5

Thomason, Richard 113
Thomson, Judith Jarvis 195, 222
Tobia, Kevin 229

INDEX

Triple Theory 3, 4, 6, 8, 9, 10–11, 14, 16–17, 18, 20, 25–6, 82, 105, 114–17, 135, 149, 191–4, 229–30
trolley cases 12–13, 20, 21, 22, 23–5, 110, 195
Tunnel 110–11, 214–16, 218

utilitarianism, hedonic 102

war 16, 22–3
way of thinking (WOT) 7, 29, 40–9
Williams, Bernard 6, 60, 63, 67, 75, 78 n. 29, 108, 168 n. 4
Wolf, Susan 1, 4, 6, 10–20, 24–6, 190, 193–4
Wood, Allen 1, 4–5, 6, 10–11, 20–6, 194–5